Preparing Literature Reviews

Qualitative and Quantitative Approaches

Third Edition

M. Ling Pan

Pyrczak Publishing

P.O. Box 250430 • Glendale, CA 91225

"Pyrczak Publishing" is an imprint of Fred Pyrczak, Publisher, A California Corporation.

Although the author and publisher have made every effort to ensure the accuracy and completeness of information contained in this book, we assume no responsibility for errors, inaccuracies, omissions, or any inconsistency herein. Any slights of people, places, or organizations are unintentional.

Project Director: Monica Lopez.

Cover design by Robert Kibler and Larry Nichols.

Editorial assistance provided by Cheryl Alcorn, Randall R. Bruce, Brenda Koplin, Jack Petit, Erica Simmons, and Sharon Young.

Printed in the United States of America by Malloy, Inc.

ISBN 1-884585-76-0

Contents

Continued →

Introduction to the Third Edition

A literature review is an original work based on a critical examination of the literature on a topic. The reviewer should evaluate the available evidence as well as relevant theories (while noting gaps in the literature) and create a synthesis that provides a comprehensive overview of the literature.

Preparing an adequate literature review is far from being a mechanical process. Instead, it is part science and part art. "Science" comes into play because there are usually a considerable number of original research reports to be evaluated when preparing a review on a given topic. Since all research is subject to error, a reviewer should examine the research critically and make evaluations in order to arrive at conclusions based on the strength of the research evidence.

"Art" comes into play because making sense of a body of literature requires subjective judgments regarding which sources to emphasize, how to combine the information from various sources, and how to account for gaps in knowledge on a topic so that a cohesive synthesis of the literature results.

Qualitatively Oriented versus Quantitatively Oriented Reviews

This book covers the basics for preparing both qualitative (i.e., narrative) and quantitative reviews. These do not constitute a dichotomy. Rather, literature reviews exist on a continuum from very highly qualitative (with little mention of statistics or the research methods used to obtain them) to very highly quantitative (with the final synthesis based on the mathematical averaging of results across various studies reported by different researchers).

Most beginning students should consider writing a qualitative review in which statistical material is very judiciously selected for inclusion in the review. This book shows how to select and interpret such statistical material and how to present it in qualitatively oriented reviews.

Qualitative and quantitative reviews have a great deal in common, so almost all the material in this book (Chapters 1 through 14) is relevant, regardless of the reviewer's orientation to the issue of quantification.

Chapters 15 and 16 present the basics of a highly quantitative approach called meta-analysis. In a meta-analysis, results from previous research are combined mathematically in order to arrive at a grand "average," indicating the strength and direction of results over a number of studies conducted by various researchers. Even students who will not be preparing meta-analytic reviews should study these chapters carefully since knowledge of the basics of meta-analysis will help in properly interpreting the results of published meta-analytic reviews, which may be cited in qualitative reviews.

About the End-of-Chapter Exercises

There are no right or wrong answers to the end-of chapter exercises. Instead, the questions in the exercises are designed to encourage students to reconsider the basic points in the chapters as students prepare literature reviews. The questions may also be used as the basis for classroom discussions.

The Checklist of Guidelines

Beginning on page 109, the Checklist of Guidelines presents a comprehensive list of the guidelines presented throughout this book. It can be used in several ways. First, it can be used as an index to help students quickly locate material read earlier. Second, it can be used as a checklist of reminders to reconsider when writing and revising.a review. Third, instructors can use it for easy reference when commenting on students' literature reviews. For instance, instead of writing out a criticism (either positive or negative), an instructor can refer to the checklist to quickly locate appropriate guidelines in order to write statements such as "Please improve this section. See Guideline 8.5," or "Good application of Guideline 9.2."

About the Model Literature Reviews

Nine model literature reviews are presented near the end of this book. They are "models" in the sense that they are well-written examples that illustrate various ways to evaluate, discuss, and synthesize literature. Note, however, that no one model fits all purposes. For instance, a literature review written for inclusion in a doctoral dissertation normally would be more extensive and detailed than one written as a senior project by an undergraduate.

Model Literature Reviews 1 through 3 are qualitatively oriented and were written as "stand-alone" reviews (i.e., not as introductions to larger documents such as theses).

Model Literature Reviews 4 through 6 are also qualitatively oriented. They were written as introductions to reports on original research. As such, their function is to establish the context for and the need for the research being reported.

Model Literature Reviews 7 through 9 are examples of meta-analyses, which are highly quantitative reviews.

A common set of questions appears at the end of all the model literature reviews. These are designed to stimulate classroom discussions of the reviews.

About the Examples

Throughout the book are a large number of examples to illustrate the guidelines. The examples that have references are quoted from published sources. The remaining examples were written by the author to parallel types of material frequently encountered in literature reviews. In some cases, these examples illustrate undesirable techniques that should be avoided. Instead of quoting such examples (and potentially embarrassing the authors), examples that are similar to those that appeared in recent literature reviews were created.

About the Third Edition

In order to place more emphasis on the process of writing, the material relevant to preparing the first draft has been expanded into five new chapters: Chapter 7 (Preparing a Topic Outline for the First Draft), Chapter 8 (Writing the First Draft: Basic Principles), Chapter 9 (Writing the First Draft: Optional Techniques), Chapter 10 (Writing the First Draft: Statistical Issues in Qualitative Reviews), and Chapter 11 (Building Tables to Summarize Literature).

In addition, new examples have been incorporated throughout the book in order to keep it up-to-date.

Acknowledgments

Dr. Gene Glass of Arizona State University, Tempe, Dr. Deborah M. Oh of California State University, Los Angeles, and Dr. Richard Rasor of American River College provided many helpful comments to this book. Although these individuals made important contributions to the development of this book, errors and omissions, of course, remain the responsibility of the author.

Contacting the Author

I encourage you to share with me your criticisms of this book. You can communicate with me via my publisher. The mailing address is shown on the title page of this book. Also, you can send e-mails to me in care of the publisher at info@pyrczak.com.

M. Ling Pan
Los Angeles, California

Notes:

Chapter 1

Introduction to Qualitative and Quantitative Reviews

A literature review is a *synthesis* of the literature on a topic. To create the synthesis, various diverse and sometimes conflicting ideas and findings in the literature need to be evaluated and combined to create a new, original work that provides an organized overview of the state of knowledge on a topic.

Abstracts versus Literature Reviews

An abstract is a brief summary of a published work. Most research articles in professional journals begin with abstracts, typically about 100 to 150 words in length. Stringing together a series of abstracts on a given topic does *not* create a literature review since such a string of elements fails to organize and show how various elements in the literature relate to each other.

Overview of Steps in Preparing a Literature Review

The following steps are described in more detail in the remaining chapters of this book. These steps apply to both qualitative and quantitative reviews. The distinction between the two types of reviews is explored later in this chapter.

Step 1: Select a Topic

The first step is to select a topic. In most cases, this is an interactive process in which the initial search of the literature reveals how much and what types of literature exist on a topic. Based on this information, the initial topic may need to be narrowed, broadened, or adjusted. At the same time, the needs of the audience for whom the review is being written will influence the selection of a topic.

Step 2: Locate and Read Literature for an Overview

The second step is to locate literature on the selected topic and read it with an eye toward getting a broad overview of which issues have been thoroughly covered, which ones need more investigation, which principles seem most firmly established and/or most widely accepted as being valid, and, perhaps most important, which theories have a bearing on the topic being reviewed.

Step 3: Establish Specific Purposes

Third, the reviewer should establish specific purposes for the literature review. For instance, Box 1A on the next page shows some possible purposes. Note that the purposes should be put in writing, which can later be incorporated into the introduction to the literature review. In addition, a student who is preparing a literature review for a class might share the written purposes with the instructor in order to get feedback on their appropriateness before beginning to write the review.

Box 1A *Sample purposes for a literature review on Treatment X.*

The purposes of this literature review are to:

1. trace the history of scientific developments, including relevant theories, that resulted in the development of Treatment X,

2. summarize and evaluate the legal and ethical issues involving the implementation of the treatment,

3. estimate the overall degree of effectiveness of the treatment by evaluating the experiments in which the treatment was compared with a placebo, and

4. describe possible fruitful areas for future research based on the research conducted to date.

Step 4: Evaluate and Interpret the Literature

Next, the literature needs to be evaluated and interpreted. Many reviewers give high evaluations to sources that present the results of rigorous scientific studies. At the same time, many reviewers give high evaluations to studies that provide crucial insights even if the underlying methods for collecting data are mildly, or even seriously, flawed. In addition, all authors of literature reviews should pay special attention to literature that presents, tests, and/or builds on the theories related to their topics.

Step 5: Synthesize the Literature

Fifth, the literature needs to be synthesized. This is done by first grouping various sources according to their similarities and differences, while considering possible explanations for differences (and contradictions) in the literature. Note that a synthesis very often will not result in a single, straightforward conclusion. Instead, it might consist of speculation on how the pieces of evidence found in the literature fit together along with some tentative conclusions and a discussion of their implications. This often leads to suggestions for future research that might produce a more definitive understanding of the topic.

Step 6: Plan and Write the First Draft

Most reviewers begin by introducing the topic and establishing its importance (e.g., indicating how many people are affected by the issue under review). Then, they prepare a topic outline with major headings and subheadings and write the review following the outline.

Step 7: Have the First Draft Evaluated and Revise It

The first draft of a literature review should be evaluated by others. Of course, an evaluation by an expert is highly desirable. However, note that a well-written review should be comprehensible to even nonexperts, such as other students, who can often provide valuable feedback. Revising (and, in some cases, entirely rewriting) a review in light of this feedback is a crucial step in producing a literature review of high quality.

This book covers the preparation of both qualitatively oriented and quantitatively oriented reviews. The following guidelines help distinguish between the two types of reviews.

✤ Guideline 1.1
Quantitatively oriented reviewers place more emphasis on precise statistical results than do qualitatively oriented reviewers.

The main distinction between the quantitatively oriented and qualitatively oriented reviews lies in the extent to which specific statistics are used in creating a synthesis. Reviewers who write quantitatively oriented reviews base their synthesis and conclusions more closely on specific statistical values than those who write qualitatively oriented reviews. For instance, compare the statement in Example 1.1.1 with the one in Example 1.1.2. Note that the statements in both examples refer to the same three published experiments.

Example 1.1.1
Sample statement that might appear in a quantitatively oriented review:

The three experiments in which Drug A was compared with a placebo yielded mean reductions on the Pain Relief Scale of 2.1, 3.3, and 4.0 points on a scale from 0 (no pain) to 20 (extreme pain). All three were statistically significant at the $p < .05$ level. The mean (i.e., arithmetic average) of these three means is 3.1, which is the best estimate of the effectiveness of Drug A. Hence, Drug A appears to produce a small but significant reduction in pain.[1]

Example 1.1.2
Sample statement that might appear in a qualitatively oriented review:

In each of the three experiments in which Drug A was compared with a placebo, there was a small but significant reduction in pain reported by those who took the drug, as indicated by self-reports on the Pain Relief Scale. On this 20-point scale, the average for the experimental group was a few points lower than the average for the placebo group. Thus, Drug A appears to be effective but of limited value in reducing pain.

In summary, authors of highly quantitatively oriented reviews tend to cite precise statistical values, while authors of qualitatively oriented reviews often make only general references to statistical findings.

✤ Guideline 1.2
If the main thrust of a review is the mathematical combination of statistics, the review is called a "meta-analysis" or "meta-analytic review."

The prefix "meta-" means *going beyond* or *transcending*. Thus, meta-analysis refers to a statistical analysis that goes beyond or transcends previous statistical analyses. For instance, the author of Example 1.1.1 above used the meta-analytic technique of averaging results across three studies.

The use of meta-analytic techniques (such as averaging means or correlation coefficients across studies) is most likely to be found in quantitatively oriented reviews. There is no reason, however, why the author of a primarily qualitatively oriented review could not occasionally use such a technique to make his or her review more quantitatively oriented than it otherwise would be. Thus, readers who are planning to write qualitatively oriented reviews should carefully study the material on meta-analysis in the last two chapters of this book.

✤ Guideline 1.3
Qualitative and quantitative reviews have many common features.

The authors of both qualitatively oriented and quantitatively oriented reviews have an obligation to cover certain common ground, including the following:

---

[1] The *mean* is the most popular average. Combining statistical results across experiments, as illustrated in Example 1.1.1, is called *meta-analysis*, which is the topic of the last two chapters of this book.

a.   introducing the topic and defining key terms,

b.   establishing the importance of the topic,

c.   providing an overview of the amount of available literature and its types (e.g., theoretical, statistical, speculative),

d.   describing how they searched for relevant literature,

e.   discussing their selection of literature to include in their review (especially if there is much literature on the topic and not all of it could be covered),

f.   pointing out gaps in the literature (i.e., areas that are not covered by the literature),

g.   pointing out consistent findings across studies,

h.   describing and, if possible, reconciling discrepancies in the results of various studies,

i.   arriving at a synthesis that organizes what is known about the topic, and

j.   discussing possible implications and directions for future research.

These and many other important issues in the preparation of both qualitatively oriented and quantitatively oriented literature reviews are covered in the remaining chapters of this book.

✍ Guideline 1.4
Many literature reviews are a blend of qualitatively oriented and quantitatively oriented approaches.

Many literature reviews employ a blend of techniques. That is why the term "oriented" is used throughout this book. It would be difficult to find in print a purely qualitative review (one without even some general references to statistical results) or to find a purely quantitative review (one without a qualitative narrative component that helps readers interpret the statistical aspects of the literature being cited).

✍ Guideline 1.5
Read both qualitatively oriented and quantitatively oriented reviews in preparation for writing a new review.

One of the best ways to learn how to write in any genre is to read many examples of it. Whether students are planning to write a qualitatively oriented or a quantitatively oriented review, they should make a point of reading at least several examples of each very early in the planning stages. A good place to start is to read Model Literature Review 1, which is an example of a qualitatively oriented review. Note that Model Literature Reviews 7 through 9 are examples of meta-analyses, which are highly quantitative reviews. (The model literature reviews are near the end of this book.)

Timeline Considerations

Determine how much time is available before the final draft of your literature review is due, and prepare a *written* timeline. Begin by allocating about one-tenth of your available time to each of the ten steps described near the beginning of this chapter. This will account for 70 percent of your time while keeping 30 percent in reserve in case one of the steps takes longer than anticipated.

Exercise for Chapter 1

1. A classmate asks you to critique the first draft of a literature review she has written for a class assignment. While reading the draft, you realize that the classmate has, for the most part, simply summarized one study after another—each summarized in its own paragraph. Based on the information in this chapter, what advice would you give her?

2. Have you written a literature review in the past? If yes, was it qualitatively or quantitatively oriented? Explain.

3. If you wrote a qualitatively oriented review in the past, did it synthesize literature *or* did it only summarize the literature (e.g., did it present only a series of abstracts)? Explain.

4. Have you selected a preliminary topic for the literature you will be writing? If yes, briefly describe the topic and the reason for your interest in it. (You may want to return to this question and revise your answer after reading the next chapter.)

5. At this point, are you leaning toward preparing a qualitatively *or* quantitatively oriented literature review? Read at least one of the model qualitative literature reviews (Reviews 1, 2, 3, 4, 5, or 6) and one of the highly quantitative meta-analytic reviews (Reviews 7, 8, or 9) near the end of this book before answering this question.

Notes:

Chapter 2

Selecting a Topic for Review

This chapter presents guidelines for making a preliminary selection of a topic to review. After searching for literature (covered in the next chapter), the topic may need to be adjusted depending on the amount of literature available for review. For instance, if there is a very large amount of literature on the preliminary topic, it may need to be narrowed to make it more manageable.

✍ Guideline 2.1
Consider the audience's expectations and/or requirements.

If the primary audience is a professor (or a committee of professors), read carefully any handouts on the literature review assignment, and make careful notes of oral directions that are given. If there is a maximum page length, consider selecting a topic that is narrow enough to permit writing an in-depth review within the page limit.

When writing for possible publication in a journal, study literature reviews in the journals to which the review might be submitted. Often, journals print guidelines for potential authors in each issue.

✍ Guideline 2.2
Consider personal interests.

Reviewers often write reviews on topics of personal interest. While consideration of personal interests is important, make sure that the topic selected is well within the boundaries expected by the audience (such as the professor who will be grading the review).

✍ Guideline 2.3
Examine textbooks for topic ideas.

Content-area textbooks provide overviews of the state of knowledge in academic and professional areas. Most broad topics in textbooks are too broad as the basis for in-depth literature review because there is often too much literature on them. However, many subtopics may provide suitable ideas for topic selection.

✍ Guideline 2.4
Scan titles and abstracts of articles in professional journals.

Scanning the titles of journal articles and their abstracts (i.e., summaries of articles that are usually published near the beginning of articles) in the general area of interest may yield interesting ideas for topics for literature reviews. Many students who have not read professional journals widely have been surprised at the wide variety of interesting topics covered in these journals.

✍ Guideline 2.5
Consider selecting a theory as the topic for a literature review.

In the literature review on any topic, it is desirable to consider and describe any theories that have implications for understanding the topic. In addition, a reviewer might write a review that focuses on a single theory. Such a review might cover issues such as the origins of the theory, the areas in which the theory has been applied, and the extent to which research has validated the theory. Content-area textbooks describe major theories. Less well-known and emerging theories can be identified through a literature search, a possibility that is considered in the next chapter.

For theories on which there has been much research, a reviewer might focus on the application of the theory to a single applied field such as social work or nursing.

♮ Guideline 2.6
Consider reviewing the literature on instrument(s) or assessment procedure(s).

When conducting empirical research, researchers use instruments such as tests, personality scales, questionnaires, and interview schedules. For widely used instruments, there is usually a substantial body of literature, in which researchers explore their validity and reliability.

Suppose, for instance, a researcher is interested in the construct called "anxiety." Instead of reviewing literature on the sources and correlates of anxiety, a reviewer might review the literature on a particular measure of anxiety such as the Beck Anxiety Inventory (BAI), which has been widely used to study anxiety. The review might cover (a) the history of attempts to measure anxiety (and its historical as well as current definitions), (b) the development of the BAI, and (c) the results of studies on the BAI's validity and reliability.

♮ Guideline 2.7
Consider reviewing literature on the effectiveness of a particular program.

Thousands of formal programs have been launched to deliver educational, psychological, and social services. A review of the literature on a particular program might yield valuable insights regarding its effectiveness.

♮ Guideline 2.8
Consider brainstorming a list of possible topics.

The basic premise of brainstorming is to produce ideas uncritically. Brainstorming usually works best when conducted by a small group, so a group of students might be formed for this activity. Group members generate ideas (often in response to ideas suggested by others in a back-and-forth oral dialogue) without criticizing each other's ideas since criticism can inhibit spontaneity and creativity.

At some later point, of course, a reviewer will need to critically evaluate the ideas generated by a brainstorming session in order to select an appropriate topic for review. Sometimes, combining various ideas generated during brainstorming will produce a useful topic.

♮ Guideline 2.9
Consider narrowing a broad topic by adding delimitations.

A delimitation is a restriction on a topic. For instance, a broad topic such as "compliance with physicians' directions by patients" could be delimited in a number of ways. Examples 2.9.1 through 2.9.4 show some possibilities. Note that by adding delimitations, a reviewer is making a topic more narrow. Avoid the temptation to add so many delimitations that the topic becomes too narrow.

Example 2.9.1
Sample topic delimited by age of patients:
Compliance with physicians' directions by elderly patients.

Example 2.9.2

Sample topic delimited by type of compliance:

Compliance with physicians' directions regarding medications.

Example 2.9.3

Sample topic delimited by type of disease:

Compliance with physicians' directions by patients with diabetes.

Example 2.9.4

Sample topic with two delimitations (type of compliance and type of disease):

Compliance with physicians' directions regarding medications by patients with diabetes.

A common way to delimit a topic is to restrict it by using one or more demographic variables. A demographic variable is a background variable with two or more categories. By selecting one or more of the categories and using them as delimitations, a topic can be narrowed.

The first column in Box 2A shows some demographic variables widely examined in research. The second column gives samples of categories that might be used when delimiting a topic. The first demographic variable in the box is "age"; its use was illustrated in Example 2.9.1 above. The second one is "education, classification." For instance, a topic might be delimited to children who have been classified as "gifted."

Box 2A *Sample demographic variables and categories.*

Sample demographic variables for delimiting topics:	Sample categories that might be used to delimit topics:
age	elderly
education, classification	gifted
education, highest level of	college graduate
education, type of	vocational
employment, length of	newly hired
employment status	employed part-time
ethnicity/race	Caucasian
extracurricular activities	competitive sports
gender	male
group membership	union member
health, mental disorder	depression
health, overall status	poor health
health, physical disease	diabetes
household composition	intact family with children
income, household	$20,000 to $35,000
income, personal	high income
language preference	Spanish
marital status	divorced
nationality, current	Canadian
national origin	Mexico
occupation	nurse
place of birth	Korea
political activism	votes regularly
political affiliation	Independent
relationship status	divorced
religion, affiliation	Greek Orthodox *Continued* →

residence, place of	New York City metropolitan area
residence, type of	homeless
sexual orientation	heterosexual
size of city/town/area	large urban area
socioeconomic status (SES)	middle SES

✍ Guideline 2.10
Select a topic with an eye toward future goals and activities.

For college students, the most common future goals and activities are their career aspirations and their plans for future academic pursuits. When applying for admission to an advanced degree program, a student may be asked to provide a writing sample. If the literature review is on a topic related to the program, it might be an excellent sample to submit.

✍ Guideline 2.11
Put possible topics in writing.

Initial topic ideas might be expressed as short phrases, sentences, or paragraphs, which should be put in writing. It is often helpful to put the written topic ideas away for a day or two and then reconsider them.

Presenting written topic ideas to a professor will help avoid miscommunication regarding the suitability of a topic for a literature review written as a term project. The feedback a professor (or a committee of professors) provides on topic ideas may assist greatly in refining them.

Concluding Comments

The next two chapters deal with searching for literature on a topic. Be prepared to refine and modify the initial topic idea in light of the available literature. If there is too little literature on a topic, it may need to be broadened; if there is too much, it may need to be narrowed.

Exercise for Chapter 2

1. If your audience is your professor (or a committee of professors), have they described their expectations regarding topic selection? Write down any questions about expectations that you want to ask at the next class meeting. (See Guideline 2.1.)

2. Write very brief descriptions of at least two preliminary topic ideas in which you have a personal interest. (See Guideline 2.2.)

3. Evaluate each idea you wrote down for Question 1 on a scale from 5 (highly appropriate for the intended audience that will be reading your review) to 1 (highly inappropriate).

4. Have you examined any textbooks for possible topic ideas? If yes, did this help you identify possible topics? Explain. (See Guideline 2.3.)

5. Have you scanned titles and abstracts in professional journals for topic ideas? If yes, did this help you identify possible topics? Explain. (See Guideline 2.4.)

6. At this point, are you interested in reviewing the literature on a theory? Explain. (See Guideline 2.5.)

7. At this point, are you interested in reviewing the literature on instrument(s) or assessment procedure(s)? Explain. (See Guideline 2.6.)

8. At this point, are you interested in reviewing the literature on the evaluations of a program? Explain. (See Guideline 2.7.)

9. Have you brainstormed topic ideas with other students? If yes, was brainstorming useful? Explain. (See Guideline 2.8.)

10. Name a broad topic in which you are interested. Delimit it by using one category of one of the sample demographic variables in Box 2A in this chapter. (See Guideline 2.9.)

11. Can you think of demographic variables that are not included in Box 2A but which might be important in your field? If so, name them. (See Guideline 2.9.)

12. Do you have any specific future goals and/or activities that might influence your selection of a topic? If so, describe them. (See Guideline 2.10.)

13. Have you put your initial topic ideas in writing? If yes, have you shared them with your professor? (See Guideline 2.11.)

Notes:

Chapter 3

Searching for Literature in Professional Journals

The processes of searching for literature and refining a topic idea are intertwined because the amount of literature found on a topic will determine whether it needs to be broadened (to find more literature) or to be narrowed (to retrieve less literature). In addition, as the literature on a topic is examined, related topics that are of even greater interest than the original topic may be identified.

The use of databases designed to assist in locating academic literature, such as professional journals, is described below.

PsycARTICLES and *PsycINFO*

Some of the examples in this chapter are from the *PsycARTICLES* database, which is published electronically by the American Psychological Association (APA). At the time of this writing, it contains more than 25,000 searchable full-text articles (i.e., the complete articles, not just summaries) from 42 journals published by APA and allied organizations. APA also publishes *PsycINFO*, which contains abstracts (i.e., summaries) of more than 1.5 million references to both APA and non-APA journal articles and books.

Access to these databases is free of charge to students through most college and university libraries.

ERIC

Some of the examples in this chapter are from the *ERIC* database, which is published electronically by the Educational Resources Information Center. At the time of this writing, it contains references to more than one million records that provide citations for journal articles, books, conference papers, and so on.

ERIC defines "education" in its broadest sense (i.e., *not* as a field devoted only to classroom and curriculum issues). For instance, a sociology student interested in reviewing literature on the homeless could do a "simple search" (with no restrictions to the search) in *ERIC*, which, at the time of this writing, retrieved references to 1,682 documents on the homeless. Restricted to only journal articles (i.e., a "restricted search," not a "simple search"), references to 736 journal articles were retrieved.[1]

Access to the *ERIC* system is free to all Internet users. Its home page can be accessed by visiting www.eric.ed.gov, where there is information about its services, history, and how to conduct effective searches for relevant literature.

Other Databases

Other major databases include *Sociological Abstracts* (formerly *SocioFile*), *Linguistics and Language Behavior Abstracts*, *Social Work Abstracts*, *Business Source Plus*, *Health Source Plus*, as well as *MEDLINE/PubMed*. Most college and university libraries maintain subscriptions to the online versions of these databases. In addition, there are highly specialized databases (not

---

[1] To restrict a search to only journal articles, click on "Advanced Search" on the home page. Then click on the box to the left of "Journal Articles."

listed here). These can be identified through library handouts and/or consultation with a reference librarian.

ꙮ Guideline 3.1
Use the database's Thesaurus to identify appropriate descriptors (search terms).

If the database has a thesaurus of keywords on which it is structured, search the thesaurus for relevant terms to use in a search. For instance, in the *ERIC* database, the Thesaurus can be accessed by clicking on the Thesaurus tab at the top of the home page.

A thesaurus can be useful in identifying search terms (known as "descriptors") that will produce the most fruitful search. For instance, entering the term "problem drinking" in the Thesaurus (and clicking through the links on the screen) results in the identification of "alcohol abuse" as the appropriate descriptor. Going back to the home page and conducting a search using "alcohol abuse" yields 4,740 references, while the less appropriate term "problem drinking" results in a less comprehensive search, yielding only 552 references.[2]

Note that the *ERIC* Thesaurus suggests related terms, broader terms, and narrower terms, which may help in pinpointing a literature search.

ꙮ Guideline 3.2
Use the Boolean operators NOT, AND, and OR.

By using the Boolean logical operators (NOT, AND, and OR), a reviewer can broaden or narrow a search.[3] For instance, consider the results of four searches shown in Example 3.2.1, which were conducted in the *PsycARTICLES* database. The example makes it clear that the operators NOT as well as AND *reduce* the number of references found while OR *increases* the number.

Example 3.2.1
Number of journal articles identified using NOT, AND, and OR:

Term entered in database restricted to the years 2000 to the year this was written:	Number of journal articles identified:
depression	5,977
depression NOT treatment	1,909
depression AND treatment	4,070
depression OR treatment	10,609

Boolean operators can also be used to delimit a search to selected demographics. (See Guideline 2.9 in Chapter 2.) For instance, searching only for "anxiety" in the *ERIC* database yields 7,656 references. Searching for "anxiety" AND "children" yields 1,491 references.

ꙮ Guideline 3.3
Consider using truncated terms.

Using truncated terms in an electronic search can increase the number of references retrieved.

---

[2] Searching for "problem drinking" yields only those references in which both words appear in close proximity. In contrast, searching for the *ERIC* descriptor "alcohol abuse" locates all sources that discuss the issue, regardless of whether the descriptor is used by the authors.
[3] To access the Boolean operators in *ERIC*, first click on "Advanced Search" on the home page. In APA databases, first click on "Fielded Search."

In *PsycARTICLES*, a term can be truncated by using an asterisk. For instance, a search for the truncated term "Mexic*" yields all references that contain words that start with the letters "mexic," such as Mexico, Mexican, and Mexicans. This broadens a search. For instance, searching *PsycARTICLES* using the term "Mexico" (without truncation) yields 107 journal articles, while using the truncated term retrieves 168 articles.

♭ Guideline 3.4
Consider restricting the search to the title field.

When too many references are retrieved, restricting a search to the titles (in the advanced search mode in *ERIC* or the fielded search mode in APA) can greatly reduce the number. For instance, in *ERIC*, searching for the term "anxiety" (without a restriction) yields 9,916 references. With the restriction that the term "anxiety" must appear in the title yields a much smaller 2,535 references.[4]

While this technique may delete some useful references, it yields only references that were sufficiently focused on anxiety (as opposed to being used as an incidental term) that the authors chose to include the term "anxiety" in the titles.

♭ Guideline 3.5
Search for theoretical literature.

Because the development and testing of theories is a major activity in the social and behavioral sciences, it is desirable to discuss relevant theories in literature reviews on most topics. Theoretical literature can be located by searching for a topic term AND the term "theory" (with AND as a Boolean operator; see Guideline 3.2). For instance, for the topic term "aging," *PsycARTICLES* yields 1,226 references. Searching for "aging" AND "theory" yields 321 references, which are the ones most likely to contain a discussion of theories that relate to aging.

Guideline 2.5 in Chapter 2 suggests the possibility of writing a review on a theory. Entering the name of a theory as a search term will usually yield references on that particular theory. For instance, a *PsycARTICLES* search using the term "social learning theory" yields 1,949 references for the past three years.[5]

♭ Guideline 3.6
Consider searching for the works of a particular author.

Many prolific researchers conduct research on a selected topic over a period of decades. This results from the fact that the insights on a topic gained from one study often lead to the development of new hypotheses on the same topic that the same researchers investigate in subsequent studies. To locate the literature authored by such a researcher (and trace the history of that author's work on the topic), restrict a search to the author field (i.e., from the drop-down menu in the advanced search mode of *ERIC*, select "author" and type in the author's name). For instance, Albert Bandura has conducted research on self-efficacy for many years. By selecting the "author" field from the drop-down menu in *ERIC* and typing in "Bandura" coupled with "self-efficacy" (using AND as a Boolean operator; see Guideline 3.2), seven journal articles that Bandura authored or coauthored on self-efficacy from 1977 through 2005 are identified.

---

[4] In some databases, a search can also be restricted to the abstracts (i.e., summaries) of literature.
[5] The past three years is the default in the fielded search mode of *PsycARTICLES*.

⅋ **Guideline 3.7**
Consider searching a citation index.

Using some of the suggestions for searching literature described above, suppose a reviewer found a pivotal journal article by Smith that was published several years ago. By using a citation index, the reviewer can identify other literature in which Smith's article has since been cited. This literature might provide alternative perspectives on Smith's article written by other writers; some might critique it, others might report successful and unsuccessful attempts to replicate Smith's research, while still others might provide evidence for and against Smith's theory, and so on. Obviously, there is great potential for obtaining valuable references by using a citation index.

Most academic libraries maintain subscriptions to major citation indices such as the *Social Science Citation Index*, the *Science Citation Index*, and the *Arts and Humanities Citation Index*. These can be searched electronically at libraries that maintain subscriptions to them.

⅋ **Guideline 3.8**
Examine the references cited in the literature that has been located.

Research articles typically begin with literature reviews. Examine the literature citations in the articles for references that may not have been located in other ways.

⅋ **Guideline 3.9**
Maintain a written record of how the literature search was conducted.

Suppose a reviewer reaches the conclusion that "few experimental studies have been published on the XYZ phenomenon" and includes the conclusion in a literature review. Such a statement might be challenged by a professor who is familiar with relevant experimental studies that the reviewer failed to locate. By being able to state specifically which databases were searched *and* how they were searched, the reviewer can deflect criticism that he or she had been careless in conducting the search.[6]

Exercise for Chapter 3

Directions: Answer the following questions after you search a database. Note that if you are completing this exercise at home without access to a database subscribed to by a college library, search *ERIC* (www.eric.gov), which is available free of charge to all Internet users.

1. Which database did you use for this exercise?

2. Did you consult the database's Thesaurus? If yes, was it useful? Explain. (See Guideline 3.1.)

3. Did you use Boolean operators when searching? If yes, which ones were used? Were they useful? Explain. (See Guideline 3.2.)

4. Did you search using truncated terms? If yes, were the truncated terms useful? Explain. (See Guideline 3.3.)

---

[6] Reviewers who prepare highly quantitative literature reviews known as "meta-analyses" are expected to describe in their reviews how they searched for relevant literature. This is discussed in the last two chapters of this book.

5. Did you conduct a search while restricting the search to the title field? If yes, was it useful? Explain. (See Guideline 3.4.)

6. Did you search for theoretical literature? If yes, did you find useful references? Explain. (See Guideline 3.5.)

7. Did you search for the works of a particular author? If yes, was relevant literature identified? Explain. (See Guideline 3.6.)

8. Did you search a citation index? If yes, was it useful? Explain. (See Guideline 3.7.)

9. Did you examine the references cited in the literature you located? If yes, did this help you identify additional useful literature? Explain. (See Guideline 3.8.)

10. Did you maintain a written record of how the search was conducted? Why? Why not? (See Guideline 3.9.)

Notes:

Chapter 4

Retrieving and Evaluating Information from the Web

The focus in the previous chapter was on electronic databases designed to help users access academic literature—especially articles published in professional journals. This chapter focuses on using more general Web sources for retrieving information that might be included in a literature review.

✋ Guideline 4.1
Web sources are often more up-to-date than professional journals.

When writing literature reviews, writers often need up-to-date information. Because of the ease of electronic publishing, the Web is more likely to have such information than conventionally printed materials. Note that it is not uncommon for a printed journal article or book to be published a year or more after it was written. Despite this delay, professional journals are usually the primary sources of detailed information on how investigators conducted their research, so they remain premier sources of information for literature reviews.

✋ Guideline 4.2
Information on current issues can often be found using general search engines.

A general search engine such as www.Google.com can be used to locate information that might be included in a literature review. Consider the topic of smoking during pregnancy. A quick search using the search term "women smoking pregnancy" retrieved 4,210,000 sites with related information. The fourth site in the list, maintained by the March of Dimes, contains the information shown in Example 4.2.1.

Example 4.2.1
Sample topic delimited by age of patients:

In the United States more than 20 percent of women smoke. According to the World Health Organization, a similar number of women in other developed countries smoke, and about 9 percent of women in developing countries smoke. Many of these women smoke while they are pregnant. This is a major public health problem because, not only can smoking harm a woman's health, but smoking during pregnancy can lead to pregnancy complications and serious health problems in newborns.[1]

✋ Guideline 4.3
FedStats.gov is an important source of statistical information.

Often, literature reviews begin with current statistics on how many people (and/or the percentage of people) are affected by the topic of the literature review, and up-to-date statistics are often available at www.FedStats.gov.

---

[1] Retrieved from http://www.marchofdimes.com/professionals/14332_1171.asp on January 2, 2007.

Statistics from more than 100 federal agencies can be accessed at www.FedStats.gov.[2] Prior to establishment of this Web site, individuals needed to search for statistics agency-by-agency. While the FedStats site still allows users to do this, they can also search by *topic* and the FedStats search engine will automatically search all agencies for relevant links to federal statistics. This is important for two reasons: (1) A user does not have to search each agency separately, and (2) an agency that a user is not aware of may have statistics relevant to his or her topic.

For example, conducting a search by first clicking on <u>Topic links – A to Z</u> produces an alphabetical list of topics. Box 4A shows the topics under the letter C.

Box 4A *FedStats links for the letter C.*

Cancer:
-- *Atlas of Cancer Mortality in the United States*
-- Breast
-- Cervical
-- Lung
-- Mortality maps
-- Prostate
Charitable trusts
Children:
-- Administration for Children programs and services
-- Adoption
-- *America's Children* (ChildStats)
-- Behavior and social environment indicators
-- Child care
-- Child support enforcement
-- Cigarette smoking
-- Delinquency and victimization
-- Delinquency case records (data and analysis software package)
-- Juvenile arrests
-- Juveniles as offenders
-- Juveniles as victims
-- Juveniles in court
-- Juveniles in detention and corrections
-- Drug use
-- Economic security indicators
-- Education indicators
-- Foster care
-- HeadStart
-- Temporary Assistance for Needy Families
Health:
-- Child and infant
-- Indicators
-- Insurance
-- Population and family characteristics
-- Nutrition
-- WIC
Civil justice statistics
Coal
Commodity flow
Common cold
Communications:
-- Broadcast radio and television
-- Cable television providers by community served (size 9M)
-- Telephone industry and telephone usage
-- Wireless communications services
Computer and Internet use
Construction
Industry tax statistics:
-- Corporations
-- Exempt organizations' unrelated business
-- Partnerships
-- Sole proprietorship
Consumer Credit
Consumer product safety
Consumer Price Indexes
Consumption, energy
Corporations
Country profiles
Crime (See also *Law enforcement*):
-- Characteristics of crime
-- Children
-- Crime in schools
-- Crimes reported to the police
-- Criminal offenders
-- Drugs
-- Firearms
-- Hate
-- Homicide
-- Prison inmates
-- Terrorism
-- Victims
-- Violent
Criminal justice:
-- Corrections
-- Capital punishment
-- Inmates
-- Jails
-- Prisons
-- Probation and parole statistics
-- Courts and sentencing
-- Court organization
-- Criminal case processing
-- Pretrial release and detention
-- Sentencing
-- Criminal record systems
Continued →

---

[2] Be sure to go to www.FedStats.*gov* and *not* www.FedStats.*com*. The latter is *not* a government site.

-- Employment and expenditure	**Crops:**
-- Federal justice statistics	-- Crop progress and weather, weekly
-- Indigent defense statistics	-- Data by county
-- Law enforcement	-- Data by state, historic
-- Campus law enforcement	-- Field
-- Federal law enforcement	-- Fruits and nuts
-- State and local law enforcement	-- Vegetables
-- Prosecution	

Clicking on the "Foster care" link under "Children" produces hundreds of statistics, including the sample in Box 4B. This sample illustrates the level of detail typical in the federal government's databases.

Box 4B *A sample of the large number of statistics on "Foster care" at www.FedStats.gov.*

What was the race/ethnicity of the children who entered care during FY 2005?			What were the outcomes for the children exiting foster care during FY 2005?		
AI/AN–Non-Hispanic	2%	7,036	Reunification with Parent(s) or Primary Caretaker(s)	54%	155,608
Asian–Non-Hispanic	1%	2,454	Living with Other Relative(s)	11%	31,362
Black–Non-Hispanic	26%	80,430	Adoption	18%	51,323
Hawaiian/PI–Non-Hispanic	0%	1,031	Emancipation	9%	24,407
Hispanic	18%	56,603	Guardianship	4%	12,881
White–Non-Hispanic	47%	144,679	Transfer to Another Agency	2%	6,440
Unknown/Unable to Determine	3%	8,126	Runaway	2%	4,445
Two or More–Non-Hispanic	3%	10,642	Death of Child	0%	534

✍ Guideline 4.4

State government Web sites are a source of local statistics.

The main Web pages for various states can be accessed by using the postal service's state names abbreviations in URL addresses such as www.ga.gov (for Georgia) and www.ca.gov (for California). While the organization of the home pages varies greatly from state to state, they contain links that can lead to a variety of statistical information, which can be useful when local statistics are needed for a literature review.

In addition, there are links to descriptions of a variety of government-funded programs. This information can be valuable for individuals who are reviewing literature on programs, a possibility suggested in Guideline 2.7 in Chapter 2.

✍ Guideline 4.5

Use the raw statistics from governmental agencies, not statistics filtered by special interests.

Some individuals (such as politicians) and groups (such as advocacy groups) with special interests may understandably be selective in choosing which government statistics to report and interpret on their Web sites. Hence, it is usually best to obtain the original government reports either in print or via the Web.

✍ Guideline 4.6

Consider consulting the Library of Congress's Virtual Reference Shelf on the Web.

The Library of Congress maintains a Web site titled the Virtual Reference Shelf. It is an excellent site for general references such as dictionaries, general history, abbreviations, genealogy, and so on. It can be found at www.loc.gov/rr/askalib/virtualref.html.[3] Box 4C shows the main links on the home page of the site.

As an example, a reviewer might click on "Education," and then on "Education Reference Desk." Then, clicking on "School Safety" (a link under Educational Management), links to 25 Internet sites that deal with school safety and violence are provided. Some of these links are to important reports on the topic such as the report titled School Survey on Crime and Safety, which is based on a nationally representative sample of 3,000 public schools. Other links are to groups and organizations such as the National School Safety Center. In addition, one link is to PAVNET, which is an online library of information about violence and youth-at-risk, representing data from seven different federal agencies.

Box 4C *Links on the home page of the Library of Congress's Virtual Reference Shelf.*

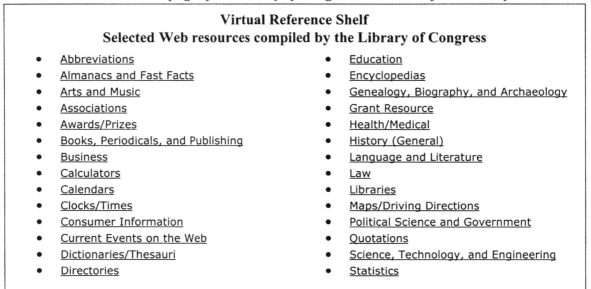

Virtual Reference Shelf
Selected Web resources compiled by the Library of Congress

- Abbreviations
- Almanacs and Fast Facts
- Arts and Music
- Associations
- Awards/Prizes
- Books, Periodicals, and Publishing
- Business
- Calculators
- Calendars
- Clocks/Times
- Consumer Information
- Current Events on the Web
- Dictionaries/Thesauri
- Directories

- Education
- Encyclopedias
- Genealogy, Biography, and Archaeology
- Grant Resource
- Health/Medical
- History (General)
- Language and Literature
- Law
- Libraries
- Maps/Driving Directions
- Political Science and Government
- Quotations
- Science, Technology, and Engineering
- Statistics

Library of Congress Research Tools

Internet Public Library Reference Center * Other Reference Sites * In the News

✎ **Guideline 4.7**
Consider accessing information posted on the Web by professional associations.

A wide variety of associations post information (and statistics) on the Web. While reviewers may already be familiar with the major organizations in their respective fields, there are many specialized organizations that deal with specialized issues.

To identify specialized associations, following the link called "Associations" in the Virtual Reference Shelf (see the fourth link in Box 4C) can be useful. For instance, within the field of education, links to these associations can be found: Association for Childhood Education International, National Association for the Education of Young Children, and the National Head Start Association.

In addition to posting information and statistics on the Web, associations post position papers on a variety of contemporary issues relating to their fields. The positions taken by such associations might be cited in literature reviews.

---

[3] Rather than typing (and risk mistyping) long URLs, it is sometimes faster to do a quick search on a major search engine such as www.Google.com using a term such as "Virtual Reference Shelf." Use the quotation marks around the terms (e.g., "Virtual Reference Shelf") to conduct an exact phrase match.

✎ Guideline 4.8
Pay attention to the extension (gov, edu, org, com, and net) in the results of Web searches.

When a Web search using an engine such as Google.com yields hundreds or thousands of links, paying attention to the extensions such as "com" (for commercial), "gov" (for government), and "edu" (for education) can help in selecting the most promising links to visit. As a general rule, sites with "gov" and "edu" are more likely to be nonpartisan and noncommercial than other Web sites.

✎ Guideline 4.9
Consider clicking on "cached" when opening a Web site from a search engine.

When the option is available (such as in Google), it is usually more desirable to click on "cached" near the end of the description of the link than to click on the main link for a Web site. By clicking on "cached," the words used in the search will be highlighted in different colors from the other words at the Web site, making it easier to locate information on the topic(s) of interest within a Web site, especially if much material is presented at the site.

✎ Guideline 4.10
After finding a useful Web site, consider following the links that it provides.

Following this guideline may be more efficient in locating relevant materials than a general search using a search engine such as Google.

Concluding Comments

The mercurial nature of the Web is the source of both a major strength and a major weakness. The strength is that its quick "changeability" allows individuals and organizations to promptly post current information. Prior to development of the Web, the dissemination of information often had a publication lag of up to a year (or sometimes more) in traditional, hard-copy publishing. A major weakness of publishing on the Web is that almost anyone can post information (whether it is correct or not) without the editorial scrutiny that the material would typically undergo if it were being published in hard copy.

As the Web becomes an increasingly important source of information for those who review literature, it is important to establish criteria to consider when evaluating a Web-based source of information. In developing criteria, some of the considerations are:

1. Who sponsors the Web site in question? A government agency? A professional association? An advocacy group? A for-profit corporation?

2. Does the Web site present primary source material (i.e., original) or just secondary source material?

3. If secondary material provides the "factual" underpinnings of the content of a Web site, is the material analyzed thoughtfully and logically, hence, making an original contribution by presenting original interpretation(s)?

4. Does the Web site indicate when it was published on the Web and/or when it was last updated?

5. Are complete references to cited material given?

6. Does traditional, hard-copy literature that is more thorough and complete than the material published on a Web site exist? (For instance, does the Web site contain only summaries of more extensive hard-copy publications?)

7. Is the purpose of the site merely to persuade readers to take a position (such as a political position or a position that is favorable to a commercial product) rather than to provide information and well-rounded, logical interpretations?

Exercise for Chapter 4

1. Go to www.FedStats.gov and look up the topic on which you will be writing a review. Make notes on how you conducted the search. Write down a few relevant statistics, if any, that you found. (See Guideline 4.3.)

2. Look up the main Web site for the state government where you live. Explore the site. Does it contain any information on a topic that you will be reviewing? Explain. (See Guideline 4.4.)

3. Examine the Library of Congress's Virtual Reference Shelf. Explore it to see if it contains information relevant to the topic of your review. Describe your findings here. (See Guideline 4.6.)

4. Did you locate any professional associations that have posted material relevant to the topic of your review? If yes, briefly describe what you found. (See Guideline 4.7.)

5. Overall, how useful was the Web for locating information that might be used in your literature review?

Chapter 5

Evaluating and Interpreting Research Literature

This chapter covers some of the major issues in evaluating and interpreting research literature published in professional journals. It is designed for students who have not had formal training in research methods but who will need to review such material.

Readers who have taken a research methods course will already be aware of much of the material in this chapter. For these students, the guidelines will serve as a means of review of major concepts.

✆ Guideline 5.1
Be wary of sources offering "proof," "facts," and "truth" based on research.

There are certain "proofs" in mathematics and other fields that rely on deduction. Stated simply, scholars start with assumptions and derive a solution that must be true if the assumptions are correct. Also, there are everyday "facts" that all individuals can probably agree on as being true. For instance, all people who even briefly look into the matter would agree with the "fact" that more voters in California are registered as Democrats than are registered as Republicans.

However, when studying complex human behavior, researchers almost always have at least some degree of uncertainty regarding their findings for reasons explored later in this chapter. In the face of this inherent uncertainty associated with research, consumers of research should strive to arrive at defensible conclusions regarding what seems most likely to be true *based on the whole body of research on a topic*. It is worthy of note that a major purpose of literature reviews is to make sense of a body of research.

✆ Guideline 5.2
Distinguish between quantitative and qualitative research.

On the surface, *quantitative research* can be easily distinguished from qualitative research in terms of their results. In quantitative research, the results are presented as quantities or numbers (that is, statistics), while in *qualitative research*, the results are trends and themes that are described in words.

More important, quantitative researchers emphasize the generalizability of their research. They strive to use large, representative samples from which generalizations can be made regarding population parameters. They favor instruments (such as questionnaires, attitude scales, and achievement tests) that have questions with choices, which can be easily administered to large samples.

In contrast, qualitative researchers emphasize the collection of in-depth information obtained from small samples without regard to generalizability to a population. The in-depth information is frequently collected through extensive one-on-one interviews with participants.

The distinction between quantitative and qualitative research has implications for evaluating research, which are explored in some of the guidelines in this chapter. Appendix A provides more information on the distinction between the two types of research, while Appendix B provides more information relevant for evaluating qualitative research.

✎ Guideline 5.3
Quantitative researchers prefer unbiased samples.

An unbiased sample is the best way to obtain data that can be generalized to a population with a high degree of confidence. To obtain an unbiased sample, all members of a population must be identified, and then each member must be given an equal chance of being selected. This is accomplished by random sampling (such as drawing names out of a hat).

Unfortunately, many researchers work with populations whose members cannot be completely identified (e.g., the homeless). Even with populations whose members can be identified (e.g., all fifth graders in a school district), researchers may not have administrative access to the entire population. In addition, even if all are administratively accessible, some individuals often refuse to participate, creating a bias.

Despite these problems, the work of quantitative researchers who use random sampling to the extent possible should be given higher evaluations than the work of quantitative researchers who use whatever individuals happen to be readily available (e.g., a professor using the members of her class). Using research participants for this reason is called "convenience sampling." Making generalizations from convenience sampling should be done with considerable caution.

✎ Guideline 5.4
Qualitative researchers prefer purposive samples.

Since qualitative researchers do not strive to make generalizations to populations, they seldom attempt to employ random sampling. Instead, they strive for "purposive samples." Individuals for such a sample are purposively selected because they are likely to be especially good sources of information. Criteria should be established for their selection (e.g., a racially diverse sample of experienced and inexperienced teachers in an urban school setting for a study of racial tensions among faculty in the setting).

Like quantitative researchers, qualitative researchers often must study only those individuals who happen to be readily available to them (i.e., they study samples of convenience). As with quantitative research, results based on such samples should be viewed with caution.

✎ Guideline 5.5
Be cautious when a body of literature has a common sampling flaw.

It is not unusual to find an entire body of research literature on a topic that has a common sampling flaw. For instance, most research in the social and behavioral sciences is conducted by professors who often have limited resources. As a result, a large proportion of studies are conducted with college/university students who volunteer to participate. This provides no knowledge of how nonvolunteers would respond, or how individuals who are not college students would respond.

When there is a common sampling flaw in all (or most) of the studies being reviewed on a particular topic, this should be pointed out in the literature review as a weakness in the body of the research as a whole.

✎ Guideline 5.6
There is no single, perfect way to measure most traits.

Measures (often called "instrumentation") in research reports vary greatly from highly structured (such as multiple-choice achievement tests or personality scales) to highly unstructured (such as loosely structured, free-flowing interviews). While some measures of a given trait may be better than other measures, none should be presumed to be perfect.

Consider this example: A researcher is planning a study on the incidence of driving under the influence (DUI) of alcohol. Box 5A lists some measurement approaches that might be used. Note that each has drawbacks that might potentially flaw the results of the study.

Box 5A *Approaches to measurement in a study on DUI.*

Approach	Potential Drawback
Questionnaire with objective-type items asking about DUI behavior	Respondents might not be willing to admit to the behavior and may give socially desirable responses even if responses are anonymous.
	Respondents might interpret "under the influence" in various ways. The questionnaire might provide a definition, which would help reduce the problem.
Brief structured interviews	Same drawbacks as the first approach except that responses will not be anonymous, increasing the possibility of failing to admit to DUI behavior.
In-depth interviews	If rapport is established, respondents might be more likely to admit to DUI behavior.
	Subjectivity required to interpret and summarize results across a group of respondents may lead to errors in analysis.
Direct observation	Participants might behave differently if they know they are being observed (such as when leaving a bar).
	The sample of observations will probably be limited (e.g., researchers cannot follow subjects everywhere; subjects might drink in private).
Questioning significant others	They might be unwilling to "squeal" on their significant others.
	They might not be with the subjects at appropriate times (e.g., parents not going out with the adolescents on their dates).
Examining criminal records available to the public	Would yield information on *only* those who were driving under the influence *and* were stopped by police *and* were charged *and* convicted.

ᛌ Guideline 5.7
Give high evaluations to studies that use multiple measures of key variables.

Other things being equal, reviewers can have more confidence in consistent results that are obtained by using two or more measures. For instance, a researcher might use two or more of the types of measures listed in Box 5A above to measure DUI behavior.

This guideline applies to both quantitative and qualitative research.

ᛌ Guideline 5.8
Be cautious when a body of literature has a common measurement flaw.

It is not unusual to find an entire body of research literature on a topic that has a common measurement flaw. For instance, using self-reports on socially undesirable behaviors can lead to underreporting of the behaviors. If the literature on a particular type of undesirable behavior relies only on self-reports, the body of literature may contain underreporting of the behavior.

When there is a common measurement flaw in all (or most) of the studies being reviewed on a particular topic, this should be pointed out in the literature review as a weakness in the body of the research as a whole.

⬦ Guideline 5.9
Consider the reliability of measures used in research.

Reliability refers to the consistency of results. For instance, if an algebra test is administered twice to the same individuals, a reliable algebra test will provide consistent results (e.g., the individual who has the highest score the first time has the highest score the second time; the individual who has the second highest score the first time has the second highest score the second time; and so on).

Qualitatively oriented researchers often report the extent to which two or more independent individuals identified the same themes when analyzing participants' responses to loosely structured interviews. This indicates the consistency of the interpretations by two or more individuals. The level of agreement is sometimes expressed as a percentage (e.g., 95% agreement). More often, qualitative researchers simply state that agreement was reached, as illustrated in Example 5.9.1.

Example 5.9.1
Qualitative researchers' description of their agreement in interpreting data:
Each coder independently analyzed all interviews first; then, the two compared coding with each other. Disagreement was found in very few cases, but consensus was easily reached as [the coders] discussed their rationales for the coding.[1]

Other things being equal, give high evaluations to qualitative studies in which the rate of agreement among independent coders is high.

Quantitatively oriented researchers (who tend to use objectively scored measures) often report on reliability using correlation coefficients (ranging from 0.00 for no reliability to 1.00 for perfect reliability).[2] Often, reliabilities range from about 0.65 to 0.85, indicating moderate to high reliability. Note that in their research articles, quantitative researchers often address validity of the measures used in their research, which is illustrated in Example 5.9.2.

Example 5.9.2
Quantitative researchers' description of the reliability of a measure used in their research:
Consistent with this previous research, the SREIS [Self-Rated Emotional Intelligence Scale] had acceptable reliability (α = .84) in the present study, as did each of the subscales (α's > .70).[3]

Other things being equal, give high evaluations to quantitative studies in which the reliability of the measures has been established and is at acceptable levels such as .65 or higher.

⬦ Guideline 5.10
Consider the validity of measures used in quantitative research.

Validity refers to the extent to which an instrument measures what it is supposed to measure. While it is beyond the scope of this book to explore the many approaches and controversies concerning how to estimate the validity of a measure, note that quantitative researchers often ad-

---

[1] Veith, Sherman, Pellino, & Yasui (2006, p. 291).
[2] Quantitative researchers often report coefficient alpha (α), which is a special type of correlation coefficient, to indicate "reliability." It indicates the extent to which the individual items in a measure yield similar results, that is, yield results that are consistent with each other. (This is loosely analogous to reporting the extent to which researchers in qualitative studies agree with each other.)
[3] Dunn, Brackett, Ashton-James, Schneiderman, & Salovey (2007, p. 88).

dress the issue of the validity of the measures used in their research, which is illustrated in Example 5.10.1.

Example 5.10.1

Researchers' description of the validity of a measure used in their research:

The Marital Adjustment Test (MAT; Locke & Wallace, 1959) is a widely used measure of relationship adjustment with acceptable validity as well as the ability to discriminate between distressed and nondistressed couples (Crane, Allgood, Larson, & Griffin, 1990).[4]

As in the example above, researchers' descriptions of validity are usually quite brief and often contain references where additional information can be obtained.

Other things being equal, give high evaluations to quantitative studies in which the issue of the validity of the measures is satisfactorily addressed.

✎ Guideline 5.11

Consider the care with which the interview protocols were developed.

Most qualitative researchers use semi-structured or open-ended interviews. While the validity of such measures cannot be estimated statistically, the care with which the interviews were planned and executed can be judged from their descriptions. Example 5.11.1 shows the level of detail that might be expected in such a description in a report on qualitative research.

Example 5.11.1

Researchers' description of the validity of a measure used in their research:

We designed a semistructured interview protocol. In the development of the protocol, all interviewers conducted a pilot interview to examine the content and clarity of the questions and to provide interviewers with an opportunity to become comfortable with the protocol. The feedback obtained from these pilot interviews was used to modify the protocol questions. The final protocol contained a standard set of questions, and interviewers used additional probes to clarify information or encourage participants to expand their answers. The protocol contained four sections, and the interview was conducted over the course of two sessions. The opening section of the interview focused on participants' overall experiences with cultural issues in supervision. The second and third sections of the interview explored participants' specific experiences with culturally responsive and unresponsive supervision with a culturally different supervisor. Here, participants of color were asked to focus on events that occurred with European American supervisors, and European American participants were asked to focus on events that occurred with supervisors of color. For each of these incidents, we asked participants to discuss events that had personal meaning and that had significance to their training experiences as a counselor. Within these sections, we also asked about the quality of the supervision relationship prior to the event, the effect of the event on the supervisee, the supervision relationship, satisfaction with supervision, and the outcome of the clinical case(s). A follow-up interview was scheduled for about 2 weeks after the initial interview and before data analysis was begun. This second interview offered the researcher the opportunity to clarify any information from the first interview and to explore additional reactions of the participant that may have arisen as a consequence of the initial interview.[5]

Other things being equal, give high evaluations to qualitative studies in which the interview protocols are described in detail.

---

[4] Rhoades, Stanley, & Markman (2006, p. 556).
[5] Burkard et al. (2006, pp. 290–291).

↳ Guideline 5.12

Consider quality control measures in qualitative research.

Qualitative researchers use a variety of techniques to assure readers that the results represent more than just the idiosyncratic views imposed by a single researcher in the interpretation of the data. Two common techniques are *peer review* (having an outside researcher review the entire research process) and *member checking* (having the participants in the research review the researcher's interpretations for accuracy). See Appendix B for more information on these and other measures qualitative researchers often take to increase the quality of their research.

↳ Guideline 5.13

Consider researchers' self-critiques of their own research methods.

Researchers often point out the major flaws in their research methodology. Typically, these are flaws that the researchers could not overcome because of limited resources such as time, access to participants, and so on. Very often, these are referred to as "limitations" and are usually discussed briefly near the end of research articles in the Discussion section.

Example 5.13.1 shows a discussion of limitations, which appeared in the Discussion section of a research article in an academic journal. It illustrates the usefulness of following this guideline in order to identify methodological weaknesses that might otherwise be overlooked by reviewers.

Example 5.13.1

Sample statement by researchers regarding the limitations of their study:

There were some limitations to this study. First, we provided adolescent participants with specific smoking categories (i.e., casual or addicted smoker) rather than allowing them to provide their own categories, which may have caused some confusion among adolescents not familiar with such terms. Another possible limitation is the fact that we only evaluated adolescents who had never smoked even a puff of a cigarette and thus were unable to explore how experiences with cigarette smoking affect discrimination of types of smokers.... Finally, the racial distribution is not necessarily representative of the United States as a whole. African Americans are relatively underrepresented in this sample, while Asians are overrepresented.[6]

In addition, researchers often will point out major methodological strengths of their studies, especially if they were the first to have these strengths (e.g., the first study on a topic that used a random sample from a population).

Paying close attention to self-critiques of research methodology helps reviewers evaluate the research reports that will be cited in literature reviews.

↳ Guideline 5.14

Be cautious when quantitative researchers refer to causality.

For quantitative researchers, the gold standard for investigating cause-and-effect relationships is to conduct experiments in which participants are assigned at random to treatment groups such as experimental and control groups.

Lower-quality experiments such as an experimental group consisting of an existing group (e.g., Teacher Smith's class getting Treatment X) being compared with another existing group

---

[6] Rubinstein, Halpern-Felsher, Thompson, & Millstein (2003, p. 661).

(e.g., Teacher Doe's class, which gets no treatment) offer less convincing evidence of causal links than experiments with random assignment.

Quantitative researchers sometimes look to the past for factors that may have led to an existing condition. This is called causal-comparative or ex post facto research. For instance, the histories of high school dropouts might be compared with the histories of those who graduated for possible causes of dropping out. Such research can be tricky to interpret given the large number of causal factors that may be at play in complex behavior.

Other things being equal, experiments with random assignment to treatment groups should be given higher marks for exploring causality than other types of quantitative research.

✎ Guideline 5.15
Be cautious when qualitative researchers refer to causality.

Qualitatively oriented researchers seldom conduct experiments. Instead, to explore causality, they take an in-depth look at their participants through intensive interviews, open-ended questionnaires, observations, and so on.

Note that self-reports can be difficult to interpret when attempting to identify causal variables not only because participants might not tell the truth about certain aspects of their lives, but also because they might not have the self-insights to understand why they do what they do (i.e., the causes of their behavior). For instance, a group of juvenile inmates in jail might be interviewed by a qualitatively oriented researcher to study the causes of their delinquent behavior. It is the qualitatively oriented researcher's job to question the participants in such a way that the researcher ferrets out information on causation even if the participants are not aware of it or are unable to verbalize it directly. This can be a daunting task.

In well-crafted qualitative research reports dealing with causality, researchers typically discuss various causal explanations and the degree of success they had in ruling out some in favor of one or more other explanations. It is important to pay careful attention to such discussions when preparing literature reviews.

✎ Guideline 5.16
Assess the strengths of trends across studies when evaluating literature.

Because it is safe to assume that all research is flawed, it is important when writing a review to consider the trends across the body of research on a topic and give greater emphasis to the methodologically stronger studies than to weaker ones.

✎ Guideline 5.17
Recognize the limitations of significance testing.

Quantitatively oriented researchers typically conduct significance tests. As a result, they make statements such as "the mean (average) for Group A is significantly higher than the mean for Group B ($p < .05$)."[7] Saying that it is significantly higher is equivalent to saying it is reliably higher. It is *not* equivalent to saying that the difference is large. In other words, a researcher is saying that a reliable difference has been detected, not that the difference is necessarily large or important.

Because this concept may be difficult to understand at first, consider this example: Suppose that a disgruntled employee decides that he will clock in to work exactly 30 seconds late each day. Because management is strict about punctuality, the other workers clock in before or

_____

[7] Note that "$p < .05$" indicates that there are only 5 chances in 100 that the researcher is in error in making the statement that the difference is statistically significant.

just on time. This happens day after day for months on end. At some point, a large enough sample of days would be observed that a significance test would declare the difference in clock-in times between the disgruntled employee and the other employees to be statistically significant just because it is a reliable phenomenon, not because the difference (30 seconds) is large enough to be of any practical consequence.

This is an important guideline because it is not uncommon to find researchers discussing their "statistically significant" results as though they were large enough to be of practical significance. Always examine the absolute size of the difference (e.g., the difference between the reported percentages or averages).

Additional Reading

This chapter presents only a brief overview of some of the basics for evaluating research. While there are a large number of high-quality textbooks on research methods available, *Evaluating Research in Academic Journals: A Practical Guide to Realistic Evaluation*[8] is highly recommended for its accessibility to novice researchers and its emphasis on straightforward, clearly explained evaluation criteria.

Exercise for Chapter 5

Directions: Select a research article you have located for possible citation in your literature review and answer the following questions about it. (Note that your instructor may want to assign a single research article for all students in the class to evaluate using the following question.)

1. What is the title of the article?

2. Is the article an example of quantitative or qualitative research?[9] (See Guideline 5.2.)

3. Was the sample selected at random? Was it a purposive sample? Did the researchers use a sample of convenience? (See Guidelines 5.3 and 5.4.)

4. What is your overall evaluation of the quality of the sample? (See Guidelines 5.2 through 5.5.)

5. Did the researcher use multiple measures of a key variable? (See Guidelines 5.6 and 5.7.)

6. Does the researcher offer evidence of the reliability of the measures? (See Guideline 5.9.)

7. If the research is quantitative, does the researcher offer evidence of the validity of the measures? (See Guideline 5.10.)

8. If the researcher used interviews, is the interview protocol described in detail? (See Guideline 5.11.)

---

[8] Pyrczak, F. (2008). Available through special order through bookstores and at www.Pyrczak.com.
[9] While it is relatively rare, some researchers report on the use of both approaches in a given article.

9. If the research is qualitative, did the researcher use peer review or member checking? (See Guideline 5.12.)

10. Does the researcher explicitly describe strengths and weaknesses of his/her own research? (See Guideline 5.13.)

11. Does the researcher refer to causality? Is the research a good vehicle for exploring causality? (See Guidelines 5.14 and 5.15.)

12. Does the researcher report the results of significance tests? If yes, does the researcher imply that any significant differences are necessarily large? Explain.

13. What is your overall evaluation of the article you used for this exercise?

Notes:

Chapter 6

Taking Notes and Avoiding Unintentional Plagiarism

In this chapter, the term "taking notes" is defined very broadly to include not only writing notes on paper (or cards), but also underlining or highlighting on photocopies, using Post-It® flags, as well as making notes using a word processor.

Since failure to take good notes can lead to unintentional plagiarism, the issue of plagiarism is also included in this chapter.

✎ Guideline 6.1
Group sources into broad categories before taking notes.

Grouping the related articles together will help in getting an overview of the literature on a topic and will make note-taking easier.

Grouping can be in a variety of ways, such as in terms of methodology (e.g., group surveys separately from experiments), in terms of participants (e.g., group studies of adults separately from studies of adolescents), or in terms of theories (e.g., group those based on theory A separately from those based on theory B).

✎ Guideline 6.2
Within each category, group sources chronologically.

Because a reviewer may want to make notes on the history of how thinking on a topic has changed over time, it is usually best to read and take notes on the oldest sources first.

✎ Guideline 6.3
Use colored highlighters to mark photocopies.

Using a different color for different types of elements will make it easy to locate and retrieve specific types of information. For instance, yellow might be used for statistics that help establish the importance of the problem, green might be used to highlight definitions of key terms, and pink might be used to highlight major findings, and so on.

✎ Guideline 6.4
Give each source a unique identifier such as the surname of the first author.

The identifiers could also be numbers such as 1, 2, and 3. Write these directly on the first page of the photocopy of each source. Using identifiers can make note-taking more efficient and effective, which is explored in the next two guidelines.

✎ Guideline 6.5
Label the tops of note cards with the unique identifiers.

This will make it easy to go back to the original source if the notes are not complete or if additional information is needed while writing.

✤ **Guideline 6.6**

Consider building a table that summarizes key points in the literature.

One way to organize material initially is to build a table in which the unique identifiers (e.g., authors' names; see Guideline 6.4) are listed in the first column and special characteristics of each source are listed in the other columns.[1]

Example 6.6.1 shows a simple table summarizing five experiments. An important advantage of a table like the one in the example is that patterns that might otherwise be overlooked may become obvious in the table. For instance, from the table it is clear that the three studies that had significant differences (all in favor of the experimental group) were conducted with random assignment, which is highly desirable in an experimental study.

Example 6.6.1

A sample "notes table," which helps organize literature and provide an overview:

Identifier	Level of Education	Type of Measure	Number of Participants	Type of Assignment	Outcome
Applegate (2004)	College	Questionnaire	25 E, 20 C	Random	Sig. in favor of E
Brown (2005)	College	Interview	10 E, 10 C	Intact Groups (Nonrandom)	Diff. not sig.
Jones (2005)	General Adult Population	Observation	30 E only	(No control group)	Diff. not sig.
Chang (2006)	High School	Questionnaire	50 E, 50 C	Random	Sig. in favor of E
Solis (2007)	College	Questionnaire	110 E, 115 C	Random	Sig. in favor of E
Note. E = Experimental Group; C = Control Group; Diff. = difference; Sig. = statistically significant.					

It is often desirable to build more than one table. For instance, one table might be built for experiments on the topic, another for surveys, and yet another for qualitative studies.

While tables can also be built for inclusion in a literature review, which is a possibility discussed in Chapter 11, the purpose at this point is to build rough tables to get an overview of the literature.

✤ **Guideline 6.7**

Make more extensive notes on more important studies.

This guideline is suggested since a reviewer might want to discuss important studies in more detail than those that are of lesser importance.

✤ **Guideline 6.8**

Avoid including quotations in the notes.

The purpose of a literature review is to present the reviewer's synthesis of the literature on a topic in his or her own words. Thus, it is usually inappropriate to include direct quotations from the literature in a literature review.

---

[1] Tables are easy to build with modern word processing programs. For example, when using Microsoft® Word, click on "Table" at the top of the screen, then click on "Insert." From that point on, the procedure for building a table will be obvious. If a large number of columns is needed, switch from "portrait" to "landscape" (which will turn the page on its side so that it is wider than it is long) by clicking on "File," then "Page Setup," then "Landscape," and then "OK."

The main exception to this guideline is for technical material (such as a technical definition) whose precise meaning might be lost in paraphrase.

✎ Guideline 6.9
Pay special attention to definitions while taking notes.

If different authors use different definitions of the variables relating to the topic being reviewed, the differences may need to be taken into account in the literature review. One possibility is to consider whether studies with one type of definition tend to have one type of result while those with another definition tend to have a different type.

✎ Guideline 6.10
Make notes on researchers' descriptions of the limitations of their research methodology.

Authors of research articles often describe the limitations of their studies. While this may be done anywhere in their articles, they typically discuss them in the Discussion section near the end of their articles. Such limitations should be considered when drawing conclusions from research literature. (See Chapter 5 on evaluating research reports.)

✎ Guideline 6.11
When in doubt, cite the source.

Failure to cite a source for an original idea constitutes plagiarism even if the idea (or point of view) is logical and makes common sense. Even "obvious ideas" belong to the person who first uttered or wrote them. The citation decision chart in Box 6B on the next page should be helpful in determining whether or not to cite material.

✎ Guideline 6.12
If someone else's idea is rephrased, the original source should be cited.

The definition of plagiarism in Box 6A makes this guideline clear. Italics have been added for emphasis.

Box 6A   *A definition of plagiarism.*[2]

> "Plagiarism is the failure to distinguish the student's own words and ideas from those of a source the student has consulted. *Ideas derived from another, whether presented as exact words, a paraphrase, a summary, or quoted phrase, must always be appropriately referenced to the source*, whether the source is printed, electronic, or spoken. Whenever exact words are used, quotation marks or an indented block indicator of a quotation must be used, together with the proper citation in a style required by the professor [or other audience such as a journal editor]."

---

[2] From Harris (2001, p. 132). Copyright © 2001 by Pyrczak Publishing. All rights reserved. No duplication permitted without written permission from the publisher. Reprinted with permission.

Box 6B *Citation decision chart.*[3]

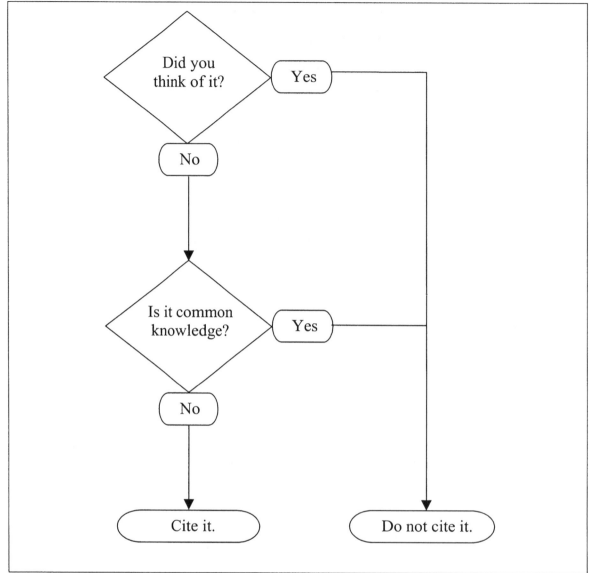

♥ **Guideline 6.13**

Failure to indicate clearly the beginning *and* end of summarized literature may lead to charges of plagiarism.

It is common in literature reviews to summarize another writer's ideas in more than one paragraph. When doing this, make sure to clearly identify the common source for the material in each paragraph. Example 6.13.1 illustrates how this can be done. Notice that the source (Smith) is identified in each of the three paragraphs.

Example 6.13.1
Three paragraphs that summarize material from a single source (source identified in each paragraph; bold added for instructional purposes):

With the development of new telescopic methods, **Smith** (2006) was able to show that the coloration of the moon is....

Smith also pointed out that knowing the correct coloration of the moon helps scientists in three important ways....

Earlier studies failed to identify the correct coloration because of two serious flaws in their methodology, according to **Smith**. First, they....

Keeping accurate notes on the sources of all ideas and clearly indicating the sources in the literature review will preclude charges of plagiarism.

Exercise for Chapter 6

1. Did you group sources into broad categories before taking notes? If yes, how many categories? (See Guideline 6.1.)

2. Did you read sources in chronological order? Did this help you understand the history of the topic? Explain. (See Guideline 6.2.)

3. Did you build summary tables? If yes, did it help you identify patterns that might otherwise have been overlooked? Explain. (See Guideline 6.6.)

4. How many direct quotations did you write in your notes? How many of them do you plan to use in your review? (See Guideline 6.8.)

5. Did you make notes on definitions found in the literature? Explain. (See Guideline 6.9.)

6. Did researchers discuss the limitations of their research in their reports? (See Guideline 6.10.)

7. How confident are you in your ability to avoid unintentional plagiarism? (See Guidelines 6.11 through 6.13.)

Notes:

Chapter 7

Preparing a Topic Outline
for the First Draft

At this point, you should have selected a topic, collected literature on the topic, evaluated the literature that reports the results of research, and made notes on the literature. The next step is to plan the first draft of the literature review.

✢ Guideline 7.1
The first element in the topic outline is the Introduction.

Elements to cover in the Introduction are described below. Note that in a thesis or dissertation, the Introduction is usually a separate chapter (Chapter 1) from the Literature Review (Chapter 2).

✢ Guideline 7.2
Essential elements in the Introduction are (1) identifying the topic and (2) establishing its importance.

Establishing the importance of a topic can be done by discussing the numbers or percentages of individuals affected by the topic (usually with citations to literature) and/or by discussing the importance of the topic to certain individuals or groups.

Note that it is not necessary for large numbers of individuals to be affected in order for a problem to be important. For instance, a rare disease may have a devastating impact on the individuals affected.

✢ Guideline 7.3
Consider providing definitions of key terms in the Introduction.

Providing definitions of key terms is especially important when (1) some readers may not be familiar with the terms and (2) when conflicting definitions have been used in the literature. Note that conflicting definitions might be the source of conflicting results of studies.

Noting definitions of key terms was mentioned in Guidelines 6.3, 6.8, and 6.9 in the previous chapter.

✢ Guideline 7.4
In the Introduction, consider describing the strategies used to locate literature on the topic.

This should describe the databases that were searched and the specific terms that were used in the search. While this element is almost always included in highly quantified literature reviews (known as meta-analyses; see the last two chapters of this book), it is also desirable in literature reviews written as term projects since it allows professors to judge the care with which the literature was searched.

✥ Guideline 7.5
Consider commenting on the extent and nature of the literature in the Introduction.

Comments such as those in Example 7.5.1 in the Introduction help set the stage for the review.

Example 7.5.1
Comment on the extent and nature of the literature:

The literature on Topic X is quite extensive, with more than two dozen studies published in the last few years. With only two exceptions, which are experiments, all the studies are regional or local surveys.

✥ Guideline 7.6
Consider describing the objectives and organization of the literature review near the end of the Introduction.

Consider concluding the introduction with a statement of the objectives of the review and a brief description of the material that will be covered in the review. Example 7.6.1 illustrates this guideline. The authors included it at the end of the introduction to a published literature review. Note that the authors of the example use the personal pronoun "we." While this is acceptable, it is much more common to use the passive voice (e.g., "The theoretical basis is discussed" instead of "We discuss the theoretical basis").

This guideline is especially appropriate for long literature reviews.

Example 7.6.1
Description of the objectives and organization of a literature review:

Our objectives in the present review are to provide an integrated overview of current knowledge regarding the link between burnout and CVD [cardiovascular disease] risk and cardiovascular-related events and to describe plausible pathways of this link. In addition, we propose potentially promising avenues for future research in this area. We start with the theoretical basis for distinguishing between stress, chronic stress, and burnout. We then discuss the concept of burnout and distinguish between burnout and related affective dysfunctions, mainly depression. Evidence that suggests burnout and depression may be differentiated at the physiological level is introduced in a later section of our review. We present the evidence concerning the effects of burnout on cardiovascular health. We then present the potential mechanisms linking burnout and CVD. Finally, we discuss the implications and directions for future research.[1]

✥ Guideline 7.7
Discuss theories; if the discussion is extensive, consider presenting it in a separate section.

If the material on theories is limited, it may be integrated into the Introduction or elsewhere in the review. If the material is extensive and crucial to understanding the literature review, consider presenting it in a separate section with its own heading within the review, as well as possible subheadings if more than one theory is to be discussed.

Example 7.7.1 shows the topic outline for a literature review, as discussed up to this point in this chapter.

Example 7.7.1
Topic outline for the elements covered through Guideline 7.7:

I. Introduction
  A. Identify the topic
  B. Establish the importance of the topic

---

[1] Melamed, Shirom, Toker, Berliner, & Shapira (2006, p. 328).

       1. Number of individuals affected
       2. Impact on individuals
    C. Definitions of key terms
    D. Literature search strategies
    E. Description of the extent and nature of the literature
    F. Overview of the organization of the rest of the review
  II. Theoretical considerations
    A. Theory X
    B. Theory Y

✏ Guideline 7.8
Group notes to identify major topics and subtopics for the body of the literature review.

Group notes according to commonalities in order to identify major topics as well as subtopics for the topic outline for the body of the review. Try several different groupings before settling on one.

Note that a particular source may fall into more than one grouping. For instance, if there is a group on job burnout among women and another group on job burnout among men, a research article that explores burnout among both women and men might be included in both groups.

The nature and organization for the body of a literature review will vary greatly from one review to another depending on the nature and extent of the literature on the topic. Example 7.8.1 shows the outline for a review on internalized oppression among Filipinos and Filipino Americans, which is referred to by ethnic scholars as "colonial mentality" resulting from colonization of the Philippines.

Example 7.8.1
Sample topic outline for the body of a review (following the introduction and theory sections):

III. Frameworks
    A. Psychological Impact of Oppression
    B. Colonialism
    C. Summary of Frameworks
IV. Filipino Americans and CM [Colonial Mentality]
    A. Filipino American Population
    B. Primer on the Philippines' Colonial History
       1. Colonialism Under Spain
       2. Colonialism Under the United States
    C. CM Discourse in the Filipino American Community
    D. Dimensions of CM
       1. Denigration of the Filipino Self
       2. Denigration of the Filipino Culture and Body
       3. Denigration Against Less-Americanized Filipinos
       4. Tolerance of Oppression
    E. Quantifying CM

✏ Guideline 7.9
Consider including a summary at the ends of long sections of a review.

Note that point III.C. in Example 7.8.1 calls for a summary of the preceding material regarding frameworks.

✎ Guideline 7.10

Consider including a summary at the end of the body of a literature review.

For long reviews, a summary at the end of the body of the review can help readers focus on the main points of the review.

✎ Guideline 7.11

In a review that serves as the introduction to a research report, conclude the review with statements of research hypotheses or purposes.

Most research articles published in professional journals begin with literature reviews. These reviews should end with explicitly stated research hypotheses (e.g., "It is hypothesized that X is greater than Y") or research purposes (e.g., "The purpose is to explore the differences between X and Y"). Obviously, the research hypotheses or purposes should flow logically from the literature that has been reviewed. (In a research report, the literature review is followed by a section describing the research methods used to conduct the research.)

✎ Guideline 7.12

Conclude a "stand-alone" review with a Discussion section that provides conclusions, implications, and suggestions for future research.

A "stand-alone" review is a complete document—not the introduction to a larger work such as a research report.

A reviewer typically needs to draw conclusions despite inconclusive evidence in the literature as well as gaps (i.e., areas that have not been studied). Readers will want to know what the reviewer's educated opinions are on the state of knowledge on the topic of the review.

Based on the conclusions, a reviewer may suggest implications, which should focus on direct actions individuals and groups should take based on the reviewer's conclusions. For instance, a review on the educational needs of homeless children might lead to implications concerning specific actions school personnel might take when working with such children.

Having carefully considered and synthesized the research on a topic, the reviewer is in an especially good position to make suggestions for possible fruitful areas for future research. Often, these suggestions center on gaps in the literature such as groups of people and variables that have not been studied to date. Note that the suggestions should be specific; it is not useful to make only simple statements such as "More research is needed."

✎ Guideline 7.13

There is no single standard format for a topic outline for a literature review.

While an effective review may be written without faithfully following the suggestions in this chapter, students are urged to consider carefully the guidelines presented here because they provide framework that will assure that important elements have not been inadvertently omitted.

Example 7.13.1 shows the topic outline for a stand-alone literature review, as described in this chapter. By reading the model literature reviews near the end of this book, students will discover alternative frameworks for organizing reviews.

Example 7.13.1
Topic outline through Guideline 7.13:
I. Introduction
   A. Identify the topic
   B. Establish the importance of the topic

        1. Number of individuals affected
        2. Seriousness of the impact on individuals
    C. Definitions of key terms
    D. Literature search strategies
    E. Description of the extent and nature of the literature
    F. Overview of the organization of the rest of the review
II. Theoretical considerations
    A. Theory X
    B. Theory Y
III. Body of the Review[2]
    (This may consist of multiple headings and subheadings; see Example 7.8.1.)
IV. Summary
    (Summary of Part III)
V. Discussion
    A. Conclusions
    B. Implications
    C. Suggestions for Future Research

Exercise for Chapter 7

1. In the topic outline for your review, do you plan to include all the points (A through F) in Part I, the Introduction? (See Example 7.13.1 above.)

2. In the topic outline for your review, do you plan to include a separate section on theoretical material? (See Part II in Example 7.13.1 above.)

3. Have you tried grouping and regrouping notes to identify major topics and subtopics for the body of the review? If yes, list the topics in the order in which they will be covered. (See Examples 7.8.1 and 7.13.1 above.)

4. Do you plan to include a summary of the body of the review? Note that this is especially appropriate for long literature reviews. (See Part IV in Example 7.13.1 above.)

5. Will your outline include any major deviations from the one shown in Example 7.13.1? Explain.

---

[2] In a meta-analysis (see the last two chapters of this book), the body of the literature review consists of an Analysis section that describes the statistical analysis of the results of previous studies and a Results section that presents the results of the analysis.

Notes:

Chapter 8

Writing the First Draft: Basic Principles

Having prepared a topic outline (see Chapter 7), the next step is to begin writing the first draft. This chapter covers basic writing strategies for organizing and presenting the material found in the literature. Chapter 9 describes optional techniques that may be used when writing literature reviews, while Chapter 10 discusses issues regarding the presentation of statistical material in qualitative reviews.

✤ Guideline 8.1
Fill in the topic outline with brief notes, including unique identifiers.

Guideline 6.4 in Chapter 6 suggests labeling each piece of literature with a unique identifier, such as a number or the surname of the first author. Before beginning to write, fill in the outline with notes that indicate the material that will be presented under each heading (and subheading) as well as which sources (indicated with identifiers) will be used. This is illustrated in Example 8.1.1, where the identifiers for pieces of literature are indicated by numbers (e.g., #2 and #5).

Example 8.1.1
Portion of topic outline with brief notes:

I. Introduction
  A. Identify the topic
  B. Establish the importance of the topic
    1. Number of individuals affected
        #2: *Number of adolescents*
        #5: *Number of adults*
        #10: *Difficulty in determining the number (i.e., self-reports)*
    2. Impact on individuals
        #4, 8, and 15: *Impact on physical health*
        #5: *Impact on psychological health*
        #12: *Costs of clinical treatment*

Note that a given reference may appear under more than one topic or subtopic. For instance, in the example above, reference #5 appears under two subtopics. This results from the fact that reference #5 has two types of information (number of adults affected and impact on psychological health).

This guideline is especially important when there is a large amount of literature to be organized.

✤ Guideline 8.2
Write an essay that moves logically from one point to another. Do not write a string of annotations.

Write an essay that moves logically from topic to topic (following the topic outline) with references cited as needed.

An annotation is a summary of a piece of literature. Most academic literature has already been annotated, and the annotations have been published both in print and on the Web. Rewriting and presenting a string of annotations is not a literature review because it fails to synthesize the literature.

✥ Guideline 8.3
When appropriate, cite two or more sources for a single point.

Note that various sources may be grouped such as sources #4, #8, and #15 for the impact on physical health in Example 8.1.1 above.

Example 8.3.1 shows a statement from a literature review that cites three sources for a single point.

Example 8.3.1
Three sources given for a single point:

Preliminary research has found that young African American women are particularly interested in and engaged in science—at least during the high school years (Hanson & Palmer-Johnson, 2000; Mau et al., 1995; National Center for Educational Statistics, 2000a). In spite of this interest....[1]

✥ Guideline 8.4
Avoid very long strings of references for a single point.

When a large number of sources support a single point, consider whether differentiations can be made among them. If so, differentiate among them in the review in order to break up the string.

Example 8.4.1
Long string of references for a single point (not recommended):

Numerous evaluations have indicated that Program X is superior to Program Y (Doe, 2002; Smith, 2003; Black, 2004; Jones, 2004; Solis, 2005; Williams, 2005; Hinds, 2005; Lindsay & Jones, 2006; Blacksmith, 2006; Hinds, 2006; Sherod & Washington, 2006).

Improved Version of Example 8.4.1
Differentiations among references (recommended):

Numerous evaluations have indicated that Program X is superior to Program Y. Specifically, Program X appears to be superior in terms of student retention (Doe, 2002; Smith, 2003), in terms of student attitudes (Black, 2004; Jones, 2004; Solis, 2005), and achievement of short-term goals (Williams, 2005), as well as long-term goals (Hinds, 2005; Lindsay & Jones, 2006; Blacksmith, 2006; Hinds, 2006; Sherod & Washington, 2006).

✥ Guideline 8.5
Use quotations very sparingly.

A reviewer should strive to write a review that flows smoothly and is cohesive. Frequent use of quotations can produce a choppy review that is uneven in style. Thus, quotations should be used very sparingly.

A major exception is when citing technical information (such as a technical definition), whose meaning might be significantly changed in paraphrase.

---

[1] Hanson (2007, p. 4).

❧ Guideline 8.6
Support statements indicating that a topic is timely.

Avoid asserting that the topic of a literature review is timely unless the statement is supported. For instance, avoid making statements such as "Recently, there has been renewed interest in Topic A" or "Topic A is of increasing interest" without indicating the timeframe and supporting evidence.

Example 8.6.1
Vague statement regarding timeliness (no support and no specific timeframe):

Over recent years, there has been renewed interest in Topic A.

Improved Version of Example 8.6.1
Statement on timeliness with support and specific timeframe:

The renewed interest in Topic A is indicated by a 30% increase in funding for studies on the topic by the National Science Foundation over the past three years.

❧ Guideline 8.7
Emphasize stronger studies over weaker ones.

One of the reasons for evaluating the quality of research literature (see Chapter 5) is to identify those studies that deserve more attention than others in a literature review. For instance, if there are three experiments on a topic but only one used random assignment to experimental and control conditions, emphasize the results of the latter by providing more information on its results than the results of the other two.

❧ Guideline 8.8
Point out important strengths and weaknesses of the research being cited.

While it is not necessary (nor is it desirable) to write a detailed critique of the strengths and weaknesses of each study cited in a literature review, studies on a given topic or subtopic can sometimes be critiqued as a group, as illustrated in Example 8.8.1.

Example 8.8.1
Critique of a group of studies:

Cambodian refugees are often viewed as under-using mental health services despite considerable unmet need, although virtually all data are from small samples or from samples where representativeness is uncertain.... In perhaps the most rigorous examination of this issue, Blair (2001) found that....[2]

In addition, the strength of individual studies can be indicated by providing information that points to their specific strengths and weaknesses. For instance, the authors of the excerpt in Example 8.8.2 note that the results were obtained using a large sample.

Example 8.8.2
Strength of a study indicated:

Additionally, there is evidence suggesting that adolescent mothers have a higher incidence of engaging in particularly serious forms of inappropriate parenting such as child abuse. A study using 1,997 mothers ranging from 16 to 46 years of age at the time of

---

[2] Modified from Marshall et al. (2006, p. 1829).

their child's birth reported that the younger the mother was when she gave birth, the greater the likelihood of physical child abuse (Connelly & Straus, 1992).[3]

✎ Guideline 8.9
Use tentative language when describing the results of weak studies.

All research is subject to error (see Guideline 5.1 in Chapter 5), with some studies providing more definitive results than others. When reviewers discuss points for which the research evidence is clearly weak, it is desirable to use tentative language (i.e., language that clearly indicates that the underlying research is not conclusive).

Examples 8.9.1 and 8.9.2 illustrate the use of tentative language.

Example 8.9.1
Statement with tentative language (with italics added for instructional purposes):

There is evidence that religious participation is important for elderly African Americans (Black, 1999; Chatters & Taylor, 1994). Furthermore, religious service attendance *appears to contribute* to quality of life and good health for substantial proportions of elderly people (Levin, 1994; McFadden, 1996; Neill & Kahn, 1999) and....[4]

Example 8.9.2
Statement with tentative language (with italics added for instructional purposes):

Research on two-parent families *suggests* that fathers are more involved with sons than with daughters (Harris & Morgan, 1991).[5]

✎ Guideline 8.10
Use language that distinguishes between the results of studies and speculation.

In literature reviews that focus on the results of research, use language that alerts readers to points that are based on speculation (rather than research). This can be done by using terms such as "speculated," "suggested," "argued," "proposed," and "commented." The author of Example 8.10.1 follows this guideline by using the terms "argued," "proposed," and "comments."

Example 8.10.1
Statement with terms indicating speculation (italics added for instructional purposes):

Buss (1987) *argued* that people are not randomly exposed to their life experiences. He *proposed* that individuals selectively seek or avoid certain experiences or situations and may evoke responses from those around them, sometimes unintentionally. Furthermore, people may alter, influence, and manipulate the environments in which they have chosen to live. Buss's *comments* point to an important limitation of....[6]

✎ Guideline 8.11
Point out consistent findings in a body of literature.

When there is consistency in the findings of the literature on a given topic or subtopic, it is important to point this out since confidence is greater in a consistent finding across studies than in a finding reported in a single, isolated study. This guideline is followed in Examples 8.11.1 and 8.11.2.

---

[3] Middlemiss & McGuigan (2005, p. 212).
[4] Roff et al. (2006, p. 246).
[5] Bronte-Tinkew, Moore, & Carrano (2006, p. 853).
[6] Shih (2006, p. 434).

Example 8.11.1

Consistent finding noted:

In an array of previous studies, researchers have convincingly documented higher levels of alcohol use and adverse consequences among students who are members of fraternities compared with other college students, and to same-aged peers not attending college (Larimer, Anderson, Baer, & Marlatt, 2000; Marlatt, Baer, & Larimer, 1995; Wechsler, Kuh, & Davenport, 1996; Sher, Bartholow, & Nanda, 2001). Larimer et al. (2000) noted in a review of this extensive literature that these findings date back to the 1950s. Heavy drinking has become a normative part of fraternity culture....[7]

Example 8.11.2

Consistent finding noted:

One consistent finding in the depression literature is that women are two times more likely to experience depression than are men (e.g., Angold & Rutter, 1992; Nolen-Hoeksema & Girgus, 1994).[8]

Note that in Example 8.11.2, the author uses "e.g." to indicate that she is citing only examples of the supporting sources.

✤ Guideline 8.12
Point out contradictions and inconsistent findings in a body of literature.

Contradictions and inconsistent findings often point to areas in which additional research is needed to arrive at more definitive conclusions.

✤ Guideline 8.13
Identify gaps in the literature.

For each subtopic in a literature review, point out any obvious gaps. These may be reiterated in the Conclusions section of the literature review (see Point V.A., in Example 7.13.1 in Chapter 7). This is illustrated in Examples 8.13.1 and 8.13.2.

Example 8.13.1

A statement about a gap in the literature:

Although there is an abundance of research on homeless older adults and a growing body of research on homeless adolescents, very little research to date addresses the population of homeless-emerging adults (i.e., 18 to 25 years of age...).[9]

Example 8.13.2

A statement about a gap in the literature:

Lack of attention to demographic variables is another limitation of the research on psychosocial outcomes of adult children of parents with mental illness. In fact, the only demographic variable examined in these studies was child gender....[10]

---

[7] Caudill et al. (2006, p. 141).
[8] Shih (2006, p. 434).
[9] Tyler & Johnson (2006, p. 134).
[10] Mowbray, Bybee, Oyserman, MacFarlane, & Bowersox (2006, p. 100).

✎ Guideline 8.14
Indicate when previous literature reviews are being cited.

A published literature review is a fundamentally different type of source than a published report of original research. Readers will assume that results cited from the literature are from original research reports unless indicated otherwise.

This guideline was followed in the second sentence in Example 8.11.1 above. Referring to a previous review can be done in two ways: either as part of a sentence as in Example 8.14.1, or in parentheses, as in Example 8.14.2.

Example 8.14.1
Review article indicated as part of a sentence:

A **review of literature** on comparisons of couples exposed to high and low levels of stressors indicates that stressful work experiences have been associated with greater marital conflict, lower marital support, and more marital dissatisfaction (see Perry-Jenkins, Repetti, & Crouter, 2000).[11]

Example 8.14.2
Review article indicated parenthetically:

In comparisons of couples exposed to high and low levels of stressors, stressful work experiences have been associated with greater marital conflict, lower marital support, and more marital dissatisfaction (see Perry-Jenkins, Repetti, & Crouter, 2000, for a **review**).[12]

✎ Guideline 8.15
Indicate the degree of certainty in the conclusions.

In the Conclusions subsection of a literature review (see Point V.A. in the topic outline in Example 7.13.1), use expressions that indicate the degree of certainty with which the conclusions were reached. Box 8A shows some sample expressions for varying degrees of certainty. For instance, consider the research on the effects of smoking tobacco on health. The conclusion that smoking is harmful could be stated with almost absolute certainty given the large number of definitive studies on this topic. At the other extreme, conclusions regarding the effectiveness of a new instructional devise that was tried out with only a few students in each of several studies would lead to very tentative conclusions.

Box 8A *Expressions indicating degrees of certainty in conclusions reached.*

Degree of Certainty	Sample Expressions
Almost absolutely certain	The results of extensive experimental research leads to the firm conclusion....
	The evidence from all major studies overwhelmingly supports the conclusion that....
Close to certain	The body of literature on XYZ strongly indicates the following conclusions....
	Continued →

---

[11] Loosely based on Story & Repetti (2006, p. 690).
[12] Ibid.

Fair degree of certainty	The four studies to date confirm the major premises of the ABC theory, pointing to the validity of the theory. This conclusion should be tempered by the limited number of studies....
Rather uncertain	The inconsistencies in the results of the studies on this topic make reaching firm conclusions problematic. Still, the best of the studies seem to suggest that....
Very uncertain	Some very preliminary evidence offered by pilot studies leads us to the very tentative conclusion that....

✠ Guideline 8.16
Implications should be specific.

Implications should usually be stated in the Implications subsection of the Discussion section (see point V.B. in the topic outline in Example 7.13.1 in Chapter 7).

The more specific the implications are, the more helpful they will be to readers of a review. When possible, avoid vague statements of implications such as: "Counselors should be more sensitive to the needs of individuals who are alcohol dependent." Note that this statement fails to indicate specifically what counselors need to do in order to be "more sensitive."

Example 8.16.1 follows this guideline by suggesting that a particular treatment is not realistic and that treatment by other providers should be explored.

Example 8.16.1
A statement of specific implications in the Conclusions:

Although studies have shown that physicians can be trained in brief motivational interviewing techniques for smoking cessation, expecting primary care providers [physicians] to deliver sophisticated cognitive-behavioral and social influence counseling is probably unrealistic. More work needs to be done to...provide access to these services...by someone other than the physician or to provide them in electronic formats.[13]

✠ Guideline 8.17
Suggestions for future research should be specific.

Having carefully considered and synthesized the research on a topic, a reviewer is in an especially good position to make suggestions for possible fruitful areas for future research. It is recommended that these suggestions be stated at the end of the review in the Discussion section (see point V.C. in Example 7.13.1 in Chapter 7).

Example 8.17.1 illustrates this guideline.

Example 8.17.1
A statement of specific implications in the Conclusions:

Although the evidence reviewed in this article has clearly drawn a link between social and physical pain, it has also highlighted some apparent discrepancies that require further research attention. As discussed earlier, some work suggests that social exclusion is related to decreased pain sensitivity, whereas other work suggests that social inclusion is related to decreased pain sensitivity. Clearly, future research is needed both to repli-

---

[13] McVea (2006, p. 561).

cate the experimental results with human participants and to help understand the mechanisms by which perceptions of social standing can influence sensitivity to pain.[14]

Exercise for Chapter 8

1. Did you follow Guideline 8.1? If yes, how helpful was it in organizing the literature before writing?

2. With which of the guidelines in this chapter were you already familiar before reading the chapter? (List the guideline numbers.)

3. Are there any guidelines in this chapter that you will not be following? Explain.

---

[14] MacDonald & Leary (2005, p. 217).

Chapter 9

Writing the First Draft: Optional Techniques

This chapter describes optional techniques that may be used when writing literature reviews.

The guidelines that refer to the Introduction in this chapter are referring to Point I in the topic outline in Example 7.7.1 in Chapter 7.

✍ Guideline 9.1
Consider presenting a historical frame of reference in the Introduction.

Reviewers sometimes briefly describe important historical developments regarding the way their topic has been conceptualized and studied. Typically, this is done in the Introduction to the review.[1] Note that showing that a topic has been studied over a long period of time helps to establish its importance.

The authors of Example 9.1.1 began their literature review with the historical material shown in the example.

Example 9.1.1

A brief historical overview presented in the first paragraph of a review:

It has long been recognized that surgery can be a very stressful experience for children. In fact, this phenomenon has piqued the interest of clinical researchers for more than 60 years. For example, Pearson (1941) observed significant emotional reactions in young children undergoing anesthesia and surgery. Eckenhoff (1953), in a retrospective study of more than 600 children, identified a link between "unsatisfactory" anesthetic inductions…and postoperative negative personality changes. Today, approximately 4 million children undergo anesthesia….[2]

✍ Guideline 9.2
Consider pointing out landmark or seminal studies in the Introduction.

A landmark or seminal article is one that planted the seeds for later studies on the issue. Such a study can be described as part of a historical overview (see Guideline 9.1).

The authors of Example 9.2.1 began their literature review with the description of a landmark study.

Example 9.2.1

A landmark study described in the first paragraph of a review:

Across the lifespan, caregiving has typically occurred within the context of the family. A landmark study by Townsend (1957)…explored the social problem of caring for the elderly at home. The findings of this study led to the coining of the term *strain of illness*, referring to the excessive physical or mental demands of caregiving imposed on

---

[1] If the historical review is extensive, consider including it as a separate subtopic in the Introduction.
[2] Wright, Stewart, Finley, & Buffett-Jerrott (2007, pp. 52–53).

the family structure or resulting in a caregiver's change in employment. Almost 50 years after Townsend's seminal work, care of the elderly...continues to be a widespread, growing social concern.[3]

The authors of Example 9.2.2 began their literature review with the description of a study they characterize as "seminal."

Example 9.2.2

A seminal study described in the first paragraph of a review:

In their seminal article, Taylor and Brown (1988) presented evidence that most people regard themselves more positively than they regard peers and that such self-enhancement fosters better mental functioning. More recent research...provided additional support for this view....[4]

✤ Guideline 9.3
In the Introduction, consider describing how the literature search was conducted.

Naming the databases that were consulted and the search terms that were used can help readers judge the care with which the literature search was conducted. While this guideline is almost universally followed by those who prepare highly quantitative reviews known as "meta-analyses" (see the last two chapters in this book), it can also be informative in qualitative reviews.

Example 9.3.1 illustrates how this guideline might be followed. Note that the reviewers also indicate the dates of publication used in the search.

Example 9.3.1

Naming the database and search terms used:

The *PsycINFO* computer database identified workplace harassment research published from 1987 through 2005. The search terms were *abuse, abusive supervision, aggression, bullying, harassment, incivility, interpersonal conflict, mistreatment, mobbing, petty tyranny,* and *social undermining*. The reference sections of the articles identified during this step were reviewed to find additional articles. Authors who had recently published research on workplace harassment were also contacted to request copies of unpublished manuscripts.[5]

✤ Guideline 9.4
In the Introduction, consider describing inclusion/exclusion criteria (if any) used when selecting literature.

When planning a review on a topic on which there is a very large amount of literature, reviewers sometimes limit the amount of literature to review by establishing criteria that must be met for a source to be included. In addition, they sometimes describe criteria that would lead to the exclusion of some sources. When this is done, the criteria should be indicated.

Example 9.4.1 illustrates this guideline by listing inclusion criteria.

Example 9.4.1

Stating the inclusion criteria:

[To be included in the review], the studies were required to meet the following criteria: (a) selection of participants with psychological problems or maladaptive behavior, (b)

---

[3] Halm, Treat-Jacobson, Lindquist, & Savik (2006, p. 426).
[4] Zuckerman & O'Loughlin (2006, p. 751).
[5] Bowling & Beehr (2006, pp. 1001–1002).

random assignment of participants to treatment conditions, (c) mean participant age of 3–18 years, and (d) posttreatment assessment of the psychological problem(s) or maladaptive behavior for which participants were selected and treated.[6]

♄ Guideline 9.5
In the Introduction, consider paraphrasing and citing the source(s) for definitions.

Key terms should be defined in the introduction. (See Point I.C. in the topic outline in Example 7.7.1 in Chapter 7.)

Reviewers often paraphrase definitions found in the literature. Even if these definitions seem to be "common sense" or "logical," the source should be cited if paraphrased definitions are included in a review. For instance, the reviewers who presented the definition in Example 9.5.1 paraphrased it from four sources, which are cited in parentheses.

Example 9.5.1
Quoting an authoritative definition:

Social support is defined as information from others that one is loved and cared for, esteemed and valued, and part of a network of communication and mutual obligations (Cobb, 1976; Cohen & Willis, 1985; Seeman, 1996; Taylor, in press).[7]

♄ Guideline 9.6
In the Introduction, consider quoting authoritative and/or technical definitions.

As indicated by Guideline 6.8 in Chapter 6, quotations should be used very sparingly in literature reviews. An exception is authoritative and technical definitions whose precise meaning might be lost in paraphrase. The reviewers who wrote Example 9.6.1 quoted a definition developed by an authoritative source. Notice that for definitions that are more than a couple of lines long, indentation should be used, as illustrated in the example.

Example 9.6.1
Quoting an authoritative definition:

In partnership with the World Health Organization (WHO), researchers from various countries adopted the following definition of QOL [quality of life]:

> Quality of life is the individuals' perception of their position in life in the context of the culture and value systems in which they live and in relation to their goals, expectations, standards, and concerns. It is a broad-ranging concept affected in a complex way by the persons' physical health, psychological state, level of independence, social relationships and their relationship to salient features of their environment. (World Health Organization Quality of Life [WHOQOL] group, 1995, p. 1405).[8]

---

[6] Weisz, Jensen-Doss, & Hawley (2006, p. 674).
[7] Kim, Sherman, Ko, & Taylor (2006, p. 1596).
[8] Paskulin & Molzahn (2007, p. 12).

✣ Guideline 9.7
Consider emphasizing content over authorship when citing references.

In the Harvard method, citations to literature are provided by citing the surname(s) of the author(s) followed by the year of publication.[9] The reference list at the end of the literature review is arranged alphabetically by surnames when this method is used.

Surnames of authors can be integrated into the sentences or placed in parentheses at the end of the sentences or paragraphs. Notice in Example 9.7.1 that the first version emphasizes authorship by mentioning the authors' names first; the second one emphasizes content of the statement by putting the surnames of authors in parentheses at the end of the sentence.

Example 9.7.1
Statement emphasizing authorship (use sparingly):

Graefe and Lichter (1999) and Manning (2001) report that cohabitating parents' relationships do not last as long as those of married parents, putting their children at a higher risk for poverty and multiple family transitions.

Statement emphasizing content:

Cohabitating parents' relationships do not last as long as those of married parents, putting their children at a higher risk for poverty and multiple family transitions (Graefe & Lichter, 1999; Manning, 2001).[10]

As a general rule, content should be emphasized except when the authorship is important, such as when referring to an important theorist or a landmark research report that is widely identified with its author.

✣ Guideline 9.8
Consider using "e.g." when there are a large number of sources for a single point.

When there are a large number of references for a single point, consider citing only some of the most important and/or most recent as examples by using "e.g." in the citation. The use of "e.g." is illustrated in Example 9.8.1.

Example 9.8.1
Use of "e.g." to cite examples of supporting literature:

In fact, racial prejudices are often so well learned that they are activated automatically upon encountering a member of relevant groups (e.g., Fazio, Jackson, Dunton, & Williams 1995; Greenwald, McGhee, & Schwartz, 1998; Olson & Fazio, 2003) and become the first piece of input on the path toward....[11]

✣ Guideline 9.9
Be generous in the use of headings and subheadings.

Short literature reviews are sometimes used to introduce reports of original research. These can often be effective without headings and subheadings. In longer reviews, headings and

---

[9] The Harvard method (also called the "author/year" method) for citing references is recommended in the *Publication Manual of the American Psychological Association*, which is the most widely used style manual in the social and behavioral sciences.

[10] Reed (2006, p. 1117).

[11] Olson & Fazio (2006, p. 421).

subheadings can help readers follow them. The topic outline (see Examples 7.8.1 and 7.13.1 in Chapter 7) can be used as a source for headings and subheadings.

As a general rule, whenever there is a large block of material (say, five or more paragraphs) that is distinct in content from the preceding material, consider adding a main heading or subheading.

When perusing the model literature reviews at the end of this book, readers will notice great diversity in the use of headings and subheadings.

✤ Guideline 9.10
Consult a style manual on formatting levels of headings.

Consult with the recommended style manual such as the *Publication Manual of the American Psychological Association* (APA) for specific guidelines for formatting various levels of headings. Some APA formats are shown in Example 9.10.1. Note that all-caps headings are *not* used. Also, note that Model Literature Review 1 uses the three levels of headings shown in the example.

Example 9.10.1
Some APA levels of headings:

Level One:

Centered Uppercase and Lowercase Heading in Bold

Level Two:

Flush Left, Italicized, Uppercase and Lowercase Heading

Level Three:

Indented with paragraph, italicized, only the first letter of the heading is capitalized.

Note that the Level Two heading is on its own line. See the heading between lines 161 and 162 on page 120. Note that a Level Three heading ends with a period, which is followed by the beginning of the paragraph on the same line. See the Level Three heading (*Parenting education.*) in line 398 on page 140 in Model Review 3 for an example.

Exercise for Chapter 9

1. Do you plan to include a historical frame of reference in the Introduction to your review? Explain. (See Guideline 9.1.)

2. Have you identified any landmark or seminal studies that you will point out? If yes, name them. (See Guideline 9.2.)

3. Do you plan to describe how the literature search was conducted? Explain. (See Guideline 9.3.)

4. Will you be using criteria to determine what literature will be covered in your review? If yes, name them. (See Guideline 9.4.)

5. Will you be using the Harvard (i.e., author/year, APA) method for citing references? If yes, will you emphasize content over authorship? Explain. (See Guideline 9.7.)

6. Will you be using "e.g." to cite examples of references that support a single point? Why? Why not? (See Guideline 9.8.)

7. Will you be using headings and subheadings in your review? Explain. (See Guideline 9.9.)

8. If you answered "yes" to Question 7, how many levels of headings will you use? (See Guideline 9.10.)

Chapter 10

Writing the First Draft:
Statistical Issues in Qualitative Reviews

The focus of this chapter is on statistical reporting in *qualitative* literature reviews. Note that the last two chapters of this book deal with reporting statistical information in highly quantitative reviews known as meta-analyses.

✤ Guideline 10.1
Consider the audience when determining the need to present statistics.

If a professor (or committee of professors) is the primary audience, his or her expectations regarding the inclusion of statistical information in a literature review should be considered.

If the goal is publication in a particular journal, examine reviews published in that journal to determine how much statistical information is included in typical reviews.

✤ Guideline 10.2
Recognize that some matters are inherently more statistical than others.

Some matters are inherently statistical. Examples are employment rates, prevalence rates (such as the prevalence of inhalant use), incidence of particular types of crime, and achievement levels on standardized tests. When discussing such matters, selective inclusion of relevant statistics from the literature can be highly appropriate.

✤ Guideline 10.3
Consider replacing vague terms with statistics when referring to quantities.

Terms such as "more," "less," "stronger," "weaker," "higher," "lower," "majority," and "minority" refer to quantities. If the quantities referred to with these terms are simple and easy to understand, consider replacing them with the specific statistics. Consider Example 10.3.1, which asserts that the suicide rate is "much higher." The statistics in the improved version of the example makes the statement more specific.

Example 10.3.1
A statement using the term "higher":

The suicide rate among American Indians age 15 to 24 years is much higher than that of other young people in the United States (Indian Health Service, 2004).

Improved Version of Example 10.3.1
A statement with the term "higher" replaced with statistics:

The suicide rate among American Indians age 15 to 24 years is more than 3 times that of other young people in the United States (37.4 versus 11.4 per 100,000; Indian Health Service, 2004).[1]

---

[1] Based on Freedenthal & Stiffman (2007, pp. 58–59).

✤ Guideline 10.4
Consider providing statistical coverage for selected studies.

Rather than providing statistical coverage for all quantitative research covered in a review, consider citing statistics for only those studies judged to be the strongest in terms of their research methodology or in terms of their importance in understanding the conclusions of the review.

✤ Guideline 10.5
Be selective when reporting statistics.

Complete statistical results are available to the interested reader in the original sources. Thus, a reviewer is not obligated to reproduce all statistical values from the originals. Instead, only a sample of important statistics should be judiciously selected. For instance, a research report being cited might have percentages for 12 different age groups of men and women (for a total of 24 percentages). A reviewer might point out only that the percentages for women ranged from 13% to 16%, while the percentages for men ranged from 12% to 14%, thus, mentioning only four of the 24 percentages in the review.

✤ Guideline 10.6
When the statistical results vary greatly, differentiate among the underlying studies.

Consider Example 10.6.1 in which the range of results (from 12% to 73%) varies greatly. Because of this variation, the statement fails to provide readers with useful information. Compare it with the improved version in which the results are differentiated in terms of the type of study that provided each result.

Example 10.6.1
Large variation (no differentiation):
Estimates of the percentage of adolescents who have experimented with Drug X vary greatly from 12% to 73% (Doe, 2006; Smith, 2007).

Improved Version of Example 10.6.1
A statement differentiating between different results:
Estimates of the percentage of adolescents who have experimented with Drug X vary greatly, with a low estimate of 12% in a nationally representative sample (Doe, 2006) to 73% in a study of a small samples of inner-city adolescents (Smith, 2007).

✤ Guideline 10.7
Consider variation when citing the results of research.

Research findings seldom apply to all individuals studied. Instead, the individuals vary in their characteristics. Be careful to use language that reflects this variation. For instance, it would be misleading to state that research shows that "low socioeconomic students are low in math achievement," since it might be taken to mean that they all are low. A more accurate statement would be that "low socioeconomic students **tend to be** low in math achievement."

Also note that an average describes the typical individual in a group. When averages are reported, the underlying scores almost always vary, so avoid making statements that imply that an average result applies to all individuals studied.

Consider Example 10.7.1, which could be interpreted to indicate that all men are lower than all women. The problem is fixed in the first improved version of the example by indicating that the result is an *average* result. It is fixed in the second improved version by indicating that the result is a *tendency* (not necessarily true of all men and all women).

Example 10.7.1
Failure to note that the result is an average with underlying variation:
Men are lower in emotional intelligence than women (Jones, 2007).

First Improved Version of Example 10.7.1
Average result is noted:
On average, men score lower in emotional intelligence than women (Jones, 2007).

Second Improved Version of Example 10.7.1
Tendency is noted:
Men tend to score lower in emotional intelligence than women (Jones, 2007).

⍦ Guideline 10.8
Consider commenting on the size of an average difference.

Pointing out whether an average difference is small, intermediate, or large can help readers understand the result. Making a judgment on size can be facilitated in three ways. First, the author of the study being cited may use language that indicates his or her judgment regarding size. Second, a reviewer can consider the scale used to measure the variable in relation to the size of a difference. For instance, a one-point difference on a five-point scale (such as Strongly Agree to Strongly Disagree) might be considered moderately large, while a one-point difference on a 50-item scale might be considered very small. Third, a measure of "effect size" might be computed and interpreted. Computation and interpretation of effect sizes is considered in the last two chapters of this book.

Consider Example 10.8.1 below with the First Improved Version of Example 10.7.1 above. Notice that the word "substantially" in Example 10.8.1 indicates that the difference is large.

Example 10.8.1
Size of average difference indicated with the word "substantially":
On average, men scored substantially lower in emotional intelligence than women (Jones, 2007).

⍦ Guideline 10.9
Consider commenting on the strength of a correlation.

Correlation coefficients describe the strength and direction of a relationship between two sets of scores. They can vary from +1.00 (a perfect positive correlation) to 0.00 (no correlation) to −1.00 (a perfect negative correlation). While there are no universally accepted labels to describe the strength of relationships, these are some rough guidelines: values below about .25 (*weak*), values near .50 (*moderate*), and values above .75 (*strong*).

Example 10.9.1 indicates only that positive correlations were found. The improved version on the next page indicates that they are strong.

Example 10.9.1
Strength of relationship not indicated":
In this set of studies, the correlations between vocabulary scores and reading comprehension scores were positive.

Improved Version of Example 10.9.1
Strength of relationship indicated:

In this set of studies, the correlations between vocabulary scores and reading comprehension scores were positive and strong.

↳ Guideline 10.10
Consider reporting the values of correlation coefficients parenthetically.

Additional information about correlation can be provided by reporting the values of the correlation coefficients parenthetically, as illustrated in Example 10.10.1.

Example 10.10.1
Values of r given in parentheses:

In this set of studies, the correlations between vocabulary scores and reading comprehension scores were positive and strong (values of r ranging from .79 to .82).

↳ Guideline 10.11
It is seldom necessary to mention "statistical significance."

As indicated in Guideline 5.17 in Chapter 5, the fact that a difference is statistically significant indicates only that it is reliable—not necessarily that it is large.

When reviewers of research literature point out that a difference was found, readers of the review will assume that it is a statistically significant difference. Thus, reviewers typically do not point out that such a difference is statistically significant.

As a corollary, it is not necessary to present values associated with significance testing such as *t*, *F*, chi-square, *df*, and *p*.

↳ Guideline 10.12
With rare exceptions, avoid reproducing tables of statistical values in a review.

Research reports frequently contain tables of statistical values. These tables usually contain more statistics than are needed for readers of reviews to get an overview of the overall results. Thus, reviewers very rarely reproduce statistical tables from the literature.

↳ Guideline 10.13
Consider building tables to present selected statistics.

Tables can be an effective way to organize and present large amounts of material. The next chapter covers building tables for inclusion in a literature review. These may contain some selected statistics, but they are not reproductions of statistical tables from the literature.

Concluding Comments

The extent to which a qualitative review is quantified with statistics is a matter of judgment. A reviewer should consider the needs of his or her audience as well as the purpose of the review. Including some judiciously selected statistics in a review can preclude the criticism that the review is too broad and general and, hence, fails to fully support the conclusions. In contrast, a qualitative review that is riddled with a multitude of statistics can make it difficult for readers to obtain a clear overview of the material being reviewed.

Exercise for Chapter 10

1. Is your topic (or some of your subtopics) inherently statistical? Explain. (See Guideline 10.2.)

2. Examine Example 10.3.1. Do you agree that the improved version is superior? Explain.

3. Have you identified some studies for which you plan to provide more detailed statistical coverage than for other studies? Explain. (See Guideline 10.4.)

4. Overall, to what extent do you plan to cite specific statistics in your review?

Notes:

Chapter 11

Building Tables to Summarize Literature

Tables can be an effective way to present a summary of information that can be easily scanned by readers.[1]

⤷ Guideline 11.1
Consider building a table to show selected statistics from an important study.

As indicated in Guideline 10.4 in the previous chapter, one technique to consider when writing qualitative reviews is to present statistical material only for especially important studies being reviewed. Even when just the highlights of statistical material are included in the narrative, the narrative may be difficult to follow if it is cluttered with numbers.

Consider Example 11.1.1, which presents selected statistics within a paragraph. Example 11.1.2 shows the same statistics in a table, which is much easier to read.

Example 11.1.1
Statistics presented in a narrative (more difficult to follow than the same statistics tabled in Example 11.1.2):

The most rigorous evaluation of the program was conducted by Doe (2007). During the first three years, students from five schools participated, while students from eight schools participated during the last year for which data are available. The number of students participating for each respective year were 94, 110, 111, and 143. During the first three years of the program (i.e., 2002–2003, 2003–2004, and 2004–2005), the dropout rate consistently declined. During these years, the dropout rates were 22.5%, 20.4%, and 17.2%, respectively. During the last year (2005–2006), the dropout rate (18.5%) inched up, possibly because of the addition of three schools to the program during that year.

Example 11.1.2
Same statistics as in Example 11.1.1 (tabular form in this example is superior to the narrative form in Example 11.1.1):

Table 1. *Numbers of schools, students, and dropout rates by year.*

School Year	Number of Schools	Number of Students	Dropout Rate (%)
2002–2003	5	94	22.5
2003–2004	5	110	20.4
2004–2005	5	111	17.2
2005–2006	8	143	18.5

---

[1] Guideline 6.6 in Chapter 6 suggests building tables to get an overview of the literature while preparing a topic outline. Tables prepared for that purpose can be rough and informal. This chapter deals with building formal tables for inclusion in a literature review.

✤ Guideline 11.2
Table numbers and highlights of the tables should be mentioned in the narrative.

Tables should not be presented in isolation. Instead, highlights of a table should be mentioned in the narrative, while mentioning the table number where additional details can be found. For instance, for the table in Example 11.1.2 on the previous page, a brief narrative such as the one in Example 11.2.1 could be used.

Example 11.2.1
Narrative for the table in Example 11.1.2:

The most rigorous evaluation of the program was conducted by Doe (2007). As indicated in Table 1 above, during the first three years, the dropout rate consistently declined. During the last year, the dropout rate inched up, possibly because of the addition of three new schools to the program during that year.

✤ Guideline 11.3
Consider building a table to show statistics derived from a variety of studies.

One of the most effective uses of tables in literature reviews is to present results from a variety of studies in a single table, which allows readers to scan to compare results from study to study. This guideline is illustrated in the table in Example 11.3.1.

Example 11.3.1
A table summarizing the statistical results of various studies:

Table 1
Recidivism Rates for Prisoners Participating in Rehabilitation Programs

Source:	Type of Program	Number of Participants	Recidivism Rates (%)
Black (2004)	Individual counseling	22	13.5
Smith (2006)	Job skills training	76	43.2
Jones (2005)	Academic skills instruction	221	49.6
West (2007)	Group counseling	55	29.3

✤ Guideline 11.4
Consider the order in which to present studies in tables.

One way to order studies is alphabetically by researchers' last names, which is done in Example 11.3.1. This is especially appropriate for tables that contain information on a large number of studies. An alphabetical list allows readers to quickly locate studies mentioned in the narrative. For instance, if the narrative says "West (2006) was the only study employing group counseling," readers can skip to the bottom of an alphabetically arranged table to obtain information from the table about West's study.

Studies can also be arranged in chronological order by year of publication. This is especially appropriate if the reviewer wants to point out trends in results across time.

A third arrangement that is sometimes useful is to list the studies in order of the magnitude of the results (e.g., put the study with the highest recidivism rate in the top row, the study with the next highest rate in the second row, and so on).

ꙮ Guideline 11.5
Tables can be used to present material other than statistical results.

While tables are especially appropriate for presenting statistical results, tables can be used to summarize other characteristics of the literature as long as the characteristics can be stated very concisely; tables are usually inappropriate for presenting long narrative material.

The authors of Example 11.5.1 searched the literature for pain observation scales used with older adults with cognitive or communication difficulties. They identified 13 such scales, which they summarized in the table (only a portion of which is shown in the example).

Example 11.5.1
A table summarizing the characteristics of pain observation scales:[2]

Table 1

Structural Characteristics of Pain Observation Scales

Scale:	Target Population	No. of Items	Categories*	Response Category	Score Range
Pain Behavior Method	Cognitively impaired	5	1, 2, 4	Presence or absence	0–5
Assessment for Discomfort in Dementia	Patients with moderate to severe dementia	5	1, 2, 3, 4, 5, 6	Presence or absence	0–5
Abbey Pain Scale	Patients with end-stage dementia	6	1, 2, 3, 4, 5, 6	4-point scale	0–18

*Note: 1 = facial expression; 2 = motor behavior; 3 = social behavior or mood; 4 = vocalization; 5 = eat or sleep pattern; 6 = physiological indicators

ꙮ Guideline 11.6
Use homogeneous content for each table.

Tables are easier to build and are easier for readers to follow when the content of each table is homogeneous. For instance, one table could be used to summarize results from experiments, while another could be used to summarize the results of surveys; one table could be used to summarize the results for adolescents, while another could be used to summarize the results for adults; and so on.

ꙮ Guideline 11.7
Consider establishing inclusion criteria for tables.

When there is a very large number of sources that might be summarized in a table, consider keeping the table reasonably short by establishing inclusion criteria. For instance, if there are 40 experiments on a topic, consider building a table for only the 12 that meet the criterion of having random assignment to experimental and control groups.

---

[2] Modified from van Herk, van Dijk, Baar, Tibboel, & de Wit (2007, p. 36).

♭ Guideline 11.8
Avoid the overuse of tables.

While tables are an effective way to provide readers with an overview of selected material, they do not synthesize material. The emphasis in a literature review should be on the narrative that relates the various elements in the literature to each other. Overuse of tables can distract from this emphasis.

♭ Guideline 11.9
Give each table a number and descriptive title (i.e., caption).

A table number (e.g., Table 1) allows the reviewer to refer to the table in the narrative by number (e.g., "As indicated in Table 1, the....").
A table's title (often called the "caption") should indicate the contents of the table.

♭ Guideline 11.10
Consult a style manual for guidelines on formatting tables.

Style manuals such as the *Publication Manual of the American Psychological Association* (APA) often provide specific advice on formatting and labeling tables. The tables in this chapter are consistent with APA style. For instance, the table numbers appear on a separate line from the captions, and the captions are in italics.

♭ Guideline 11.11
Learn how to build tables using a word processing program.

Complex word processing programs have table-building features that make building tables relatively easy. For instance, in Microsoft Word, click on "Table" at the top of the screen, then click on "Insert" (from the drop-down menu) and then click on "Table" (from the next drop-down menu.) At this point, a dialog box will appear which asks for the number of columns and rows. After entering the desired numbers, click on "OK" to insert a table in the document.
The width of rows can be adjusted by dragging the vertical lines to the left or right using the mouse. Additional formatting tools can be accessed by clicking on "View," then on "Toolbars," and then on "Tables and Borders." Running the cursor across the icons in the Tables and Borders toolbar will produce pop-ups that indicate the function of each icon.

Exercise for Chapter 11

1. At this point, do you plan to include any tables in your literature review?

2. If "yes" to Question 1, will any tables be used to present statistics from a single important study? (See Guideline 11.1.)

3. If "yes" to Question 1, will any tables be used to present statistics derived from a variety of studies? (See Guideline 11.1.)

4. If "yes" to Question 1, will any tables be used to present material other than statistical results? (See Guideline 11.5.)

5. Have you consulted a style manual for guidelines on formatting tables? If yes, was the style manual useful? Explain. (See Guideline 11.10.)

6. How experienced are you with building tables using a word processing program? If you are experienced, do you have any suggestions for less-experienced students? Explain. (See Guideline 11.11.)

Notes:

Chapter 12

Revising and Refining the First Draft

Having written the first draft, review it while considering the following guidelines.

↳ Guideline 12.1
Put the first draft aside and reread it after a couple of days.

Material that seemed clear when it was written will often seem less so when it is reread a couple of days later.

↳ Guideline 12.2
Check the structure of each paragraph; keep it simple.

The purpose of scientific writing is to communicate information clearly and unambiguously. Thus, it is perfectly acceptable in scientific writing to write paragraphs that follow the simplest model for paragraph writing: Write a topic sentence first, and then write sentences that provide details that support the material in the topic sentence.

↳ Guideline 12.3
Consider breaking long paragraphs into two or more shorter ones.

Long paragraphs can be hard to follow. Often, the material in a long paragraph can be more effectively presented in two or more shorter ones. For instance, instead of using one very long paragraph to discuss a relevant theory, consider using three: (1) a paragraph to define and illustrate the theory, (2) a paragraph to discuss literature that supports the theory, and (3) a paragraph to discuss literature that casts doubt on the theory.

↳ Guideline 12.4
Consider using transitional terms between paragraphs and within paragraphs.

Example 12.4.1 shows the beginnings of three sequential paragraphs in a literature review. Notice how the transitional terms, which are italicized in bold, help make smooth transitions from one paragraph to the next.

> **Example 12.4.1**
> *The beginnings of three paragraphs. Paragraphs 2 and 3 contain transitional terms* ***(italicized in bold)***:
>
> A considerable body of theory suggests that elected public officials in a democracy have reason to pay attention to public opinion. Rational choice theorists, for example, have long argued that....
>
> Empirically, ***too***, there is substantial scholarly evidence of rather close connections between citizens' opinions....
>
> ***Moreover***, there has been an enormous increase in policy-related polls and surveys of public opinion....

In his book on rhetoric and style in writing, Harris (2003) makes a number of suggestions regarding the use of transitional terms, four of which are shown in Box 12A.

Box 12A *The use of transitional terms.*[1]

> 1. Use transitions between paragraphs to signal connections (addition, contrast, and so forth) between idea segments. Use transitions within paragraphs to signal a change from one sentence to another or from one section of the paragraph to another.
>
> 2. Use sufficient transitions to provide coherence (holding together, like glue) and continuity (making the thought process easy to follow). Less experienced writers tend to supply too few transitions.
>
> 3. Avoid using too many strong transitions. Be careful to avoid littering your writing with *however* and *nevertheless*. Strong transitions should be used sparingly.
>
> 4. Transitions become stronger when they are placed at the beginning (or end) of a sentence, milder (or less strong) when they are moved into the sentence. Generally, moving transitions into the sentence is the better choice.

Box 12B provide examples of transitional terms, which Harris has classified according to function (e.g., "addition" and "comparison") as well as according to strength (i.e., "milder" and "stronger"). While they are especially important for making transitions from one paragraph to another, they can also be used to make transitions within paragraphs.

Box 12B *Transitional terms that can be used to provide coherence.*[2]

	Milder		**Stronger**	
Addition	a further x	next	additionally	first, second
	also	nor	again	further
	and	other	besides	furthermore
	and then	then	equally important	in addition
	another	too	finally, last	moreover
Comparison	a similar x	just as...so too	comparable	likewise
	another x like		in the same way	similarly
Contrast	and yet	rather	alternatively	nonetheless
	but	still	at the same time	notwithstanding
	but another	though	conversely	on the contrary
	or	yet	even so	on the other hand
	otherwise		for all that	otherwise
			however	still
			in contrast	
			instead	
				Continued →

---

[1] Harris (2003, p. 35). Reproduced with permission.
[2] Harris (2003, p. 36). Reproduced with permission.

Time	after	now	at last	immediately
	afterward	recently	at length	meanwhile
	before	shortly	at that time	presently
	earlier	soon	currently	subsequently
	first, second,	then	eventually	thereafter
	third	today	finally	
	later	tomorrow		
	next			
Purpose	because of this x	to do this	for that reason	to this end
			for this purpose	with this object
Place	beyond	nearby	adjacent to	in the front
	here	there	at that point	on the other side
			in the back	opposite to
Result	and so	then	accordingly	in consequence
	so		as a result	therefore
			consequently	thereupon
			hence	thus

Transitional terms can also be used within paragraphs to make clear the relationships among the ideas in the paragraphs.

✎ Guideline 12.5
Double-check to be sure there is a sufficient number of headings and subheadings.

Make sure that there is a sufficient number of headings and subheadings to guide the reader through the review. As a general rule, be generous in the use of headings and subheadings.

✎ Guideline 12.6
Double-check to make sure that all cited material has been referenced.

Check each citation in the body of the review against the reference list to be sure that none of the references have been inadvertently omitted. Preparation of a reference list is covered in Chapter 14.

✎ Guideline 12.7
Check for the overuse of quotations.

As indicated in Guideline 8.5, quotations should be used very sparingly in a literature review. When revising, reconsider each quotation to determine whether its contents could be as effectively presented in paraphrase.

✎ Guideline 12.8
Check for the overuse of rhetorical questions.

A rhetorical question is one that the writer answers immediately (i.e., it is not a question that the reviewer expects readers to answer). Reviewers sometimes use these questions as the topic sentences of paragraphs. While occasional use can provide variety in paragraph beginnings, too many rhetorical questions can be distracting.

Example 12.8.1 shows the use of a rhetorical question at the beginning of a paragraph.

Example 12.8.1
A paragraph that begins with a rhetorical question (use very sparingly):
What does research say about the validity of the Doe Anxiety Scale? The research on this question is extensive. In perhaps the most comprehensive study to date....

⍦ Guideline 12.9
Consider deleting truisms.

A "truism" is something all educated people probably know and believe. As such, truisms add no important information to a literature review. The first sentence in Example 12.9.1 is a truism that should be deleted.

Example 12.9.1
First sentence is a truism that should be deleted:
Without a doubt, good nutrition is very important. The 1990 Nutrition Labeling and Education Act (NLEA) requires food manufacturers to....

⍦ Guideline 12.10
Remove any material meant to be clever or amusing.

Scientific writing is serious writing, and readers will be interested in a serious analysis of the material on the topic. Attempts to be clever or amusing will detract from this.

⍦ Guideline 12.11
Consider deleting anecdotal material.

Sometimes reviewers describe personal incidents or other anecdotes. While such evidence can be relevant in a literature review, it is one of the weakest forms of scientific evidence and should be used exceedingly sparingly.

⍦ Guideline 12.12
Make sure the tone is neutral and nonemotional.

Statements designed to appeal to emotions are inappropriate in literature reviews.

⍦ Guideline 12.13
Have the first draft critiqued by others.

Other individuals such as fellow students can provide a fresh eye for catching mechanical and stylistic errors. When asking for a critique, it is especially important to ask those who will be critiquing to mark any material that is unclear in meaning.

Exercise for Chapter 12

1. Did you set aside your first draft and reread it a couple of days later? If yes, was it useful to do this? (See Guideline 12.1.)

2. Did you check each paragraph for simple structure? (See Guideline 12.2.)

3. Did you break some long paragraphs into two or more paragraphs? (See Guideline 12.3.)

4. Did you check for transitions to make paragraphs flow from one to the next? (See Guideline 12.4.)

5. Did you check to make sure there is a sufficient number of headings and subheadings? (See Guideline 12.5.)

6. Did you double-check to make sure all cited material has been referenced? (See Guideline 12.6.)

7. Did you check for overuse of quotations? (See Guideline 12.7.)

8. Did you check for overuse of rhetorical questions? (See Guideline 12.8.)

9. Did you check for and delete truisms? (See Guideline 12.9.)

10. Did you remove material meant to be clever or amusing? (See Guideline 12.10.)

11. Did you consider deleting anecdotal material? If yes, did you delete any? (See Guideline 12.11.)

12. Did you check to make sure the tone is neutral and nonemotional? (See Guideline 12.12.)

13. Did you have the first draft critiqued by others? If so, how useful were their comments? Explain. (See Guideline 12.13.)

Notes:

Chapter 13

Writing Titles and Abstracts

This chapter covers guidelines for writing effective titles and abstracts for literature reviews.

The function of titles and abstracts is to help readers identify reviews that are of interest to them.

✤ Guideline 13.1
A title should be brief.

Typically, the title of a literature review published in academic journals consists of about 10 to 14 words. Example 13.1.1 shows some titles of typical length.

Example 13.1.1
Titles of typical length for literature reviews published in academic journals:

Helping Adults with Diabetes: A Review of Evidence-Based Interventions[1]
　–10 words

The Role of Parent-Child Play in Children's Development[2]
　–9 words

Prevention and Treatment of Posttraumatic Stress Disorder in the School Setting[3]
　–11 words

✤ Guideline 13.2
Consider referring to groups of variables in a title.

If a review contains a discussion of many variables, consider writing a title that refers to the variables in groups instead of by their individual names. For instance, Example 13.2.1 refers to five individual variables. In the Improved Version, only two *groups* of variables (i.e., social benefits and physical benefits) are mentioned.

Example 13.2.1
A lengthy title improved by referring to variables in groups:
Benefits of Physical Education for Primary Grade Students: Friendship Bonding, Cooperation with Peers, Physical Stamina, Strength, and Body Weight

Improved Version of Example 13.2.1
Title improved by referring to variables in groups:
Social and Physical Benefits of Physical Education for Primary Grade Students

---

[1] DeCoster & Cummings (2005, p. 259).
[2] Blundon & Schaefer (2006, p. 1).
[3] Kruczek & Salsman (2006, p. 461).

✥ Guideline 13.3
A title should be a statement—not a complete sentence.

The titles under the previous two guidelines illustrate this guideline because they do not have subjects and verbs to make them complete sentences. Note that because they are not sentences, they should not end with periods.

✥ Guideline 13.4
Avoid stating conclusions in a title.

A title should indicate what was reviewed, not the conclusions of the review. This is because the conclusions of a review are usually complex, which precludes an accurate representation of them in a statement as short as a title.

Example 13.4.1
A title that states a conclusion (not recommended):

Behavioral Preparation Programs, Music Therapy, and Acupuncture Are Strategies That Alleviate Preoperative Anxiety in Children

Improved Version of Example 13.4.1
Title improved by referring to the topic of the review:

Prevention and Intervention Strategies to Alleviate Preoperative Anxiety in Children[4]

✥ Guideline 13.5
Avoid using a "yes–no" question as a title.

Almost any topic being reviewed is sufficiently complex that a simple "yes" or "no" answer would be an oversimplified conclusion. Thus, writers should avoid writing titles that imply that the conclusion of the review is "yes" or "no." In Example 13.5.1, the title is in the form of a question. The Improved Version refers to the same variables in a statement.

Example 13.5.1
A title in the form of a question (not recommended):

Do Depression and Anxiety Interfere with Smoking Cessation Efforts?

Improved Version of Example 13.5.1
Title improved by using a statement:

The Influence of Depression and Anxiety on Smoking Cessation Efforts

✥ Guideline 13.6
Consider using a subtitle to indicate that the document is a review.

Consider using the terms "review," "meta-analysis,"[5] or some derivative of them in a subtitle. Using these terms will help readers who are trying to locate reviews (as opposed to reports of original research). Example 13.6.1 contains titles that follow this guideline.

Example 13.6.1
Three titles with subtitles indicating that the document is a review:

Family Violence in the Military: A Review of the Literature[6]

---

[4] Based on Wright, Stewart, Finley, & Buffett-Jerrott (2007, p. 52).
[5] Meta-analyses are highly quantitative reviews, which are described in the last two chapters of this book.
[6] Rentz et al. (2006, p. 93).

Example 13.6.1 (*Continued*)

Effectiveness of Acupuncture for Migraine: Critical Literature Review[7]

Effectiveness of Secondary Pregnancy Prevention Programs: A Meta-Analysis[8]

An exception to this guideline is when writing for a journal that publishes only literature reviews (e.g., *Psychological Bulletin*). For such journals, the terms "review" and "literature review" are usually omitted from titles. Because meta-analysis is a relatively new set of techniques, however, it is customary to mention the term "meta-analysis" in subtitles, even in journals that publish only reviews.

✎ Guideline 13.7
A typical abstract should be relatively brief.

Most abstracts are brief. For instance, the *Publication Manual of the American Psychological Association* recommends that an abstract not exceed 120 words.

Note that some journals require longer abstracts for all articles they publish. In addition, some universities require longer abstracts for theses and dissertations.

✎ Guideline 13.8
An abstract should indicate the general topic of the review.

The abstracts shown below in Examples 13.9.1, 13.9.2, and 13.10.1 illustrate this guideline.

✎ Guideline 13.9
An abstract should indicate the scope of the review.

An abstract should indicate the types of material covered by the review (i.e., the scope). For instance, the abstract in Example 13.9.1 indicates that only qualitative literature (not quantitative research) is reviewed and that the review addresses four themes.

Example 13.9.1

An abstract that indicates the scope of the review:

With an aging population, concerns for road safety point to a growing need for research into the driving attitudes and habits of older adults. In this review of the qualitative literature, we have identified 25 studies that used focus groups or interviews to learn about the experiences and concerns of older drivers. The review addresses four themes: (1) The importance of driving; (2) negative aspects of driving; (3) the process of driving cessation; and (4) views of transportation alternatives. An understanding of these topics can help to improve program and research planning for the transportation needs of older adults.[9]

Of course, it is not necessary to use a numbered list to follow this guideline, as illustrated in Example 13.9.2 in which the scope is clearly indicated in the last sentences of the abstract.

Example 13.9.2

An abstract that indicates the scope of the review:

Many parents of children with autism spectrum disorders (ASD) report that their children have feeding problems. A body of literature targeted toward parents of children with ASD includes information about possible interventions for this problem. Most intervention suggestions within this literature have been only anecdotally reported to be effective; few research studies have addressed maladaptive feeding behaviors in children with ASD. This review synthesizes current research regarding the types of feeding problems and

---

[7] Griggs & Jensen (2006, p. 491).
[8] Corcoran & Pillai (2007, p. 5).
[9] Gardezi et al. (2006, p. 5).

interventions used with children with ASD. In addition, the authors briefly discuss the literature on treating feeding problems in other populations as a means of comparison. They also point out differences in empirically supported treatments and treatments used by parents for aberrant feeding behaviors in children with ASD.[10]

✎ Guideline 13.10
If space permits, general conclusions and findings may be stated in the abstract.

While an abstract is too short to include a detailed description of the conclusions and the findings in the literature that supports them, it is acceptable to include statements indicating the nature and direction of the conclusions (and specific findings) if space permits. In Example 13.10.1, the reviewers mention the topic and describe the scope of the review in the first three sentences. Then they discuss the findings of the review.

Example 13.10.1
An abstract that includes conclusions:

Family violence, including both child maltreatment and spouse abuse, is a public health concern in both military and civilian populations. However, there is limited knowledge concerning violence in military families relative to civilian families. This literature review critically reviews studies that examine child maltreatment and spouse abuse among military families and compares family violence in military versus nonmilitary populations. Physical abuse and neglect compose the majority of the reported and substantiated cases of child maltreatment in military families, followed by sexual abuse and emotional abuse. On the other hand, physical abuse represents more than 90% of all substantiated cases of spouse abuse in military families, followed by emotional abuse, neglect, and sexual abuse. Mixed results were found when comparing military and nonmilitary families in terms of child maltreatment and spouse abuse, in part because of a lack of consistency in policies and practices between military and civilian agencies.[11]

✎ Guideline 13.11
It is acceptable to cite specific statistics in the abstract of a meta-analysis.

Meta-analytic reviews, which is the topic of the last two chapters, produce statistics such as d. Including their values in an abstract can be informative. Example 13.11.1 illustrates how this can be done. (The computation and interpretation of d are described in the last two chapters of this book.)

Example 13.11.1
An abstract of a meta-analytic review that includes statistics (i.e., values of d*)*:

The prevailing view in popular culture and the psychological literature is that White women have greater body dissatisfaction than women of color. In this meta-analysis, 6 main effect sizes were obtained for differences among Asian American, Black, Hispanic, and White women with a sample of 98 studies, yielding 222 effect sizes. The average d for the White-Black comparison was 0.29, indicating that White women are more dissatisfied, but the difference is small. All other comparisons were smaller, and many were close to zero. The findings directly challenge the belief that there are large differences in dissatisfaction between White and all non-White women and suggest that body dissatisfaction may not be the golden girl problem promoted in the literature. Implications for theory and treatment are discussed.[12]

---

[10] Ledford & Gast (2006, p. 153).
[11] Rentz et al. (2006, p. 93).
[12] Grabe & Hyde (2006, p. 622).

Exercise for Chapter 13

1. Write a title for your literature review. Check to see that it is consistent with Guidelines 13.1 through 13.6.

2. Write an abstract of your review. Check to see that it is consistent with Guidelines 13.8 through 13.10.

3. Does your abstract contain more than 120 words? If yes, is a longer abstract acceptable to your audience (e.g., your professor)?

Notes:

Chapter 14

Preparing a Reference List

The guidelines in this chapter for preparing reference lists are consistent with the principles in the *Publication Manual of the American Psychological Association* (APA), which is the most frequently used style manual in the social and behavioral sciences. The APA Manual can be purchased at most college and university bookstores and is available for purchase online at www.apa.org.

✣ Guideline 14.1
Place the reference list at the end of the review under the main heading "References."

The main heading of "References" should be centered and in bold. It is the last element in a review except for author contact information or appendices, if any.

✣ Guideline 14.2
A reference list for a literature review should refer only to publications cited in the literature review.

Writers often have some sources that, for one reason or another, were not cited in their reviews. References for these uncited materials should *not* be included in the reference list at the end of a literature review.

✣ Guideline 14.3
List references alphabetically by surname of the author.

For sources with multiple authors, use the surname of the "first author" (i.e., the first author mentioned at the beginning of the source).

✣ Guideline 14.4
Use hanging indents for the second and subsequent lines of references.

A hanging indent is created when the first line is *not* indented but the subsequent ones are indented, as in Example 14.4.1, where the surnames of the authors stand out in the left margin of the list.

Example 14.4.1
Three references in alphabetical order with hanging indents:

Apple, D. W. (2006). Experimental evidence of the XYZ phenomenon. *The Journal of New Developments, 55,* 99–104.

Boy, C. C. (2007). New evidence on the validity of the XYZ phenomenon. *Journal of Psychological Renderings, 44,* 454–499.

Catty, F. B., & Jones, C. M. (2007). The XYZ phenomenon reexamined. *Journal of Social and Economic Justice, 167,* 19–26.

⤷ Guideline 14.5
Learn how to create hanging indents using a word processor.

Modern word processing programs make it easy to create hanging indents. For instance, to create a hanging indent in Microsoft Word:

1. Type a reference as a paragraph without any indents.

2. Click on the reference with the right mouse button, and then click on "Paragraph." A dialog box will appear.

3. Within the dialog box, click on the down-arrowhead to the right of "Special," and then click on the word "Hanging." (Note that at this point, Word will suggest a size for the indent under the word "By.")

4. Click OK.[1]

⤷ Guideline 14.6
Italicize the titles of journals and their volume numbers.

As most students know from basic composition classes, the titles of books should be italicized. Likewise, the titles of journals should be italicized.

Typically, all the issues of a journal for a given year constitute a volume. Volume 1 consists of all issues the first year a journal was published, Volume 2 consists of all issues the second year, and so on. Within each volume, all numbers are sequential. In other words, the first page of the first issue of a year is page 1. For the next issue of the year, the page numbers pick up where the previous issue left off. For instance, if the first issue for a year ends on page 98, the second issue of the year will begin with page 99.

In light of the above, it is clear that all a reader needs in order to locate an article is the title of the journal as well as the volume number and page numbers. Issue numbers are not essential for this purpose.

Volume numbers should be italicized. (Issue numbers do not need to be included in a reference.)

Example 14.6.1 has both the title of the journal (*Urban Education*) and its volume number (*42*) italicized.

Example 14.6.1

A reference with the journal title and volume number italicized:

Jeynes, W. H. (2007). The relationship between parental involvement and urban secondary student academic achievement: A meta-analysis. *Urban Education, 42,* 82–110.

⤷ Guideline 14.7
Pay particular attention to capitalization.

Style manuals specify when to capitalize in reference lists. For instance, in APA style, only the first letter of the first word in the main title (and subtitle, if any) of an article title are capitalized. This is true even though all important words in the titles of articles *in the journals themselves* are capitalized. This illustrates that some matters of style cannot be logically deduced; attention to details in a style manual is required.

---

[1] If the default size suggested by Word is too large or small, right-click again on the reference, click on "Paragraph" again, and change the number of inches under "By."

✎ Guideline 14.8
Pay particular attention to punctuation.

Failure to use proper punctuation in a reference list could lead to corrections on a student's review. In APA style for journals, for instance, there should always be a period after the close of the parentheses around the year of publication as well as at the end of the journal title and at the end of the reference.

✎ Guideline 14.9
Do not add extraneous material such as abbreviations for page numbers.

Page numbers in APA style are the last two numbers in a reference. APA style does not use abbreviations such as "pp." for page numbers; nor does it use the word "Volume" or the abbreviation "Vol. no."

✎ Guideline 14.10
Provide the date and URL in references for material published on the Internet.

Because material published on the Web may be modified from time to time, it is important to indicate the date on which material from the Internet was retrieved. Also, be sure to provide the full URL (such as www.example.com/retrieve) as well as any other identifying information such as the name of the author, if known. This Guideline is illustrated in Example 14.10.1.

Example 14.10.1
A reference to material retrieved from the Internet:

Jones, A. A. (2006). Some new thoughts on material evidence in the XYZ matter. Retrieved January 2, 2007, from www.newexample.org/specimen.

✎ Guideline 14.11
Format references to books in accordance with a style manual.

Example 14.11.1 shows a reference to a book formatted in APA style.

Example 14.11.1
A reference to a book in APA style:

Doe, B. D., & Smith, V. A. (2007). *The big book of little thoughts* (2nd ed.). New York: New Template Press.

✎ Guideline 14.12
Double-check the reference list against the citations in the body of the review.

In addition to checking to see that all cited material is referenced in the reference list, check to see that spelling of the authors' names is the same in both places. Also, check to see that the years of publication in the citations and in the reference list are consistent.

Concluding Comment

To cite a type of source not covered in this chapter, consult a comprehensive style manual such as the APA Manual, which specifies how to cite many types of specialized sources such as a newsletter article, an unpublished paper presented at a professional meeting, a published technical report, an edited book, and so on.

Exercise for Chapter 14

1. Examine the reference lists in the journal articles you collected for your literature review. What percentage of the reference lists are in APA style?

2. Will you be following APA style when preparing a reference list? If not, which style manual will you use?

3. Will you be citing any types of sources that are not covered in this chapter (e.g., a newsletter)? If yes, have you consulted a style manual to determine how to cite it? Was the style manual useful? Explain.

Chapter 15

Introduction to Meta-Analysis

The prefix "meta-" means "more comprehensive; transcending others." A meta-analysis is a statistical analysis that transcends others by mathematically combining the results of studies conducted by various researchers to obtain an overall combined result (a statistical synthesis).[1] Although this chapter discusses only the basics of meta-analysis, the information in it can be used to make important contributions to synthesizing data on a topic. Chapter 16 provides more advanced material on meta-analytic techniques.

Whether students are writing qualitative or quantitative literature reviews, they should master the material in this chapter since a basic understanding of meta-analysis is needed to properly interpret the results of meta-analyses, which students might find in the literature they are reviewing.

The discussion under Guideline 15.1 provides a concrete example of what is meant by "meta-analysis" and how it can be used to synthesize the results from two or more studies reporting percentages.

✤ Guideline 15.1
Meta-analysis can be used to synthesize percentages reported in various studies.

The raw statistics from three national polls (conducted by three different researchers) on public attitudes toward the XYZ issue are presented in Box 15A. In each case, the pollster has reported the number of people surveyed and the percentage who said "yes" when asked a question about the issue. The three pollsters obtained three different percentages, as shown in the box. Such differences are to be expected because of sampling error (each pollster used only a sample of the entire national population). Based on the three samples, what is the best estimate of the percentage of the population that would answer "yes" if everyone in the population were polled?

Box 15A *Results of three national polls on the XYZ issue.*

Poll 1	**Poll 2**	**Poll 3**
Number of people interviewed: 595	Number of people interviewed: 1,028	Number of people interviewed: 1,440
Percentage who answered "yes": 72%	Percentage who answered "yes": 51%	Percentage who answered "yes": 50%

To answer the question, a reviewer might be tempted to simply sum the percentages (72% + 51% + 50% = 173%) and divide the sum by the number of polls (173% ÷ 3 = 57.66%, which rounds to 58%). However, notice that Polls 2 and 3 had many more respondents than Poll 1. Hence, the results of Polls 2 and 3 are probably more reliable than Poll 1. As a result, Polls 2 and 3 should be given more weight in determining the average percentage.

The first step in giving more weight to polls with larger numbers of respondents is to calculate the total number of respondents in all three polls, which is done in Column 2 of Box 15B (595 + 1,028, + 1,440 = 3,063).

---

[1] An alternative meaning of "meta-" is "occurring later" or "occurring after." This meaning also applies to meta-analysis because a meta-analysis occurs after the original studies on which it is based have occurred.

The second step is to calculate the total number of respondents who answered "yes" in each poll. For instance for Poll 1, 72% of the 595 respondents answered "yes." To get the number who answered "yes," multiply the decimal equivalent of 72% (0.72) times the total number (595), which yields 428. In Column 4, the same procedure is used for all three polls. The sum of Column 4 in the box indicates that a total of 1,672 (428 + 524 + 720) answered "yes."

Box 15B *First steps in calculating a weighted percentage.*

Column 1	Column 2	Column 3	Column 4
	Total number of respondents.	Percentage who said "yes."	Calculate the number who said "yes" by multiplying.
Poll 1	595	72%	(595)(0.72) = 428
Poll 2	1,028	51%	(1,028)(0.51) = 524
Poll 3	1,440	50%	(1,440)(0.50) = 720
Sum of Column 2 = 3,063		**Sum of Column 4 = 1,672**	

At this point, a quantitative reviewer could report that 1,672 of the 3,063 respondents in the three studies answered "yes." Such a report would be a report on a meta-analysis (i.e., a statistical synthesis of the results of the three studies).

The values of 1,672 and 3,063 can be used to calculate a single percentage for the three studies combined. Specifically, the result of dividing the part (1,672) by the whole (3,063) and multiplying by 100 will yield the percentage. Thus: 1,672/3,063 = 0.5459 × 100 = 54.59%, which rounds to 55%.[2]

Notice that a simple average of 58% was obtained on the previous page by adding the three percentages and dividing by three (i.e., giving the three studies equal weight). A weighted average as calculated here (55%) is a better estimate than the simple average since polls with more respondents are given more weight. Thus, in a report on a meta-analysis of the three polls, a reviewer could make a statement such as: "The combined percentage for the three studies, weighted for sample size, is 55%."

A more elaborate statement regarding the example being discussed here is shown in Example 15.1.1.

Example 15.1.1
Sample statement of results of the meta-analysis of percentages:

Three national polls were conducted on public attitudes toward XYZ. The results of the polls are shown in Table 15.1 on the previous page. Note that the percentages of respondents that responded "yes" vary from 50% in the poll with the largest sample to 72% in the poll with the smallest sample size. The average percentage, weighted to take account of differences in sample size, is 55%, which indicates that a majority of the population is in favor of XYZ. This percentage is based on a total sample of 3,063 respondents.

Note that a major advantage of meta-analysis is that it provides an average result that is based on a larger sample than was used in any of the individual studies on which it is based. In this case, the best (weighted) estimate is 55%, which is based on the answers of 3,063 respondents, which is twice as large as the answer of 50% from the single poll with the largest sample (Poll 3, which had 1,440 respondents).

---

[2] Note that percentages are usually reported to whole numbers in the popular media. In academic journals, they are often reported to one or two decimal places.

ꙮ Guideline 15.2
Meta-analytic reviewers place more emphasis on precise statistical results than do qualitative reviewers.

Box 15C shows examples of how the results of the three polls considered above might be handled by writers of literature reviews with two different qualitative orientations: highly qualitative, with no mention of specific statistics, and moderately qualitative, with some mention of specific statistics. Compare these qualitative statements with the meta-analytic statement in Example 15.1.1 on the previous page.

Box 15C *Examples of qualitative statements.*

Highly Qualitative (no mention of specific statistics)	Moderately Qualitative (some statistics reported)
In the three national polls on the XYZ issue, a majority answered "yes," indicating that a majority of the population is in favor of it.	In the three national polls on the XYZ issue, between 50% and 72% answered "yes," indicating that a majority of the population is in favor of it.

ꙮ Guideline 15.3
Meta-analytic and qualitative reviews should have similar introductions.

Both highly qualitative and highly quantitative reviewers should begin their literature reviews by covering the same types of material, such as the material in points I and II in Example 7.7.1 in Chapter 7, a portion of which is reproduced here in Example 15.3.1 below.

Example 15.3.1

Topic outline for the introduction to both qualitative reviews and meta-analyses:[3]

I. Introduction
    A. Identify the topic
    B. Establish the importance of the topic
    C. Definitions of key terms
    D. Literature search strategies
    E. Description of the extent and nature of the literature
    F. Overview of the organization of the rest of the review

Example 15.3.2 shows the beginning of a meta-analytic review. Notice that it identifies the topic (i.e., teen cigarette smoking cessation) and cites literature to establish its importance.

Example 15.3.2

The beginning of a published meta-analytic review:

There are over 1 billion smokers worldwide, and, if current trends continue, 8.4 million smokers are estimated to die annually of smoking-related deaths by 2020 (Kaufman & Yach, 2000). Cigarette smoking is the single greatest preventable behavioral cause of death. Since the 1964 report to the surgeon general on the health consequences of smoking, the public health community has played a role in focusing efforts to (a) prevent cigarette smoking initiation; (b) slow or arrest progression to regular/chronic use, with associated increases in risk of nicotine dependence; and (c) address the challenges of treating nicotine dependence syndrome to facilitate cessation of cigarette smoking and maintenance of cessation (Backinger, Fagan, Matthews, & Grana, 2003).

Tobacco use behavior includes snuff, spit, chew, and other tobacco products in addition to cigarettes. This article is limited to cigarette smoking as the most common form of tobacco use. Most tobacco-behavior-targeted efforts with teens have been directed to the prevention of regular cigarette smoking (Sussman, Lichtman, Ritt, & Pallonen, 1999). Unfortunately, at present, most teen regular smokers are likely to smoke well into adulthood (Backinger et al., 2003). Many anticigarette smoking efforts have been

---

[3] Note that if the material on theory is brief, it can be integrated into the Introduction.

expended on adult cessation programming, but relatively little effort has been directed to teen cigarette smoking cessation....[4]

✥ Guideline 15.4
Describe in detail how the literature was searched.

Guideline 9.3 in Chapter 9 suggests that reviewers "consider" describing how the literature search was conducted. It was suggested as an optional technique because many qualitative reviewers do not follow the guideline. However, Guideline 15.4 is almost universally followed by those who prepare meta-analyses, so it is not presented as an optional technique. Notice that the guideline not only indicates that the search should be described, but also that it be described "in detail."

Example 15.4.1 illustrates this guideline. Note that the researcher not only names the databases and search terms (key words) in the first paragraph, but also additional search techniques used (starting in the second paragraph).

Example 15.4.1
Portion of a detailed description of the search for literature for a meta-analysis:

An extensive literature search was conducted to collect studies that had investigated social support and burnout. The first step in the search involved the utilization of four major computer databases that abstract sources with relevance to social support, burnout, or both (*PsycInfo, Business Source Elite, JStor,* and *MEDLine*). The following key words were utilized: burnout, strain, support, cohesion, social support, supervisor support, coworker support, family, conservation of resources, and work-family conflict. The abstracts of those articles that came up as hits were checked for indications that their content would be appropriate for the meta-analysis (e.g., they had conducted an empirical study where social support and burnout were measured in some form). The electronic searches yielded 115 potential articles and dissertations, of which 103 were included in the meta-analysis because they met the inclusion criteria below.

Because many studies have included burnout and social support in their data collection without those variables serving as the primary focus of the study, I conducted a number of manual searches to supplement the computer search above. First, I reviewed the reference section of the two previous meta-analyses relevant to the topic (Lee & Ashforth, 1996; Viswesvaran, Sanchez, & Fisher, 1999). This search yielded three additional articles. Second, I conducted manual searches of....[5]

✥ Guideline 15.5
Consider describing the literature search in a separate section with its own heading.

In Model Meta-Analytic Review Number 7 near the end of this book, the authors use the heading "Search Strategy for Identification of Studies" on page 160 between lines 153–154.

✥ Guideline 15.6
Describe any efforts made to overcome the "file drawer effect" (i.e., publication bias).

Reviewers who conduct meta-analyses often concern themselves with the "file drawer effect," also known as "publication bias." The terms refer to the possibility that researchers who obtain statistically insignificant results may not submit them for publication (on the assumption that editors favor publishing research that has statistically significant results). Thus, researchers with insignificant results may be stashing their never-to-be-published data in an electronic "file drawer."

Searching for unpublished (i.e., "filed") studies is a sign of care in searching for literature for a meta-analysis. Search techniques for this purpose include searching for unpublished theses and dissertations, unpublished papers presented at professional associations, and contacting re-

---

[4] Sussman, Sun, & Dent (2006, p. 549).
[5] Halbesleben (2006, pp. 1135–1136).

searchers who have published papers on the topic to determine whether they have filed away any unpublished research reports. When a reviewer engages in these types of activities, the efforts should be described in the report of the meta-analysis.

✎ Guideline 15.7
Decide whether to exclude studies with seriously flawed research methods.

A single study can have a strong effect on the outcome of a meta-analysis, especially if the study has a large number of participants or if the study is one of only a small number of studies.

While a qualitatively oriented reviewer can mention seriously flawed studies and dismiss their importance because of their flaws, a very weak study in a meta-analysis may count as much as a very strong study that has the same number of participants. Thus, some meta-analytic reviewers choose to exclude seriously flawed studies from their meta-analyses.

While excluding weak studies from a meta-analysis is a matter of some controversy, it seems best to omit them if they are excluded on the basis of pre-established, objective criteria such as "All studies without a control group will be excluded."

Some reviewers suggest that all studies, regardless of their flaws, should be included in a meta-analysis. Their rationale is that a certain type of weakness in some studies might counterbalance another type of weakness in other studies when their results are all averaged. The possibility of such a "counterbalancing effect of weaknesses" seems most likely to happen when there is a relatively large number of studies. When there is only a small number, the results of the weakest study might overwhelm the results of the limited number of strong studies when results are combined.

When seriously flawed studies are omitted from a meta-analysis, this fact should be mentioned along with the criteria used to identify those that were omitted.

✎ Guideline 15.8
Describe any inclusion/exclusion criteria used to select among available sources for a meta-analysis.

Be specific in naming any inclusion/exclusion criteria for selecting literature to include in a meta-analysis. While this guideline was suggested in Chapter 9 as an "optional" technique, which might be followed by qualitative reviewers, this guideline is so widely followed by meta-analytic reviewers that it is strongly recommended here.

Consider Example 15.8.1. The authors name inclusion criteria first. Then they name exclusion criteria.

Example 15.8.1
Inclusion and exclusion criteria named (italics added for emphasis):

The author and another reviewer independently reviewed 25 studies that reported the effect of hospital-based CM [case management] for inclusion in the meta-analysis. Studies were *included* if they met the following *criteria*: (a) sample included adults aged 18 years and more; (b) intervention was hospital-based CM for inpatients; (c) the design was randomized experimental.... Studies in which patients were mentally ill or received out-patient services were *excluded*. In addition, studies implementing hospital-to-community-based or community-based CM were *excluded*. [6]

---

[6] Kim & Soeken (2005, p. 256).

✣ Guideline 15.9
Consider including one or more moderator variables in a meta-analysis.

A "moderator variable" is a variable used to form separate groups for separate analyses within a meta-analytic project. For instance, a frequently used moderator variable is gender. Using this variable, reviewers analyze the data separately for men and women. Differences in the effect sizes for men and women would indicate that gender "moderates" the variables (i.e., the variables operate at different levels in men and women).

In Example 15.9.1, the reviewers indicate that they used undergraduate major (academic discipline) as a moderator variable in a meta-analysis of the validity of the Graduate Record Examination (GRE).

Example 15.9.1
Academic discipline as a moderator in a meta-analysis of the validity of the GRE:

Several variables may moderate the relationship between scores on the GRE and performance in graduate school. First, the predictive validity of the GRE may vary by academic discipline. Although there are many similarities in some of the fundamental tasks required of all graduate students, there are differences in the type of training and demands of different academic areas. To investigate the impact of academic field on the predictive validity of the GRE tests, we conducted separate analyses for subsamples representing four broad disciplines: humanities, the social sciences, life sciences, and math–physical sciences.[7]

✣ Guideline 15.10
Consider incorporating a "mini" meta-analysis within a larger qualitative review.

Qualitative reviewers may consider including within a qualitative review a small meta-analysis of those studies that lend themselves to being synthesized mathematically, while keeping the main part of the review qualitative. This can be especially appropriate when the bulk of the literature on a topic is speculative, theoretical, historical, and/or anecdotal.

✣ Guideline 15.11
Consider conducting a meta-analysis using Cohen's *d*.

The mean is the most commonly reported average. It is computed by summing a set of scores and dividing the sum by the number of scores. Frequently, researchers use means to describe the average difference between two groups such as the average difference in income between high school dropouts and high school graduates.

Consider an example that illustrates the desirability of using Cohen's *d* when comparing means. Suppose there have been 15 experiments on the effects of computer-assisted instruction in algebra given to experimental groups. In each study, the control group received algebra instruction without computers. At the end of each study, algebra achievement was measured. If all experimenters used the same instruments (i.e., the same algebra tests), a meta-analytic reviewer could simply average the 15 means for the 15 experimental groups and compare the result with the average of the 15 means for the 15 control groups.

Unfortunately, there is usually wide variation from study to study in how a variable is measured. For instance, in one study, the participants might be administered a 30-item test, while in another a 120-item test might be used. Hypothetical results for such a situation are shown in Box 15D, with the means in bold.

---

[7] Kuncel, Hezlett, & Ones (2001, p. 168).

Box 15D *Results of two studies to be synthesized in a meta-analysis.*

	Experimental group	Control group
Study 1 (30 test questions)	*m* = **12.00** *s* = 4.00 *n* = 30	*m* = **7.00** *s* = 4.00 *n* = 30
Study 2 (120 test questions)	*m* = **80.00** *s* = 14.00 *n* = 30	*m* = **70.00** *s* = 14.00 *n* = 30

Interpreting the average result across the two studies (i.e., conducting a meta-analysis that mathematically synthesizes the results) is complicated by the fact that two different scales (one with a maximum of 30 and one with a maximum of 120 were used).[8]

Cohen's *d* was developed for this purpose: to express the difference between means (such as the difference between the experimental and control groups) on a common scale that is comparable from study to study and thus, can be easily interpreted.

Considering how Cohen's *d* is computed will help in understanding its meaning. To compute Cohen's *d* for each of the two studies in Box 15D above, subtract the control group mean from the experimental group mean and divide the difference by the standard deviation of the control group. These calculations are shown in Box 15E for Study 1. Note that the subscript "$_e$" stands for "experimental group" (i.e., m_e stands for the mean of the experimental group), and the subscript "$_c$" stands for "control group." As you can see, *d* = 1.25 for Study 1. The calculation of *d* for Study 2 is shown in Box 15F, in which *d* equals 0.71. Without any additional information, it is clear that Study 1 has more units of Cohen's *d* (1.25 units worth of *d*) than Study 2 (0.71 units worth of *d*).

Box 15E *Calculation of Cohen's* d *for Study 1 using statistics in Box 15D.*

	Experimental group	Control group
Study 1	m_e = 12.00 s_e = 4.00	m_c = 7.00 s_c = 4.00

Calculation of *d* for Study 1:

$$d = \frac{m_e - m_c}{s_c} = \frac{12.00 - 7.00}{4.00} = \frac{5.00}{4.00} = 1.25$$

Box 15F *Calculation of Cohen's* d *for Study 2 using statistics in Box 15D.*

	Experimental group	Control group
Study 2	m_e = 80.00 s_e = 14.00	m_c = 70.00 s_c = 14.00

Calculation of *d* for Study 2:

$$d = \frac{m_e - m_c}{s_c} = \frac{80.00 - 70.00}{14.00} = \frac{10.00}{14.00} = 0.71$$

The number of items answered correctly on the algebra tests is known as the raw score. Box 15G shows the raw-score differences as well as the differences in values of *d*. While Study 2 has a larger raw-score difference, Study 1 has a larger difference in the value of *d*. What does this

---

[8] Note that percentages, which were discussed at the beginning of this chapter, are on a standard scale (per 100) that ranges from 0% to 100%, regardless of the underlying numbers of participants in various studies.

mean? Simply this: When the results of the two studies are expressed on a common scale (i.e., *d*), the difference is larger in Study 1 than in Study 2. (The raw-score difference in Study 2 is larger only because there were more test items on the algebra test in Study 2 than in Study 1.)

Box 15G *Differences between the means of experimental and control groups expressed in terms of raw scores and in terms of d.*

	Raw-score difference	Difference in *d*
Study 1	5.00	1.25
Study 2	10.00	0.71

Here is the definition of *d*: *It is a scale on which the difference between two means is expressed in terms of standard deviation units.* (Remember that for each study, the raw-score difference between the two means was divided by the standard deviation of the control group.) Thus, for Study 1, the experimental group exceeded the control group by 1.25 standard deviation units, while in Study 2, the experimental group exceeded the control group by a smaller amount: 0.71 units.

The concluding step in conducting the meta-analysis involving mean differences is to average the two values of *d* (1.25 + 0.71 = 1.96/2 = 0.98). Thus, in a meta-analysis, a reviewer would report that *d* = .98 *for the two studies combined.*[9] The interpretation of values of *d* is discussed under the next guideline.

➭ Guideline 15.12
Use care in applying mechanical rules when interpreting values of *d*.

Cohen (1992) suggested guidelines for interpreting values of *d*. Specifically, he suggested that values of about 0.20 might be said to represent *small* effects, values of about 0.50 might be said to represent *medium* effects, and values of about 0.80 might be said to represent *large* effects. These values have been widely cited in the social and behavioral science literature and have led some reviewers who conduct meta-analyses to apply them mechanically without considering the nature of the underlying variables and the practical implications of the results.

To understand the need for care in interpreting values of *d*, consider an example. Suppose the average value of *d* across four experiments on the effects of a new drug for relieving the adverse effects of chemotherapy resulted in an average value of *d* = 0.20. Suppose furthermore that in all four studies, the differences were not only in favor of the experimental group, but all four were statistically significant, indicating that the amount of relief provided by the new drug is reliable (even though it is small).[10] Applying Cohen's guidelines mechanically would result in a conclusion that the effect is "small," without recognizing that this reliable effect (however small) might be of great importance to those suffering from the effects of chemotherapy. In other words, mechanical rules cannot take into account the physical and psychological importance of a particular finding in a meta-analysis.

---

[9] In the computational example just considered, the standard deviations were the same for both groups within each study (e.g., the values of the standard deviations of the experimental and control groups in Study 1 are both 4.00). See Guideline 16.1 in the next chapter if they are different. Also, in the example, both studies had the same number of participants. If there are unequal numbers, see Guidelines 16.2 and 16.3 in the next chapter for additional mathematical procedures and considerations.

[10] A test of statistical significance determines only whether a difference is reliable (i.e., can be counted on to occur again consistently). Although larger differences are more likely to be statistically significant, small differences can also be statistically significant (i.e., a difference can be *small and reliable*).

When interpreting the value of d, keep in mind that for all practical purposes, it is expressed on a scale that ranges from 0.00 to 3.00.[11] Furthermore, the vast majority of the cases would be expected to fall between 0.00 and 1.00, which means that it is not reasonable to expect many instances where d is greater than 1.00.

✤ Guideline 15.13
Consider the overall quality of the studies when interpreting the results of a meta-analysis.

If a reviewer has selected a topic for review on which much of the research is weak, the results of the meta-analysis should be interpreted in very tentative terms. On the other hand, there are topics on which there have been a large number of studies of high quality. When this is the case, a reviewer can have more confidence in the average effect size produced by a meta-analysis. Thus, considering the extent to which the studies included in the meta-analysis are of high quality will help in interpreting the results.

Exercise for Chapter 15

1. Examine the literature you have collected. Are any of the sources you located meta-analyses? If yes, to what extent has this chapter helped you understand them?

2. Will you be preparing a meta-analytic review? Explain the reason for your answer.

3. Read one of the model meta-analytic reviews included near the end of this book. Name the review you read and comment on your impression of the usefulness of meta-analysis for synthesizing the literature on the topic.

---

[11] Values of d can exceed 3.00, but rarely do in practice. In addition, values of d can be negative, which is discussed in Guideline 16.4 in the next chapter. What is true in the positive (e.g., the vast majority are between 0.00 and 1.00) is also true in the negative (e.g., the vast majority of the cases are between 0.00 and −1.00).

Notes:

Chapter 16

A Closer Look at Meta-Analysis

Chapter 15 covers the basics of conducting and interpreting a meta-analysis, while this chapter explores some more advanced issues.

✎ Guideline 16.1
When calculating *d*, consider using the pooled value of the standard deviation.

Guideline 15.11 in the previous chapter shows how to calculate the value of *d*. Note that the two groups in each study in the example had standard deviations with the same values (see Box 15D in which both of the standard deviations in Study 1 equal 4.00 and both of the standard deviations in Study 2 equal 14.00).

In practice, it would be highly unusual for two standard deviations in a study to be identical. When they are different, which one should be used to calculate *d* for a given study? One answer is to use the standard deviation of the control group, which is called for in the formula for *d* in the previous chapter, which is reproduced here:

$$d = \frac{m_e - m_c}{s_c}$$

Instead of using the standard deviation of the control group, reviewers who conduct meta-analyses often use what is called the *pooled standard deviation*, which is a special type of average of the two standard deviations reported in a study. The formula for calculating *d* using the pooled standard deviation is:

$$d = \frac{m_e - m_c}{s_{pooled}}$$

To use this formula, the value of the pooled standard deviation must first be computed. The procedure for doing this is shown below for the statistics in Box 16A. Note that the subscript "$_e$" stands for experimental group. Thus, n_e stands for the number of participants in the experimental group. Likewise, s_e represents the experimental group's standard deviation.

Box 16A *Statistics for illustrating calculation of the pooled standard deviation.*

Group	Mean	Standard deviation	Number of participants
Exp. group	$m_e = 35.00$	$s_e = 5.00$	$n_e = 50$
Control group	$m_c = 30.00$	$s_c = 9.00$	$n_c = 60$

$$sd_{pooled} = \sqrt{\frac{(n_e - 1)s_e^{\,2} + (n_c - 1)s_c^{\,2}}{n_e + n_c - 2}} = \sqrt{\frac{(50-1)5.00^2 + (60-1)9.00^2}{50+60-2}}$$

$$= \sqrt{\frac{(49)25.00 + (59)81.00}{110-2}} = \sqrt{\frac{1225.00 + 4779.00}{108}} = \sqrt{\frac{6004}{108}} = \sqrt{55.59} = 7.46$$

Using this value for the pooled standard deviation, d is calculated as follows:

$$d = \frac{m_e - m_c}{s_{pooled}} = \frac{35.00 - 30.00}{7.46} = \frac{5.00}{7.46} = 0.67$$

If the standard deviation for the control group (instead of the pooled standard deviation) had been used, this result would have been obtained:

$$d = \frac{m_e - m_c}{s_c} = \frac{35.00 - 30.00}{9.00} = \frac{5.00}{9.00} = 0.56$$

In the above example, the value of d obtained by using the pooled standard deviation (i.e., 0.67) is different from the value obtained by using the standard deviation of the control group (0.56), which raises the question of which method is superior. Unfortunately, there is no simple answer. While this writer prefers using the formula with the standard deviation of the control group in the denominator,[1] the majority of those who publish meta-analytic studies probably use the pooled standard deviation. In practice, a meta-analytic reviewer would not be faulted for using either method as long as the reviewer clearly states which method was used.

It is important to note that only some meta-analytic reviews deal with experiments. In a classic, simple experiment there is an experimental group that is given some special treatment (such as a new drug in pill form) while a control group is given either no treatment or a neutral treatment (such as an inert pill that looks like the pill given to the experimental group). In nonexperimental studies, groups that receive no special treatment from the researcher are compared. For instance, a study might compare the amount of job-related anxiety reported by men and reported by women. In such a case, either group could be called Group 1 and the other Group 2. Suppose that the women are called Group 1, while the men constitute Group 2. Then, the formula for the pooled standard deviation will have "1" and "2" instead of "e" and "c" as subscripts and will look like this:

$$s_{pooled} = \sqrt{\frac{(n_1 - 1)s_1^2 + (n_2 - 1)s_2^2}{n_1 + n_2 - 2}}$$

Under this circumstance, the formula for d looks like this:

$$d = \frac{m_1 - m_2}{s_{pooled}}$$

✎ Guideline 16.2
Consider weighting for differences in sample sizes when calculating an average value of d.

Under Guideline 15.1 in the previous chapter, the procedure for weighting percentages to account for differences in sample size is covered. That is, how to give more weight to samples with more participants when calculating the average of the percentages reported in various studies is covered. Here, how to calculate a weighted average value of d is covered.

Consider the values of d in Box 16B. These indicate how many standard deviations separate the experimental and control groups. For instance, the value of d for Experiment 1 (i.e., 1.50)

---

[1] By using the standard deviation of the control group, the value of d has a clear meaning: It indicates the extent to which the experimental group exceeded the control group *in terms of the control group's standard deviation*. The meaning is less clear when using the pooled standard deviation because the pooled standard deviation does not refer to either group in particular, but rather to the average.

indicates that the experimental group exceeded the control group by one and one-half standard deviation units.[2]

Box 16B *Statistics for illustrating the computation of the weighted average of d.*

Experiment	Value of d	Number of standard deviations separating the experimental and control groups' means
Experiment 1 ($n = 300$)	1.50	one and one-half
Experiment 2 ($n = 10$)	0.20	two-tenths

Notice that the results of the two experiments in Box 16B are very different (i.e., one shows an extremely large effect with a value of d of 1.50 relative to the other value of d of 0.20). Notice, too, that the sample sizes (indicated by n) are also quite different. Specifically, there were 300 participants in Experiment 1, while there were only 10 participants in Experiment 2. If the two values of d are averaged, the result would be a meta-analysis (i.e., a statistical synthesis of results of the two studies). However, computing an average by simply summing the two values of d and dividing by the number of studies (i.e., $1.50 + 0.20 = 1.70/2 = 0.85$) gives both experiments the same weight (i.e., each study counts as exactly "one out of two" as a result of dividing 1.70 by 2). However, it is usually desirable to give more weight to studies with more participants. In this case, it is desirable to give more weight to Experiment 1, which had 300 participants, than to Experiment 2, which had only 10 participants.

To calculate an average value of d that is weighted to take account of the varying numbers of participants, follow these steps:

1. Create a box such as Box 16C on the next page, and write the values of d in the second column. (Note that if values of d are not reported in some research reports, a reviewer will have to calculate these values from the means and standard deviations that are reported. See Guideline 15.11 in the previous chapter and Guideline 16.1 in this chapter for the computational procedures.)

2. Multiply the values of d by the numbers of participants (e.g., 1.50×300 for Study 1) and write the answer in the last column.

3. Calculate the total number of participants (e.g., $300 + 10 = 310$).

4. Sum the last column. (In this case, the sum is 452.00.)

5. Divide the answer to Step 4 by the answer to Step 3 (e.g., $452.00/310 = 1.458 = 1.46$).

Thus, in this example, the weighted value of d (1.46) is very much closer to the value of 1.50 reported in Study 1 than to the value of 0.20 reported in Study 2. This is true because the calculations just completed gave much more weight to Study 1 with 300 participants than to Study 2 with only 10 participants. In other words, in this example, Study 2 had little effect on the average value of d (for the two studies combined) because it had very few participants.

---

[2] Most of the cases lie near the middle in a typical distribution (such as the normal curve, where the curve is high near the middle because that is where most of the cases are). Also, there are only about three standard deviation units on each side of the mean in a typical distribution. Hence, one group being 1.5 standard deviation units higher than another is quite substantial on a scale that runs from 0.00 standard deviation units to only 3.00 standard deviation units.

Box 16C *Worksheet for computing a weighted value of d.*

	Value of d	times	Number of participants (n)	equals	Product of $d \times n$
Study 1	1.50	×	300	=	450.00
Study 2	0.20	×	10	=	2.00
			Sum = 310		**Sum = 452.00**

When a reviewer weights for differences in sample size, it should be reported in the meta-analytic review, which can be done in a single sentence such as the one shown in Example 16.2.1.

Example 16.2.1

Sample statement indicating that the values of d were weighted:

The average value of *d* was weighted to account for differences in sample size.

✤ Guideline 16.3
Be cautious when there are large variations in sample sizes.

If the sample sizes vary greatly from one study to another, a reviewer should mention this fact in the description of the results of the meta-analysis. This is especially important if there are a small number of studies with samples that are much larger than the others and the average value of *d* was weighted to take account of this.

Consider this example: Suppose a reviewer finds one study with 1,000 participants and six other studies with about 30 participants each. A weighted average value of *d* (or of percentages) will be very heavily influenced by the single study with 1,000 participants. Because the influence of the study with 1,000 is so great, whatever errors exist in this study cannot be adequately cancelled out by the other six studies because they have so little influence on the average when weighting for sample size is used. In other words, the results of the meta-analysis will be based largely on a single study (the one with 1,000 participants), making the other six studies almost irrelevant.

A solution to the problem being considered is to report the values of *d* and the number of cases for each study separately (perhaps in a table). Then, report the average value of *d* for all studies. Next, report the average value of *d* for all studies *except* the one with the very large number of participants. If these two values of *d* are quite different, the reviewer should urge readers to use caution in interpreting the results because the first value of *d* is based largely on one study (due to the weighting), while the second value of *d* is based on a number of studies that unfortunately had small sample sizes.

✤ Guideline 16.4
Interpret negative values of *d* appropriately.

A negative value of *d* will be obtained if the larger mean is subtracted from the smaller mean in the numerator of either of the formulas for *d* shown under Guideline 16.1. There are two circumstances under which the larger value will be subtracted from the smaller value. First, when an instrument yields scores on a scale on which it is desirable to have low scores, the experimental group may have a lower mean than the control group. Consider, for instance, a self-report measure of depression on which *lower scores indicate less depression* (i.e., the fewer symptoms of depression an individual reports, the lower his or her score). In an experiment designed to reduce depression in the experimental group, a researcher would expect lower scores for the experimental group than for the control group. If the expectation is reached in 12 studies, a result such as the one shown in Example 16.4.1 might be obtained.

Example 16.4.1

A statement regarding a negative value of d:

The average value of *d* weighted for varying sample sizes for the 12 studies under review equals –0.50. This indicates that, on average, the mean depression score for the 12 experimental groups is a full one-half of a standard deviation *lower* than the average control group's score.

Second, if it is widely hypothesized that one group will score higher than another, it makes sense to subtract the second group's mean from the first group's mean when calculating *d*, even if the second group's mean is higher than the first group's, resulting in a negative value. Suppose, for instance, that it is widely hypothesized that poodles are more affectionate than collies. If a study reported the opposite with poodles having a mean of 60.00 on an affection scale, while collies had a mean of 70.00 (and a pooled standard deviation of 10.00 for the two groups of dogs), a negative value of *d* [i.e., (60.00 – 70.00)/10.00 = –1.00] would be obtained. If similar results were obtained in four studies, the result of the meta-analysis could be described as shown in Example 16.4.2.

Example 16.4.2

Another statement regarding a negative value of d:

The average value of *d* weighted for varying sample sizes for the four studies under review equals –1.00. The negative value indicates that the results were the opposite of what has been widely hypothesized. In other words, the studies under consideration had an average effect size that favors collies over poodles.

✎ Guideline 16.5
Meta-analyses are often conducted by averaging correlation coefficients.

The Pearson *r* is the most commonly used correlation coefficient. It expresses the degree and direction of the linear relationship between two variables. For instance, a researcher might administer a vocabulary test and a reading comprehension test to *one* sample of participants and calculate a Pearson *r* to determine whether vocabulary knowledge and reading comprehension are related and, if so, to what degree.[3]

The Pearson *r* is expressed on a scale from –1.00 (a perfect inverse relationship) through 0.00 (total absence of a relationship) to +1.00 (a perfect direct relationship). The value of *r* is interpreted by squaring it and multiplying the square by 100%. For instance, if a researcher calculated an *r* of 0.72 for the relationship between height and weight, its square is 0.72 × 0.72 = 0.52 × 100% = 52%, which means that 52% of the differences in weight can be accounted for by the differences in height among the sample.

Because *r* is expressed on a standardized scale (i.e., it can only vary from –1.00 to +1.00), values of *r* are useful when considering relationships between variables measured on diverse scales (such as pounds for weight and inches for height). Thus, like *d*, *r* is a measure that is comparable from study to study.

Consider this example: Suppose a researcher collected 30 studies in which scores on reading comprehension tests have been correlated with scores on math word problem tests, and values of *r* are reported in each. For the meta-analysis, the researcher could report the values of *r* for the

---

[3] Note that up to this point in the discussion of meta-analysis, the comparison of two groups of participants (e.g., men and women) on one variable (e.g., job-related anxiety) have been considered. In contrast, researchers use correlation when there is only one group of participants (e.g., a group of students) and two or more variables (e.g., vocabulary knowledge and reading comprehension).

individual studies, perhaps in a table. For an overall, combined average (i.e., the meta-analytic synthesis), however, the researcher would need to perform a few calculations. The steps in the calculations are:[4]

1. Convert each value of r to a value of Z using Table 1 near the end of this book.

2. Multiply each value of Z by the number of participants in the study. Call this product "nZ."

3. Sum the values of nZ.

4. Divide the sum of Step 3 by the total number of participants in the studies.

5. Convert the Z found in Step 4 back to r, using Table 1 again.

To illustrate these steps, assume that there are only two studies with relevant values of r, which are shown in Box 16D along with other statistics. Sum the values in the last column (48.65 + 97.02 = **145.67**) and sum the number in the samples (50 + 140 = **190**). Then divide the sum of the last column by the total number in the combined samples: 145.67/190 = **0.767**. This is the weighted average value of Z. To express this as the weighted average correlation coefficient, refer to Table 1 again and read from the Z column moving left to the r column. In the table, a Z of 0.767 corresponds to an r of **0.645**. Thus, a reviewer could report that the weighted average value of r across studies is 0.645, with an underlying combined sample of 190 participants.

Box 16D   *Values of r and corresponding values of Z from Table 1. Multiply values of Z by the numbers of subjects. Sum the last column.*

	Value of r	Corresponding value of Z from Table 1 near the end of the book	times	Number of participants (n)	equals	nZ (i.e., $Z \times n$)
Study 1	0.75	0.973	×	50	=	48.65
Study 2	0.60	0.693	×	140	=	97.02
				Sum = 190		**Sum = 145.67**

✎ Guideline 16.6
A single meta-analysis can contain values of both *d* and *r*.

Some studies on a given topic may report values of d (or means and standard deviations, which permit the calculation of d) while other studies on the same topic may report values of r. In this circumstance, a researcher might report the weighted average value of d for the studies that report d, and report the weighted average value of r for the studies that report values of r. Note that there are formulas, which are beyond the scope of this book, for converting values of d to r and r to d.

✎ Guideline 16.7
Consider the meaning of confidence intervals for effect sizes.

When reviewers state values of d, they often also provide 95% confidence intervals (95% CI), which can be thought of as a "margin" to allow for in light of random errors that result from random sampling (i.e., a sample might differ from its population because only a random sample of the population was studied).

---

[4] The method shown here is the *approximate method*. To use the precise method, subtract 3 (a constant for all studies) from the number in each sample before multiplying by the value of Z. Then, follow the steps shown above, but perform the final division by the sum of the same sizes minus 3 for each sample. The approximate method and the precise method usually yield very similar results. For the example under consideration, the result using the precise method is exactly the same as the result using the approximate method: 0.645.

Consider the overall effect size of $d = .99$ (the first effect size in Table 3 on page 173 in Model Review 8). In the table, the 95% CI is shown to be 0.87–1.10. This indicates that an individual can have 95% confidence that the true effect size is between these two values (between 0.87 and 1.10).

While computation of confidence intervals is beyond the scope of this book, students who are writing for publication in a journal or preparing a thesis should consider including confidence intervals in their meta-analytic reviews.[5]

Exercise for Chapter 16

1. Will you be preparing a meta-analytic review?

2. If "yes" to Question 1 and if values of d need to be computed, will you be using the standard deviation of the control groups *or* the pooled standard deviations? (See Guideline 16.1.)

3. If you will be averaging values of d, will you be weighting to take account of differences in sample sizes when calculating the averages? (See Guideline 16.2.)

4. Do you anticipate that you will need to interpret negative values of d? Explain. (See Guideline 16.4.)

5. Will you be averaging correlation coefficients? Explain. (See Guideline 16.5.)

---

[5] An effect size calculator is available at http://www.cemcentre.org/renderpage.asp?linkID=30325017. From the home page, click on the link to Excel. Then enter the needed statistics (means, numbers of cases, and standard deviations) in the row below the example (in the white spaces). The calculator will produce 95% CIs.

Notes:

References

Blundon, J. A., & Schaefer, C. E. (2006). The role of parent–child play in children's development. *Psychology and Education: An Interdisciplinary Journal, 43*, 1–10.

Bowling, N. A., & Beehr, T. A. (2006). Workplace harassment from the victim's perspective: A theoretical model and meta-analysis. *Journal of Applied Psychology, 91*, 998–1012.

Bronte-Tinkew, J., Moore, K. A., & Carrano, J. (2006). The father–child relationship, parenting styles, and adolescent risk behaviors in intact families. *Journal of Family Issues, 27*, 850–881.

Burkard, A. W., Johnson, A. J., Madson, M. B., Pruitt, N. T., Contreras-Tadych, D. A., Kozlowski, J. M., Hess, S. A., & Knox, S. (2006). Supervisor cultural responsiveness and unresponsiveness in cross-cultural supervision. *Journal of Counseling Psychology, 53*, 288–301.

Caudill, B. D., Crosse, S. B., Campbell, B., Howard, J., Luckey, B., & Blane, H. T. (2006). High-risk drinking among college fraternity members: A national perspective. *Journal of American College Health, 55*, 141–155.

Cohen, J. (1992). A power primer. *Psychological Bulletin, 112*, 155–159.

Corcoran, J., & Pillai, V. K. (2007). Effectiveness of secondary pregnancy prevention programs: A meta-analysis. *Research on Social Work Practice, 17*, 5–18.

DeCoster, V. A., & Cummings, S. M. (2005). Helping adults with diabetes: A review of evidence-based interventions. *Health & Social Work, 30*, 259–264.

Dunn, E. W., Brackett, M. A., Ashton-James, C., Schneiderman, E., & Salovey, P. (2007). On emotionally intelligent time travel: Individual differences in affective forecasting ability. *Personality and Social Psychology Bulletin, 33*, 85–93.

Freedenthal, S., & Stiffman, A. R. (2007). "They might think I was crazy": Young American Indians' reasons for not seeking help when suicidal. *Journal of Adolescent Research, 22*, 58–77.

Gardezi, F., Wilson, K. G., Man-Son-Hing, M., Marshall, S. C., Molnar, F. J., Dobbs, B. M., & Tuokko, H. A. (2006). Qualitative research on older drivers. *Clinical Gerontologist, 30*, 5–22.

Grabe, S., & Hyde, J. S. (2006). Ethnicity and body dissatisfaction among women in the United States: A meta-analysis. *Psychological Bulletin, 132*, 622–640.

Griggs, C., & Jensen, J. (2006). Effectiveness of acupuncture for migraine: Critical literature review. *Journal of Advanced Nursing, 54*, 491–501.

Halbesleben, J. R. B. (2006). Sources of social support and burnout: A meta-analytic test of the Conservation of Resources model. *Journal of Applied Psychology, 91*, 1134–1145.

Halm, M. A., Treat-Jacobson, D., Lindquist, R., & Savik, K. (2006). Correlates of caregiver burden after coronary artery bypass surgery. *Nursing Research, 55*, 426–436.

Hanson, S. L. (2007). Success in science among young African American women: the role of minority families. *Journal of Family Issues, 28*, 3–33.

Harris, R. A. (2001). *The plagiarism handbook: Strategies for preventing, detecting, and dealing with plagiarism.* Los Angeles: Pyrczak Publishing.

Harris, R. A. (2003). *Writing with clarity and style: A guide to rhetorical devices for contemporary writers.* Los Angeles: Pyrczak Publishing.

Kim, H. S., Sherman, D. K., Ko, D., & Taylor, S. E. (2006). Pursuit of comfort and pursuit of harmony: Culture, relationships, and social support seeking. *Personality and Social Psychology Bulletin, 32*, 1595–1607.

Kim, Y.-J., & Soeken, K. L. (2005). A meta-analysis of the effect of hospital-based case management on hospital length-of-stay and readmission. *Nursing Research, 54*, 255–264.

Kruczek, T., & Salsman, J. (2006). Prevention and treatment of posttraumatic stress disorder in the school setting. *Psychology in the Schools, 43*, 461–470.

Kuncel, N. R., Hezlett, S. A., & Ones, D. S. (2001). A comprehensive meta-analysis of the predictive validity of the Graduate Record Examinations: Implications for graduate student selection and performance. *Psychological Bulletin, 127*, 162–181.

Ledford, J. R., & Gast, D. L. (2006). Feeding problems in children with autism spectrum disorders: A review. *Focus on Autism and Other Developmental Disabilities, 21*, 153–166.

MacDonald, G., & Leary, M. R. (2005). Why does social exclusion hurt? The relationship between social and physical pain. *Psychological Bulletin, 131*, 202–223.

References

Marshall, G. N., Berthold, S. M., Schell, T. L., Elliott, M. N., Chun, C.-A., & Hambarsoomians, K. (2006). Rates and correlates of seeking mental health services among Cambodian refugees. *American Journal of Public Health, 96*, 1829–1835.

McVea, K. L. S. P. (2006). Evidence for clinical smoking cessation for adolescents. *Health Psychology, 25*, 558–562.

Melamed, S., Shirom, A., Toker, S., Berliner, S., & Shapira, I. (2006). Burnout and risk of cardiovascular disease: Evidence, possible causal paths, and promising research directions. *Psychological Bulletin, 132*, 327–353.

Middlemiss, W., & McGuigan, W. (2005). Ethnicity and adolescent mothers' benefit from participation in home-visitation services. *Family Relations, 54*, 212–224.

Mowbray, C. T., Bybee, D., Oyserman, D., MacFarlane, P., & Bowersox, N. (2006). Psychosocial outcomes for adult children of parents with severe mental illnesses: Demographic and clinical history predictors. *Health & Social Work, 31*, 99–108.

Olson, M. A., & Fazio, R. H. (2006). Reducing automatically activated racial prejudice through implicit evaluative conditioning. *Personality and Social Psychology Bulletin, 32*, 421–433.

Paskulin, L. M. G., & Molzahn, A. (2007). Quality of life of older adults in Canada and Brazil. *Western Journal of Nursing Research, 29*, 10–26.

Reed, J. M. (2006). Not crossing the "extra line": How cohabitors with children view their unions. *Journal of Marriage and Family, 68*, 1117–1131.

Rentz, E. D., Martin, S. L., Gibbs, D. A., Clinton-Sherrod, M., Hardison, J., & Marshall, S. W. (2006). Family violence in the military: A review of the literature. *Trauma, Violence, & Abuse, 7*, 93–108.

Rhoades, G. K., Stanley, S. M., & Markman, H. J. (2006). Pre-engagement cohabitation and gender asymmetry in marital commitment. *Journal of Family Psychology, 20*, 553–560.

Roff, L. L., Klemmack, D. L., Simon, C., Cho, G. W., Parker, M. W., Koenig, H. G., Sawyer-Baker, P., & Allman, R. M. (2006). Functional limitations and religious service attendance among African American and white older adults. *Health & Social Work, 31*, 246–255.

Rubinstein, M. L., Halpern-Felsher, B. L., Thompson, P. J., & Millstein, S. G. (2003). Adolescents discriminate between types of smokers and related risks: Evidence from nonsmokers. *Journal of Adolescent Research, 18*, 651–663.

Shih, J. H. (2006). Sex differences in stress generation: An examination of sociotropy/autonomy, stress, and depressive symptoms. *Personality and Social Psychology Bulletin, 32*, 434–446.

Story, L. B., & Repetti, R. (2006). Daily occupational stressors and marital behavior. *Journal of Family Psychology, 20*, 690–700.

Sussman, S., Sun, P., & Dent, C. W. (2006). A meta-analysis of teen cigarette smoking cessation. *Health Psychology, 25*, 549–557.

Tyler, K. A., & Johnson, K. A. (2006). Pathways in and out of substance use among homeless-emerging adults. *Journal of Adolescent Research, 21*, 133–157.

van Herk, R., van Dijk, M., Baar, F. P. M., Tibboel, D., & de Wit, R. (2007). Observation scales for pain assessment in older adults with cognitive impairments or communication difficulties. *Nursing Research, 56*, 34–43.

Veith, E. M., Sherman, J. E., Pellino, T. A., & Yasui, N. Y. (2006). Qualitative analysis of the peer-mentoring relationship among individuals with spinal cord injury. *Rehabilitation Psychology, 51*, 289–298.

Weisz, J. R., Jensen-Doss, A., & Hawley, K. M. (2006). Evidence-based youth psychotherapies versus usual clinical care: A meta-analysis of direct comparisons. *American Psychologist, 61*, 671–689.

Wright, K. D., Stewart, S. H., Finley, G. A., & Buffet-Jerrott, S. E. (2007). Prevention and intervention strategies to alleviate preoperative anxiety in children: A critical review. *Behavior Modification, 31*, 52–79.

Zuckerman, M., & O'Loughlin, R. E. (2006). Self-enhancement by social comparison: A prospective analysis. *Personality and Social Psychology Bulletin, 32*, 751–760.

Checklist of Guidelines

Instructors may want to refer to the following checklist numbers when commenting on students' writing. Students can use this checklist to review important points as they prepare their literature reviews.

Chapter 1 Introduction to Qualitative and Quantitative Reviews

____ 1.1 Quantitatively oriented reviewers place more emphasis on precise statistical results than do qualitatively oriented reviewers.

____ 1.2 If the main thrust of a review is the mathematical combination of statistics, the review is called a "meta-analysis" or "meta-analytic review."

____ 1.3 Qualitative and quantitative reviews have many common features.

____ 1.4 Many literature reviews are a blend of qualitatively oriented and quantitatively oriented approaches.

____ 1.5 Read both qualitatively oriented and quantitatively oriented reviews in preparation for writing a new review.

Chapter 2 Selecting a Topic for Review

____ 2.1 Consider the audience's expectations and/or requirements.

____ 2.2 Consider personal interests.

____ 2.3 Examine textbooks for topic ideas.

____ 2.4 Scan titles and abstracts of articles in professional journals.

____ 2.5 Consider selecting a theory as the topic for a literature review.

____ 2.6 Consider reviewing the literature on instrument(s) or assessment procedure(s).

____ 2.7 Consider reviewing literature on the effectiveness of a particular program.

____ 2.8 Consider brainstorming a list of possible topics.

____ 2.9 Consider narrowing a broad topic by adding delimitations.

____ 2.10 Select a topic with an eye toward future goals and activities.

____ 2.11 Put possible topics in writing.

Chapter 3 Searching for Literature in Professional Journals

____ 3.1 Use the database's Thesaurus to identify appropriate descriptors (search terms).

____ 3.2 Use the Boolean operators NOT, AND, and OR.

____ 3.3 Consider using truncated terms.

____ 3.4 Consider restricting the search to the title field.

___ 3.5 Search for theoretical literature.

___ 3.6 Consider searching for the works of a particular author.

___ 3.7 Consider searching a citation index.

___ 3.8 Examine the references cited in the literature that has been located.

___ 3.9 Maintain a written record of how the literature search was conducted.

Chapter 4 Retrieving and Evaluating Information from the Web

___ 4.1 Web sources are often more up-to-date than professional journals.

___ 4.2 Information on current issues can often be found using general search engines.

___ 4.3 FedStats.gov is an important source of statistical information.

___ 4.4 State government Web sites are a source of local statistics.

___ 4.5 Use the raw statistics from governmental agencies, not statistics filtered by special interests.

___ 4.6 Consider consulting the Library of Congress's Virtual Reference Shelf on the Web.

___ 4.7 Consider accessing information posted on the Web by professional associations.

___ 4.8 Pay attention to the extension (gov, edu, org, com, and net) in the results of Web searches.

___ 4.9 Consider clicking on "cached" when opening a Web site from a search engine.

___ 4.10 After finding a useful Web site, consider following the links that it provides.

Chapter 5 Evaluating and Interpreting Research Literature

___ 5.1 Be wary of sources offering "proof," "facts," and "truth" based on research.

___ 5.2 Distinguish between quantitative and qualitative research.

___ 5.3 Quantitative researchers prefer unbiased samples.

___ 5.4 Qualitative researchers prefer purposive samples.

___ 5.5 Be cautious when a body of literature has a common sampling flaw.

___ 5.6 There is no single, perfect way to measure most traits.

___ 5.7 Give high evaluations to studies that use multiple measures of key variables.

___ 5.8 Be cautious when a body of literature has a common measurement flaw.

___ 5.9 Consider the reliability of measures used in research.

___ 5.10 Consider the validity of measures used in quantitative research.

___ 5.11 Consider the care with which the interview protocols were developed.

___ 5.12 Consider quality control measures in qualitative research.

___ 5.13 Consider researchers' self-critiques of their own research methods.

___ 5.14 Be cautious when quantitative researchers refer to causality.

___ 5.15 Be cautious when qualitative researchers refer to causality.

___ 5.16 Assess the strengths of trends across studies when evaluating literature.

___ 5.17 Recognize the limitations of significance testing.

Chapter 6 Taking Notes and Avoiding Unintentional Plagiarism

___ 6.1 Group sources into broad categories before taking notes.

___ 6.2 Within each category, group sources chronologically.

___ 6.3 Use colored highlighters to mark photocopies.

___ 6.4 Give each source a unique identifier such as the surname of the first author.

___ 6.5 Label the tops of note cards with the unique identifiers.

___ 6.6 Consider building a table that summarizes key points in the literature.

___ 6.7 Make more extensive notes on more important studies.

___ 6.8 Avoid including quotations in the notes.

___ 6.9 Pay special attention to definitions while taking notes.

___ 6.10 Make notes on researchers' descriptions of the limitations of their research methodology.

___ 6.11 When in doubt, cite the source.

___ 6.12 If someone else's idea is rephrased, the original source should be cited.

___ 6.13 Failure to indicate clearly the beginning *and* end of summarized literature may lead to charges of plagiarism.

Chapter 7 Preparing a Topic Outline for the First Draft

___ 7.1 The first element in the topic outline is the Introduction.

___ 7.2 Essential elements in the Introduction are (1) identifying the topic and (2) establishing its importance.

___ 7.3 Consider providing definitions of key terms in the Introduction.

___ 7.4 In the Introduction, consider describing the strategies used to locate literature on the topic.

___ 7.5 Consider commenting on the extent and nature of the literature in the Introduction.

___ 7.6 Consider describing the objectives and organization of the literature review near the end of the Introduction.

___ 7.7   Discuss theories; if the discussion is extensive, consider presenting it in a separate section.

___ 7.8   Group notes to identify major topics and subtopics for the body of the literature review.

___ 7.9   Consider including a summary at the ends of long sections of a review.

___ 7.10   Consider including a summary at the end of the body of a literature review.

___ 7.11   In a review that serves as the introduction to a research report, conclude the review with statements of research hypotheses or purposes.

___ 7.12   Conclude a "stand-alone" review with a Discussion section that provides conclusions, implications, and suggestions for future research.

___ 7.13   There is no single standard format for a topic outline for a literature review.

Chapter 8   Writing the First Draft: Basic Principles

___ 8.1   Fill in the topic outline with brief notes, including unique identifiers.

___ 8.2   Write an essay that moves logically from one point to another. Do not write a string of annotations.

___ 8.3   When appropriate, cite two or more sources for a single point.

___ 8.4   Avoid very long strings of references for a single point.

___ 8.5   Use quotations very sparingly.

___ 8.6   Support statements indicating that a topic is timely.

___ 8.7   Emphasize stronger studies over weaker ones.

___ 8.8   Point out important strengths and weaknesses of the research being cited.

___ 8.9   Use tentative language when describing the results of weak studies.

___ 8.10   Use language that distinguishes between the results of studies and speculation.

___ 8.11   Point out consistent findings in a body of literature.

___ 8.12   Point out contradictions and inconsistent findings in a body of literature.

___ 8.13   Identify gaps in the literature.

___ 8.14   Indicate when previous literature reviews are being cited.

___ 8.15   Indicate the degree of certainty in the conclusions.

___ 8.16   Implications should be specific.

___ 8.17   Suggestions for future research should be specific.

Chapter 9   Writing the First Draft: Optional Techniques

___ 9.1   Consider presenting a historical frame of reference in the Introduction.

___ 9.2   Consider pointing out landmark or seminal studies in the Introduction.

___ 9.3   In the Introduction, consider describing how the literature search was conducted.

___ 9.4   In the Introduction, consider describing inclusion/exclusion criteria (if any) used when selecting literature.

___ 9.5   In the Introduction, consider paraphrasing and citing the source(s) for definitions.

___ 9.6   In the Introduction, consider quoting authoritative and/or technical definitions.

___ 9.7   Consider emphasizing content over authorship when citing references.

___ 9.8   Consider using "e.g." when there are a large number of sources for a single point.

___ 9.9   Be generous in the use of headings and subheadings.

___ 9.10   Consult a style manual on formatting levels of headings.

Chapter 10   Writing the First Draft: Statistical Issues in Qualitative Reviews

___ 10.1   Consider the audience when determining the need to present statistics.

___ 10.2   Recognize that some matters are inherently more statistical than others.

___ 10.3   Consider replacing vague terms with statistics when referring to quantities.

___ 10.4   Consider providing statistical coverage for selected studies.

___ 10.5   Be selective when reporting statistics.

___ 10.6   When the statistical results vary greatly, differentiate among the underlying studies.

___ 10.7   Consider variation when citing the results of research.

___ 10.8   Consider commenting on the size of an average difference.

___ 10.9   Consider commenting on the strength of a correlation.

___ 10.10   Consider reporting the values of correlation coefficients parenthetically.

___ 10.11   It is seldom necessary to mention "statistical significance."

___ 10.12   With rare exceptions, avoid reproducing tables of statistical values in a review.

___ 10.13   Consider building tables to present selected statistics.

Chapter 11   Building Tables to Summarize Literature

___ 11.1   Consider building a table to show selected statistics from an important study.

___ 11.2   Table numbers and highlights of the tables should be mentioned in the narrative.

___ 11.3   Consider building a table to show statistics derived from a variety of studies.

___ 11.4   Consider the order in which to present studies in tables.

___ 11.5   Tables can be used to present material other than statistical results.

____ 11.6   Use homogeneous content for each table.

____ 11.7   Consider establishing inclusion criteria for tables.

____ 11.8   Avoid the overuse of tables.

____ 11.9   Give each table a number and descriptive title (i.e., caption).

____ 11.10   Consult a style manual for guidelines on formatting tables.

____ 11.11   Learn how to build tables using a word processing program.

Chapter 12 Revising and Refining the First Draft

____ 12.1   Put the first draft aside and reread it after a couple of days.

____ 12.2   Check the structure of each paragraph; keep it simple.

____ 12.3   Consider breaking long paragraphs into two or more shorter ones.

____ 12.4   Consider using transitional terms between paragraphs and within paragraphs.

____ 12.5   Double-check to be sure there is a sufficient number of headings and subheadings.

____ 12.6   Double-check to make sure that all cited material has been referenced.

____ 12.7   Check for the overuse of quotations.

____ 12.8   Check for the overuse of rhetorical questions.

____ 12.9   Consider deleting truisms.

____ 12.10   Remove any material meant to be clever or amusing.

____ 12.11   Consider deleting anecdotal material.

____ 12.12   Make sure the tone is neutral and nonemotional.

____ 12.13   Have the first draft critiqued by others.

Chapter 13 Writing Titles and Abstracts

____ 13.1   A title should be brief.

____ 13.2   Consider referring to groups of variables in a title.

____ 13.3   A title should be a statement—not a complete sentence.

____ 13.4   Avoid stating conclusions in a title.

____ 13.5   Avoid using a "yes–no" question as a title.

____ 13.6   Consider using a subtitle to indicate that the document is a review.

____ 13.7   A typical abstract should be relatively brief.

____ 13.8   An abstract should indicate the general topic of the review.

____ 13.9   An abstract should indicate the scope of the review.

___ 13.10 If space permits, general conclusions and findings may be stated in the abstract.

___ 13.11 It is acceptable to cite specific statistics in the abstract of a meta-analysis.

Chapter 14 Preparing a Reference List

___ 14.1 Place the reference list at the end of the review under the main heading "References."

___ 14.2 A reference list for a literature review should refer to only publications cited in the literature review.

___ 14.3 List references alphabetically by surname of the author.

___ 14.4 Use hanging indents for the second and subsequent lines of references.

___ 14.5 Learn how to create hanging indents using a word processor.

___ 14.6 Italicize the titles of journals and their volume numbers.

___ 14.7 Pay particular attention to capitalization.

___ 14.8 Pay particular attention to punctuation.

___ 14.9 Do not add extraneous material such as abbreviations for page numbers.

___ 14.10 Provide the date and URL in references for material published on the Internet.

___ 14.11 Format references to books in accordance with a style manual.

___ 14.12 Double-check the reference list against the citations in the body of the review.

Chapter 15 Introduction to Meta-Analysis

___ 15.1 Meta-analysis can be used to synthesize percentages reported in various studies.

___ 15.2 Meta-analytic reviewers place more emphasis on precise statistical results than do qualitative reviewers.

___ 15.3 Meta-analytic and qualitative reviews should have similar introductions.

___ 15.4 Describe in detail how the literature was searched.

___ 15.5 Consider describing the literature search in a separate section with its own heading.

___ 15.6 Describe any efforts made to overcome the "file drawer effect" (i.e., publication bias).

___ 15.7 Decide whether to exclude studies with seriously flawed research methods.

___ 15.8 Describe any inclusion/exclusion criteria used to select among available sources for a meta-analysis.

___ 15.9 Consider including one or more moderator variables in a meta-analysis.

___ 15.10 Consider incorporating a "mini" meta-analysis within a larger qualitative review.

___ 15.11 Consider conducting a meta-analysis using Cohen's *d*.

____ 15.12   Use care in applying mechanical rules when interpreting values of d.

____ 15.13   Consider the overall quality of the studies when interpreting the results of a meta-analysis.

Chapter 16 A Closer Look at Meta-Analysis

____ 16.1   When calculating d, consider using the pooled value of the standard deviation.

____ 16.2   Consider weighting for differences in sample sizes when calculating an average value of d.

____ 16.3   Be cautious when there are large variations in sample sizes.

____ 16.4   Interpret negative values of d appropriately.

____ 16.5   Meta-analyses are often conducted by averaging correlation coefficients.

____ 16.6   A single meta-analysis can contain values of both d and r.

____ 16.7   Consider the meaning of confidence intervals for effect sizes.

Model Literature Reviews

Nine model literature reviews are reproduced on the following pages. Note that there are three sets of reviews:

• Model Literature Reviews 1 through 3 are qualitatively oriented and were written as "stand-alone" reviews (i.e., not as introductions to larger documents such as theses).

• Model Literature Reviews 4 through 6 are also qualitatively oriented. They were written as introductions to reports on original research. As such, their function is to establish the context for and the need for the research being reported.

• Model Literature Reviews 7 through 9 are examples of meta-analyses, which are highly quantitative reviews.

A common set of questions appears at the end of all the model literature reviews. These are designed to stimulate classroom discussions of the reviews.

Notes:

Model Review 1

Bullying in School: An Overview of Types, Effects, Family Characteristics, and Intervention Strategies

PAUL R. SMOKOWSKI
University of North Carolina, Chapel Hill

KELLY HOLLAND KOPASZ
Social Worker, Fort Mill, SC

ABSTRACT. Bullying represents a significant problem in U.S. schools, affecting approximately one in three children. The authors discuss the dynamics, types, characteristics, and consequences of school bullying. Risk factors for engaging in bullying, being bullied, and becoming both a bully and a victim are discussed. Research indicates that bullying has serious long-term negative effects on bullies, victims, and victims who turn to bullying as a coping strategy. Longitudinal relationships between childhood bullying and victimization and adult mental health outcomes such as anxiety, depression, substance use, and conduct disorders are outlined. Prevention programs, and their relative efficacy from empirical evaluations, are also presented. Finally, implications for school-based prevention services are provided.

From *Children & Schools*, 27, 101–110. Copyright © 2005 by National Association of Social Workers. Reprinted with permission.

Over the past 30 years, clinicians and researchers have come to understand that bullying is a serious threat to healthy child development and a potential cause of school violence (Olweus, 1978). The recent
5 school shootings in the United States have prompted many professionals to consider bullying and its impact on students. In working with children and adolescents, school psychologists and social workers need to be aware of bullying behaviors, their potentially damaging
10 consequences for victims, and school-based interventions for preventing bullying, coercion, and violence.

Bullying is usually defined as a form of aggression in which one or more children intend to harm or disturb another child who is perceived as being unable to de-
15 fend himself or herself (Glew, Rivara, & Feudtner, 2000). Typically, a power imbalance exists between the bully and the victim, with the bully being either physically or psychologically more powerful (Nansel et al., 2001). Often, the perpetrator uses bullying as a means
20 to establish dominance or maintain status (Pellegrini, Bartini, & Brooks, 1999; Roberts, 2000). In addition, bullying behaviors tend to occur repeatedly (Nansel et al.). Such behaviors include name calling, physically

assaulting, threatening, stealing, vandalizing, slander-
25 ing, excluding, and taunting (Beale, 2001). Regardless of which behavior is chosen, bullying is marked by intense intimidation that creates a pattern of humiliation, abuse, and fear for the victim (Roberts, 2000).

Bullying represents a significant problem in our na-
30 tion's schools. The National School Safety Center (NSSC) called bullying the most enduring and under-rated problem in U.S. schools (Beale, 2001). One study found that approximately 10 percent of children in the United States experienced extreme victimization by
35 bullying (Perry, Kusel, & Perry, 1988). In a more re-cent national study, nearly 30 percent of the students surveyed reported being involved in bullying in the current term as either a perpetrator or a victim (Nansel et al., 2001). This translates to 3,708,284 students re-
40 porting bullying and 3,245,904 students reporting vic-timization (Nansel et al.).

Bullying can be considered the most prevalent form of youth violence and may escalate into extremely se-rious forms of antisocial behavior. For example, the
45 surgeon general's task force on youth violence exam-ined several longitudinal surveys of violent offending. They reported about 30 percent to 40 percent of male and 16 percent to 32 percent of female youths commit-ted a serious violent offense by age 17 (U.S. Depart-
50 ment of Health and Human Services [DHHS], 2001). The most chronic form of criminal offending appears to derive from an early-onset trajectory of aggressive behavior in childhood (DHHS). Bullying peers can clearly be considered one component of this early-
55 onset trajectory. A study by Brockenbrough and col-leagues (2002) also helps to link bullying and violence. These authors conducted a survey of nearly 11,000 seventh-, ninth-, and eleventh-grade students and found that one-third of bullying victims had aggressive atti-
60 tudes. The group of victims with aggressive attitudes was more likely than other victims or bullies to report that they had carried weapons to school, used alcohol, and engaged in a physical fight at school. These highly troubled aggressive victims may be at significant risk

65 of becoming school shooters or engaging in serious long-term delinquent behavior.

The majority of bullying incidents occur in or close to school; playgrounds and hallways are two of the most common sites for altercations (Beale, 2001; Glew 70 et al., 2000). Generally, bullying occurs in areas where adult supervision is minimal. Whereas some studies show that bullying peaks during the middle school years, others show that the percentage of students who are bullied is greatest around the second grade and de- 75 clines steadily through the ninth grade (Banks, 1999; Olweus, 1993).

Generally, researchers identify four types of bullies (Beale, 2001). Well-known in schools, physical bullies are action-oriented and use direct bullying behaviors 80 such as hitting and kicking. This is the least sophisticated type of bullying because of the ease in identifying these bullies. Physical bullies are most commonly boys. Over time, physical bullies become more aggressive and may continue to manifest bullying behaviors 85 into adulthood. Verbal bullies, on the other hand, use words to hurt or humiliate their victims. Bullying by this type of bully happens rapidly, making it difficult to detect and intervene. Although there are no visible scars, this type of bullying can have devastating ef- 90 fects. The third type is called relational bullies. Relational bullies convince their peers to exclude certain children. This type of bullying happens most often with girls and can lead to feelings of rejection at a time when social connection is critical (Crick & Grotpeter, 95 1995). The final type, reactive bullies, can be the most difficult to identify. These bullies tend to be impulsive, taunting others into fighting with them. Reactive bullies will fight back, but then claim self-defense.

In this article we discuss risk factors for engaging 100 in bullying, being bullied, and becoming both a bully and a victim. We also outline longitudinal relationships between childhood bullying and victimization, family dynamics, and adult mental health outcomes. Prevention programs and implications for school personnel 105 are presented.

Bullies

Characteristics of Bullies

Although bullies may differ in the type of aggression they use, most bullies share common characteristics. According to the NSSC, bullies are overly aggressive, destructive, and enjoy dominating other children 110 (Carney & Merrell, 2001; NSSC, 1995). They also tend to be hot-tempered, impulsive, and have a low tolerance for frustration (Olweus, 1993). Bullies tend to have difficulty processing social information and often interpret other's behaviors as being antagonistic, even 115 when they are not (Dodge, 1991; McNamara & McNamara, 1997). Although peers generally dislike bullies in adolescence, bullies tend to be popular with other aggressive children in earlier grades (Pellegrini, 1998). In fact, one study found that bullies reported

120 greater ease in making friends than did other children (Nansel et al., 2001). The link between bullying and peer social status requires further clarification. Some researchers have identified popular aggressive and unpopular aggressive bully subtypes (Farmer et al., 125 2002). Popular aggressive bullies socialize with other popular children and do not appear to encounter significant social stigma stemming from their aggression. Unpopular aggressive bullies are typically rejected or neglected by other children and may use aggression as 130 a way to get attention. However, with their teachers and other adults, both types of bullies tend to act aggressively and may actually frighten some of these adults because of their physical strength and defiant attitude (Olweus, 1993).

135 Most bullies have a positive attitude toward violence, particularly as a means to solve problems or get what they want (Carney & Merrell, 2001; Glew et al., 2000). Often, bullies are "rewarded" with cigarettes, money, and prestige as a result of their aggression 140 (Olweus, 1993). They also use bullying behaviors to gain or maintain dominance and tend to lack a sense of empathy for their victims (Beale, 2001). Many bullies do not realize the level of their aggression (NSSC, 1995). Researchers have also found that bullies are 145 more likely to be involved with other problem behaviors, such as drinking and smoking (Nansel et al., 2001). In addition, bullies usually lack problem-solving skills and tend to externalize their problems as a means of coping (Andreou, 2001). They also show poorer 150 school achievement and demonstrate a dislike of the school environment, particularly in middle school (Nansel et al.; also see DHHS, 2001).

Finally, a debate exists in the literature as to whether bullies suffer from low self-esteem. Some re- 155 searchers suggested that bullies have either average or lower-than-average levels of insecurity (Glew et al., 2000). In contrast, other studies showed that bullies of both primary and post-primary school age had significantly lower global self-esteem scores than children 160 who had not bullied others (O'Moore & Kirkham, 2001).

Family Background

Research suggests that the families of bullies are often troubled (Olweus, 1994). Generally, bullies' parents are hostile, rejecting, and indifferent to their chil- 165 dren. The father figure in these homes is usually weak, if present at all, and the mother tends to be isolated and may have a permissive parenting style (Curtner-Smith, 2000; Olweus, 1978); thus, supervision of the children's whereabouts or activities tends to be minimal 170 (Roberts, 1988). When parents are aware of their child's aggressive behaviors, many dismiss them as a rite of passage or as "boys being boys" (McNamara & McNamara, 1997). Research suggests that the bully's level of aggression will increase if the caretaker con-

175 tinues to tolerate aggressive behaviors toward the child's peers, siblings, and teachers (Olweus, 1993).

Discipline in these homes is usually inconsistent (Carney & Merrell, 2001). Parents of bullies tend to use power-assertive techniques to manage behavior 180 (Pellegrini, 1998; Schwartz, Dodge, & Coie, 1993). Punishment is often physical or in the form of an angry, emotional outburst and is often followed by a long period of time in which the child is ignored (Roberts, 2000). As a result, these children learn that aggression 185 can be used as a means to an end. Bullies imitate the aggressive behaviors they see at home to obtain their goals (Patterson, Capaldi, & Bank, 1991; Roberts, 2000). Some researchers refer to this coercive cycle of violence to explain the "continuous, intergenerational 190 perpetuation of aggressive behavior" (Carney & Merrell, p. 370).

Short- and Long-Term Effects of Bullying

Many bullies experience mental health difficulties. One study found that, among bullies, nearly one-third had attention-deficit disorder, 12.5 percent had depres195 sion, and 12.5 percent had oppositional-conduct disorder (Kumpulainen, Rasanen, & Puura, 2001; see also, Kaltiala-Heino, Rimpela, & Rimpela, 2000). Also, highly aggressive bullies have been found to possess personality defects such as having a positive attitude 200 toward physical aggression (Andreou, 2001; Olweus, 1978). Furthermore, one study found that bullies tend to engage in frequent excessive drinking and other substance use more often than victims or bully–victims (Kaltiala-Heino et al.). Research has found that, as 205 adults, bullies often display externalizing behaviors and hyperactivity (Kumpulainen & Rasanen, 2000). Finally, being a bully has been associated with antisocial development in adulthood (Kaltiala-Heino et al.; Olweus, 1994; Pulkkinen & Pitkanen, 1993).

210 Children who bully others often experience long-term effects and consequences as a result of their bullying. According to NSSC, a disproportionately high number of bullies underachieve in school and later perform below potential in employment settings (Carney 215 & Merrell, 2001; NSSC, 1995). In addition, studies have found that by age 30 bullies were likely to have more criminal convictions and traffic violations than their less-aggressive peers (Roberts, 2000). A 1991 study found that 60 percent of boys who were labeled 220 as bullies in grades 6 through 9 had at least one criminal conviction by age 24 and 35–40 percent of these boys had three or more convictions by this time (Glew et al., 2000; Olweus, 1995). These adults were also more likely to have displayed aggression toward their 225 spouses and were more likely to use severe physical punishment on their own children (Roberts, 2000). In addition, research suggests that adults who were bullies as children tend to have children who become bullies (Carney & Merrell; NSSC). Thus, aggressive behaviors 230 may continue from one generation to the next.

Victims

Characteristics of Victims

Victims, in contrast to bullies, are the recipients of peer abuse. The majority of bullying victims, about two-thirds, are passive or submissive; the remaining one-third appear to have aggressive attitudes (Brock235 enbrough et al., 2002). Physically, victims tend to be small in stature, weak, and frail compared with bullies; thus, victims are often unable to protect themselves from abuse (McNamara & McNamara, 1997). These physical characteristics are particularly poignant for 240 placing boys at risk of victimization. In addition, victims may have "body anxiety," fear getting hurt, and have a negative attitude toward violence. They also may be unsuccessful at sports or other physical activities (Olweus, 1993). When attacked, many victims re245 act by crying or withdrawing, especially those in lower elementary school grades.

Victims also tend to be more quiet, cautious, anxious, insecure, and sensitive than most other children and have rather poor communication and problem250 solving skills (Glew et al., 2000). As a result, these children tend to initiate conversation less than other children and lack assertiveness skills (Schwartz et al., 1993). Consequently, many victims are abandoned by other children, have few to no friends, and are often 255 found alone on the playground or at lunchtime (Olweus, 1993). One study found that victims of bullying demonstrated poorer social and emotional adjustment, greater difficulty making friends, fewer relationships with peers, and greater loneliness (Nansel et al., 260 2001). Another study found that many victims relate better to adults such as parents and teachers than their own peers (Olweus, 1993).

In addition, victims tend to suffer from poor self-esteem (O'Moore & Kirkham, 2001). They often see 265 themselves as failures—unattractive, unintelligent, and insignificant. Because of these negative cognitions, victims may wrongly blame themselves for the bullying (Carney & Merrell, 2001). Lacking sufficient self-esteem and assertiveness to stand up for themselves, 270 victims are usually not willing to report the bullying. This unwillingness to disclose their victimization may act as a signal for bullies and may cause these victims to be targeted repeatedly. Academically, victims may perform average or better in elementary school, but 275 usually tend to be less successful than other children in middle school (Olweus, 1993). This deterioration in academic performance may be due to the negative impact of the bullying experience on the victim's sense of bonding or engagement with school.

Family Background

280 Generally, victimized children come from families that tend to be overprotective and sheltering because they realize that the child is anxious and insecure. As a result, parents may avoid conflict because they believe their child would not be able to cope. However, by

285 avoiding conflict, parents fail to teach their child appropriate conflict resolution skills (McNamara & McNamara, 1997). Many parents become overly involved in their child's activities to compensate for their child's social deficiencies. Researchers believe that the
290 family's tendency to shelter their child may serve as both a cause and a consequence of bullying (Olweus, 1993).

Short-Term Effects of Victimization

Victims may gradually see themselves as outcasts and failures. Studies suggest that victimization has a
295 significant positive correlation with several internalizing disorders, such as anxiety and depression (Brockenbrough et al., 2002; Kaltiala-Heino et al., 2000). This link between victimization and internalizing disorders is particularly strong for adolescent girls and may con-
300 tribute to the development of eating disorders (Bond, Carlin, Thomas, Rubin, & Patton, 2001). One study found that attention-deficit disorder was common among victims (Kumpulainen et al., 2001). This connection with attention-deficit disorder is understand-
305 able considering that these children may feel the need to constantly monitor their environment, anxiously anticipating the next victimization episode.

Victims of bullying often suffer from one or more of the following: chronic absenteeism, reduced aca-
310 demic performance, increased apprehension, loneliness, feelings of abandonment, and suicidal ideation (Beale, 2001; Roberts & Coursol, 1996). Because the bullying most often occurs at school, many victims are reluctant or afraid to go to school and may develop
315 psychosomatic symptoms such as headaches or stomach pains in the morning. One study found that 7 percent of U.S. eighth graders stayed home at least one day a month because of bullying (Foltz-Gray, 1996). Other researchers reported that more than one in five
320 middle school students said that they avoid restrooms at school out of fear of being bullied, and another study suggested that at least 20 percent of all students are frightened during much of their school day (Glew et al., 2000; Hazler, Hoover, & Oliver, 1992).
325 Victims may also experience physical injury (bruises, cuts, and scratches), torn clothing, and damaged property as a result of the bullying. To appease bullies and avoid injury, victims may request or steal extra money from family members. At night, victims
330 may experience difficulty sleeping and have nightmares (McNamara & McNamara, 1997). Victims are more likely than non-victims to bring weapons to school to feel safe or to retaliate (Brockenbrough et al., 2002). It is more common, however, for victims to in-
335 ternalize their problems. Unfortunately, victims sometimes attempt suicide (Olweus, 1993).

Long-Term Effects of Victimization

Victims also experience negative long-term effects as a result of childhood bullying. Because victims tend to miss many days of school, their achievement level

340 tends to be lower than their peers and many do not achieve their academic potential (McNamara & McNamara, 1997). In addition, at age 23, former victims tend to be more depressed and have poorer self-esteem than non-victimized young adults (Olweus,
345 1993). Hugh-Jones and Smith (1999) found that one-half of former victims reported long-term effects of being bullied as a child, mostly affecting their personal relationships in adulthood. Researchers have indicated that male victims experience psychosocial difficulties
350 such as inhibition with women during adulthood and may have problems in their sexual relationships (Gilmartin, 1987). In extreme cases, former victims have carried out acts of retribution, including murder, against former bullies (Carney & Merrell, 2001).
355 When former victims have their own children, they may overreact to behaviors that they perceive as bullying, contributing to an intergenerational cycle of overprotection (McNamara & McNamara, 1997). This may inhibit the development of conflict resolution skills in
360 their children, placing the children at heightened risk of becoming the next generation of victims. The risk of victimization may be transferred by genetic predisposition for a small body, by the perpetuation of overprotective parenting, and by negative cognitions that chil-
365 dren internalize.

Bully–Victims

Characteristics of Bully–Victims

Also called reactive bullies or provocative victims, these children both bully others and are bullied themselves. Bully–victims are characterized by anxious and aggressive behavior (Olweus, 1995). Students indicate
370 that these children both start fights and are picked on (Schwartz, Dodge, Pettit, & Bates, 1997). This group of children is often victimized, but also tends to tease or provoke bullies (Glew et al., 2000). When bullies respond to this provocation, a physical fight may occur
375 between the children. Bully–victims fight, but then claim self-defense (Beale, 2001). Although this has been described as a common scenario for bully–victim interactions, it is only one of a number of possible altercations that might characterize aggressive bully–
380 victims. Another bully–victim scenario may be that of the humiliated school shooter who explodes in a burst of violence when he can no longer cope.

Bully–victims can be difficult to identify. Olweus (1995) found that only a minority of victims could be
385 identified as bully–victims. However, a U.S. study found that if a child is a victim, he or she has an equal chance of being a passive victim or a bully–victim (Perry, Kusel, & Perry, 1988). Brockenbrough and colleagues (2002) surveyed 10,909 students in grades 7
390 through 11 and reported that approximately 30 percent of bullying victims had aggressive attitudes (i.e., were bully–victims). They found that this group reported carrying weapons, using alcohol, and engaging in

395 physical fights more often than nonaggressive victims or nonvictims.

Bully–victims are often hyperactive and have attention problems. In the classroom they tend to annoy other students and regularly cause aggravation (Carney & Merrell, 2001). Bully–victims are often labeled as
400 "hot-tempered" and may react with hostility toward students who accidentally provoke them (e.g., bumping into the bully–victim may precipitate unwarranted retaliation [Pellegrini, 1998]). Not surprising, these children usually elicit negative reactions from other chil-
405 dren and are not socially accepted by their peers (Andreou, 2001). Furthermore, many teachers do not like bully–victims and may give the message to the class that these children deserve to be victims if they initiate negative interactions (McNamara & McNamara, 1997).
410 Most bully–victims have low self-esteem, high neuroticism, and serious deficits in problem-solving abilities (Andreou; Mynard & Joseph, 1997). One study found that bully–victims viewed themselves as more troublesome, less intellectual, less physically attractive, more
415 anxious, less popular, and unhappier than pure bullies (O'Moore & Kirkham, 2001).

Family Background

Bully–victims usually come from troubled homes. These children frequently describe their parents as inconsistent (overprotective and neglectful) and some-
420 times abusive (Bowers, Smith, & Binney, 1994). Bully–victims claim that their families are low in warmth and lack parental management skills (Pellegrini, 1998). There is some evidence that the parents of bully–victims use power-assertive techniques with their
425 children (Pellegrini). Research suggests that bully–victims learn hostile behaviors at home and use these schemas to view the rest of the world as antagonistic and untrustworthy (Bowers et al.).

Short- and Long-Term Effects of Bullying and Victimization

Most bully–victims suffer from low self-esteem and
430 have a negative self-image. The frequency of bullying and victimization episodes appears to predict feelings of self-worth (O'Moore & Kirkham, 2001). Among bully–victims in one study, 21.5 percent had oppositional-conduct disorder, 17.7 percent had depression,
435 and 17.7 percent had attention-deficit disorder (Kumpulainen et al., 2001). These bully–victim rates for oppositional-conduct disorder and depression were higher than the rates for these disorders in children who were bullies only. Another study found that bully–
440 victims, compared with bullies or victims, had the greatest risk of depressive symptoms, anxiety, psychosomatic symptoms, eating disorders, and co-occurring mental health problems (Kaltiala-Heino et al., 2000). In addition, bully–victims were at significant risk of
445 drinking and substance use as adolescents. Children who are bully–victims at younger ages not only have more psychiatric symptoms when compared with other

children, but also have more psychiatric symptoms later in life (Kumpulainen & Rasanen, 2000).
450 Because research on bully–victims is still in its infancy and this is a relatively small group of children, researchers are still trying to understand the full range of bully–victim behaviors and relationship dynamics.

Interventions and Implications for Clinical Practice in Schools

Several strategies exist for intervening in bullying.
455 Some programs focus on intervening with either the victim or the bully; others take a systemic approach, addressing bullying behavior at multiple levels. Interventions for youth violence are also noteworthy. These interventions commonly have multiple components that
460 address family and school contexts.

Bullying Prevention Programs

The Olweus Bullying Prevention Program. The Olweus Bullying Prevention Program (Olweus & Limber, 2000) is a comprehensive intervention and is probably the most widely recognized program for ad-
465 dressing bullying. The program targets students in elementary and middle school and relies on teachers and school staff for implementation. The program prompts school personnel to create a school environment that is characterized by warmth and involvement, has firm
470 limits on unacceptable behavior, consistently applies non-hostile consequences to violations of rules, and allows adults to act as both authority figures and role models.

Initially implemented in Norway, researchers re-
475 ported that the program was associated with substantial reductions, by 50 percent or more, in the frequency with which students reported being bullied and bullying others (Olweus & Limber, 2000). In addition, Olweus (1993) reported significant reductions in stu-
480 dents' reports of general antisocial behavior and significant improvements in the social climate of the school. Program effects appeared to be cumulative, with some effects stronger at 20 months follow-up than at eight months postintervention. Program replications
485 (Melton et al., 1998; Olweus & Limber, 2000; Whitney, Rivers, Smith, & Sharp, 1994) also reported positive results. Although reductions in bullying were significant, decreasing 16 percent to 35 percent, these effects were smaller than those found in the original
490 study.

The Bullying Project. The Bullying Project (Davis, 2002) is based on the Olweus research in Norway. In addition to adopting a schoolwide zero tolerance policy on bullying, students are taught how to stand up to bul-
495 lies, how to get adult help, and how to reach out in friendship to students who may be involved in bullying situations. This project also includes interventions for both the bully and the victim. With the bully, counseling is suggested, with sessions that focus on acknowl-
500 edging actions, empathy development, or restitution. For the victim, various forms of support are sug-

gested—physical protection, support group participation with other victims, or individual therapy. Expressive arts therapies are recommended so that victims can write, act out, draw, or talk about their experiences. It is critical for victimized children to articulate their thoughts and feelings so that internalized negative messages can be countered with positive ones. No formal program evaluation data is available for the Bullying Project.

Bullybusters. Bullybusters (Beale, 2001) is an antibullying campaign geared to elementary and middle school students. The main focus of the campaign is the performance of the play "Bullybusters." Students act out short skits about common bullying situations in schools to begin classroom discussions. After the skits, the principal explains to the students that the school has a zero tolerance policy for bullying and asks the students to take positive steps to alleviate bullying in the school. Bullybusters has not been formally evaluated, but teachers in the schools where the program was implemented reported that students seemed to be more willing to report bullying behaviors. Administrators in charge of student discipline also reported a 20 percent reduction of bullying incidents during the first year of the program (Beale).

Additional Intervention Strategies

Behavioral contracts and social skills training may be helpful for some bullies (Morrison & Sandowicz, 1995). Also, bullies must be aware of school policies on bullying and should be held accountable if a rule is broken. Because bullying is often committed by a group of children against a single victim, each child in the bullying group may need a chance to speak, seek support, and receive help to change his or her behavior. Bullies often need long-term counseling services (Roberts & Coursol, 1996).

Interventions for victims are less common. Many victims cope by trying their best to be invisible. School psychologists and social workers should seek out children who may be victims of bullying. This is extremely important because most victims will not come forth and ask for help. For most victims, being bullied is shameful and frightening. Victims typically want to hide and do not want to discuss this issue. For some victims, coming to talk about being bullied may cause embarrassment. Social workers and psychologists, therefore, need to be gentle and sensitive with victims, normalize the experience, and make sure the session is not humiliating for the child.

The school psychologist or social worker should work to break the victim's isolation. If the victim can make and maintain one friendship with a peer, the painful consequences of bullying would markedly decrease and long-term loss of self-esteem may be avoided. Psychologists or social workers might also try pairing the victim with an older, supportive peer in a big brother or buddy program to break the victim's

sense of isolation and loneliness. This may also provide some protection and possibly some social status for the victim. Outreach is a critical component because of the nature of bullying. It is not exaggerating to say that the school psychologist's or social worker's efforts to be a friendship broker at this critical time may have a significant impact on this vulnerable child's life that reaches well into adulthood. Generally, interventions for victims should focus on supporting the victim, providing counseling, and building friendships between the victim and supportive peers.

Bullying prevention has linkages to youth violence prevention programming. The research literature on youth violence prevention makes clear that focusing only on the behavior to be eliminated is less effective than having a simultaneous focus on constructing a positive context that is inconsistent with bullying and coercion. Multicomponent interventions that focus on the child, his or her family, the school, and the community appear to be particularly efficacious. A number of longitudinal investigations have empirically tested multi-component interventions (see for example, Conduct Problems Prevention Research Group, 1999; Hawkins, Catalano, Kosterman, Abbott, & Hill, 1999; Tremblay, Pagani-Kurtz, Masse, Vitaro, & Pihl, 1995). The *Surgeon General's Report on Youth Violence* (DHHS, 2001) is an excellent guide that classifies ineffective, promising, and model intervention programs based on empirical evidence.

In the school environment, psychologists and social workers are often in the best position to intervene at multisystem levels. School psychologists and social workers may detect bullying more easily than other school personnel because they understand the signs and symptoms of aggressive behavior and victimization that signal a bullying problem. Teachers might refer children who are involved in bullying situations to school psychologists and social workers for other reasons (for example, conduct problems, depression, and sudden drops in academic performance). School psychologists and social workers are also in a good position to help put policies into place that take a comprehensive, schoolwide approach to preventing bullying.

The key ingredient in many bullying interventions is maintaining a zero tolerance policy with swift and serious consequences for engaging in bullying. This policy makes a strong statement about what the school, as a community, is willing to endure. All other strategies sit on this foundation. Overall, psychologists and social workers should target the atmosphere of the school to ensure that students feel safe. Of utmost importance is constructing a culture of respect and recognition where bullying is not only not tolerated but is not necessary. In such a context, everyone works to ensure that there are no social payoffs for bullying and that consequences for bullying behaviors are clear, direct, and immediate. In addition, those who have previously been involved in bullying can be guided to discover alternative forms of personal power and more effective ways to obtain recognition or vent their frustrations.

620 The following proven strategies can help fashion a school culture that promotes respect, recognition, learning, safety, and positive experiences for all students:

- Reach out to victims.
625 - Set and enforce clear rules and consequences for bullying behaviors.
- Supervise students during breaks, especially on playgrounds, in restrooms, and in busy hallways.
- Engage classes in discussion and activities related to bullying so that students who might otherwise
630 watch passively become empowered to intervene and victims are allowed to have a voice without shame.
- Encourage active participation by parents and other adults, making this a community issue that is ad-
635 dressed by community action.

Conclusion

Bullying is a serious threat not only to those involved, but also to the entire school environment. With 30 percent of children reporting involvement in a bullying situation, it is obviously an urgent problem that
640 negatively affects the lives of many children (Nansel et al., 2001; Olweus, 1993). Bullying creates short- and long-term consequences for both the victim and the bully. Victims may suffer from low self-esteem, loneliness, depression, anxiety, absenteeism, and academic
645 difficulties. Some victims may resort to violence as a response to bullying, either by taking their own lives or harming other students. Bullies also experience long-term problems such as low academic achievement, mental health difficulties, substance abuse, and crimi-
650 nality later in life. In addition, students not directly involved in bullying may witness these behaviors. This large, silent majority may not feel safe at school and this, in turn, may negatively affect the learning process for many students.

655 Many interventions have been developed to deal with bullying in the school environment. However, most of these interventions have not been formally evaluated. The most prominent intervention is the Olweus Bullying Prevention Program. This program
660 takes a comprehensive approach to bullying, has been evaluated in multiple studies, and has demonstrated impressive results in reducing bullying behaviors. Although they are not focused on bullying exclusively, youth violence prevention efforts, especially multi-
665 component ones, also address important concerns (for example, social skills training, conflict resolution, and parenting training) associated with bullying, coercion, and aggression. There are excellent resources, such as the Surgeon General's Report on Youth Violence
670 (DHHS, 2001), to guide the selection of interventions.

When bullying is tolerated, the whole school environment is tainted and students are unable to learn, grow, and interact in a safe, positive atmosphere. School psychologists and social workers can help re-
675 duce bullying by implementing effective interventions and working to create a school environment that prioritizes respect, recognition, security, and growth for all students.

References

Andreou, E. (2001). Bully/victim problems and their association with coping behaviour in conflictual peer interactions among school-age children. *Educational Psychology, 21*, 59–66.

Banks, R. (1999). *Bullying in school.* Moravia, NY: Chronicle Guidance Publications.

Beale, A.V. (2001). Bullybusters: Using drama to empower students to take a stand against bullying behavior. *Professional School Counseling, 4*, 300–306.

Bond, L., Carlin, J. B., Thomas, L., Rubin, K., & Patton, G. (2001). Does bullying cause emotional problems: A prospective study of young teenagers. *British Medical Journal, 323*, 480–483.

Bowers, L., Smith, P. K., & Binney, V. (1994). Perceived family relationships of bullies, victims, and bully/victims in middle childhood. *Journal of Social and Personal Relationships, 11*, 215–232.

Brockenbrough, K. K., Cornell, D. G., & Loper, A. B. (2002). Aggressive attitudes among victims of violence at school. *Education & Treatment of Children, 25*, 273–287.

Carney, A. G., & Merrell, K. W. (2001). Bullying in schools: Perspectives on understanding and preventing an international problem. *School Psychology International, 22*, 364–382.

Conduct Problems Prevention Research Group. (1999). Initial impact of the Fast Track prevention trial for conduct problems: II. Classroom effects. *Journal of Consulting and Clinical Psychology, 67*, 648–657.

Crick, N. R., & Grotpeter, J. K. (1995). Relational aggression, gender, and social-psychological adjustment. *Child Development, 66*, 710–722.

Curtner-Smith, M. E. (2000). Mechanisms by which family processes contribute to school-age boys' bullying. *Child Study Journal, 30*, 169–187.

Davis, S. (2002). *Stop bullying now.* Retrieved February 8, 2002, from http://stopbullyingnow.com.

Dodge, K. A. (1991). Emotion and social information processing. In J. Garber & K. A. Dodge (Eds.), *The development of emotion regulation and dysregulation* (pp 159–181). New York: Cambridge University Press.

Farmer, T. W., Leung, M. C., Pearl, R., Rodkin, P. C., Cadwallader, T. W., & Van Acker, R. (2002). Deviant or diverse groups? The peer affiliations of aggressive elementary students. *Journal of Educational Psychology, 94*, 611–620.

Foltz-Gray, D. (1996). The bully trap: Young tormentors and their victims find ways out of anger and isolation. *Teaching Tolerance, 5*, 18–23.

Gilmartin, B. G. (1987). Peer group antecedents of severe love-shyness in males. *Journal of Personality, 55*, 467–489.

Glew, G., Rivara, E., & Feudtner, C. (2000). Bullying: Children hurting children. *Pediatrics in Review, 21*, 183–190.

Hawkins, J. D., Catalano, R. F., Kosterman, R., Abbott, R., & Hill, K. G. (1999). Preventing adolescent health-risk behaviors by strengthening protection during childhood. *Archives of Pediatric and Adolescent Medicine, 153*, 226–234.

Hazler, R., Hoover, J., & Oliver, R. (1992).What children say about bullying. *Executive Educator, 14*, 20–22.

Hugh-Jones, S., & Smith, P. K. (1999). Self-reports of short- and long-term effects of bullying on children who stammer. *British Journal of Educational Psychology, 69*, 141–158.

Kaltiala-Heino, R., Rimpela, R. R., & Rimpela, A. (2000). Bullying at school: An indicator of adolescents at risk for mental disorders. *Journal of Adolescence, 23*, 661–674.

Kumpulainen, K., & Rasanen, E. (2000). Children involved in bullying at elementary and school age: Their psychiatric symptoms and deviance in adolescence. *Child Abuse & Neglect, 24*, 1567–1577.

Kumpulainen, K., Rasanen, E., & Puura, K. (2001). Psychiatric disorders and the use of mental health services among children involved in bullying. *Aggressive Behavior, 27*, 102–110.

McNamara, B., & McNamara, F. (1997). *Keys to dealing with bullies.* Hauppauge, NY: Barron's.

Melton, G. B., Limber, S. P., Cunningham, P., Osgood, D. W., Chambers, J., Flerx, V., Henggeler, S., & Nation, M. (1998). *Violence among rural youth* (Final Report to the Office of Juvenile Justice and Delinquency Prevention). Charleston, SC: Author.

Morrison, G. M., & Sandowicz, M. (1995). Importance of social skills in the prevention and intervention of anger and aggression. In M. J. Furlong & D. C. Smith (Eds.), *Anger, hostility, and aggression: Assessment, prevention, and intervention strategies for youth* (pp. 345–392). Brandon, VT: Clinical Psychology.

Mynard, H., & Joseph, S. (1997). Bully victim problems and their association with Eysenck's personality dimensions in 8 to 13 year-olds. *British Journal of Educational Psychology, 67,* 51–54.

Nansel, T. R., Overpeck, M., Pilla, R. S., Ruan, W. J., Simons-Morton, B., & Scheidt, P. (2001). Bullying behaviors among US youth: Prevalence and association with psychosocial adjustment. *JAMA, 285,* 2094–2110.

National School Safety Center. (1995). *School bullying and victimization.* Malibu, CA: Author.

Olweus, D. (1978). *Aggression in the schools: Bullies and whipping boys.* London: Hemisphere.

Olweus, D. (1993). *Bullying at school: What we know and what we can do.* Cambridge, MA: Blackwell.

Olweus, D. (1994). Annotation: Bullying at school: Basic facts and effects of a school based intervention program. *Journal of Child Psychology and Psychiatry and Allied Disciplines, 35,* 1171–1190.

Olweus, D. (1995). Bullying or peer abuse in school: Fact and intervention. *Current Directions in Psychological Science, 4,* 196–200.

Olweus, D., & Limber, S. (2000). *Bullying prevention program.* Boulder, CO: Center for the Study and Prevention of Violence.

O'Moore, M., & Kirkham, C. (2001). Self-esteem and its relationship to bullying behavior. *Aggressive Behavior, 27,* 269–283.

Patterson, G. R., Capaldi, D., & Bank, L. (1991). An early starter model for predicting delinquency. In D. J. Pepler & K. H. Rubin (Eds.), *The development and treatment of childhood aggression* (pp. 139–168). Hillsdale, NJ: Lawrence Erlbaum.

Pellegrini, A. D. (1998). Bullies and victims in school: A review and call for research. *Journal of Applied Developmental Psychology, 19,* 165–176.

Pellegrini, A. D., Bartini, M., & Brooks, E. (1999). School bullies, victims, and aggressive victims: Factors relating to group affiliation and victimization in early adolescence. *Journal of Educational Psychology, 91,* 216–224.

Perry, D., Kusel, S., & Perry, L. (1988). Victims of peer aggression. *Developmental Psychology, 24,* 807–814.

Pulkkinen, L., & Pitkanen, T. (1993). Continuities in aggressive behavior from childhood to adulthood. *Aggressive Behavior, 19,* 249–264.

Roberts, M. (1988, February). Schoolyard menace. *Psychology Today,* 53–56.

Roberts, W. B. (2000). The bully as victim. *Professional School Counseling, 4,* 148–156.

Roberts, W., & Coursol, D. (1996). Strategies for intervention with childhood and adolescent victims of bullying, teasing, and intimidation in school setting. *Elementary School Guidance and Counseling, 30,* 204–212.

Schwartz, D., Dodge, K.A., & Coie, J. D. (1993). The emergence of chronic peer victimization in boys' play groups. *Child Development, 64,* 1755–1772.

Schwartz, D., Dodge, K.A., Pettit, G. S., & Bates, J. E. (1997). The early socialization of aggressive victims of bullying. *Child Development, 68,* 665–675.

Tremblay, R. E., Pagani-Kurtz, L., Masse, L. C., Vitaro, F., & Pihl, R. O. (1995). A bimodal preventive intervention for disruptive kindergarten boys: Its impact through mid-adolescence. *Journal of Consulting and Clinical Psychology, 63,* 560–568.

U.S. Department of Health and Human Services. (2001). *Youth violence: A report of the surgeon general.* Rockville, MD: Author.

Whitney, I., Rivers, I., Smith, P., & Sharp, S. (1994). The Sheffield project: Methodology and findings. In P. Smith & S. Sharp (Eds.), *School bullying: Insights and perspectives* (pp. 20–56). London: Routledge.

About the authors: *Paul R. Smokowski,* Ph.D., MSW, is assistant professor, School of Social Work, University of North Carolina at Chapel Hill. *Kelly Holland Kopasz,* MSW, is a school social worker in Fort Mill, SC.

Address correspondence to: Dr. Paul R. Smokowski, School of Social Work, University of North Carolina at Chapel Hill, 301 Pittsboro Street, CB 3550, Chapel Hill, NC 27599-3550, E-mail: smokowsk@email.unc.edu

Exercise for Review 1

Directions: Answer the following questions based on your opinions. While there are no right or wrong answers, be prepared to explain the bases for your answers in classroom discussions.

1. Did the reviewers convince you that the topic of the review is important? Explain.

2. Is the review an essay organized around topics (as opposed to a string of annotations)? Explain.

3. Is the number of headings and subheadings adequate? Explain.

4. Is the tone of the review neutral and nonemotional? Explain.

5. Overall, does the review provide a comprehensive, logically organized overview of the topic? Explain.

6. Is the conclusion/discussion at the end of the review appropriate in light of the material covered earlier? Explain.

7. Are the suggestions for future research, if any, appropriate in light of the material reviewed? Explain.

8. Are there any obvious weaknesses in this review? Explain.

9. Does this review have any special strengths? Explain.

10. What is your overall evaluation of this review on a scale from Excellent (10) to Very Poor (0)? Explain.

Model Review 2

Language Brokering: An Integrative Review of the Literature

ALEJANDRO MORALES
University of Nebraska–Lincoln

WILLIAM E. HANSON
Purdue University

ABSTRACT. This article reviews the literature in the area of language brokering. Language brokers are children of immigrant families who translate and interpret for their parents and other individuals. Results suggest that language brokers possess unique characteristics that make them suitable for their role as the family's translator and interpreter. Parents select the child language broker based on certain personal qualities. Language brokers translate and interpret a variety of documents in a variety of settings. There is not a clear understanding of the influence of language brokering on children's academic performance. There is not a clear understanding of how language brokering experiences help or harm the parent-child relationship. Further research is needed to better understand the role that language brokering plays in the lives and well-being of children.

From *Hispanic Journal of Behavioral Sciences, 27*, 471–503. Copyright © 2005 by Sage Publications. Reprinted with permission.

When immigrant families first arrive in the United States, they must adapt to their new environment, learn a new language, and to some extent, become familiar with the beliefs, values, and customs of a new culture.
5 Thus, the process of acculturation begins immediately. For many of these families, this process is stressful and difficult to handle (Baptise, 1987; Rumbaut, 1994). To help ease the burden of this transition, immigrant parents tend to rely on their children or their extended
10 family to function effectively in American society. For example, once children become familiar with the English language, they often serve as translators and interpreters for their nonfluent parents and extended family. These children, commonly referred to as *language bro-*
15 *kers,* are expected to assist their parents in very complex, "adult-like" situations—situations that may or may not be developmentally appropriate (McQuillan & Tse, 1995; Tse, 1995a, 1995b, 1996a; Valenzuela, 1999).
20 Although children have served as language brokers for centuries, relatively little empirical attention has been given to them. Only recently, for example, have social and behavioral scientists begun to seriously consider and study this important phenomenon. Reasons
25 for this are only speculative. Perhaps it's because, his-

torically speaking, psychological theorizing and research has focused primarily on individuals and groups of individuals from middle-class, European American families. Fortunately, however, many fields in the so-
30 cial sciences (e.g., psychology) have become increasingly diverse and pluralistic and, as a result, increasingly sensitive to issues that relate directly to ethnically diverse individuals, families, and communities.
Although using children to serve as translators and
35 interpreters has been widely accepted among immigrant communities, it is still a controversial issue. In the year 2002, California lawmakers introduced a bill to the state legislature prohibiting children from translating and interpreting in medical, legal, and social
40 service settings (Coleman, 2003). They argue that (a) children are not translating information accurately, (b) translating legal and medical information may negatively affect the parent-child relationship, and (c) delivering information to a child about a serious medical
45 condition may be traumatizing to the child. Dr. Anne Foster-Rosales, an obstetrician at the University of California–San Francisco Medical Center, explained, "I've been in a situation where I had to give a diagnosis of cervical cancer, and I have a 12-year-old boy in the
50 room translating" (p. 19A). Clearly, there are multiple sides to this issue, and the extent to which language brokering should be legislated is debatable. What is less debatable, however, is the need for sound, rigorous research on this understudied topic.
55 Researchers define language brokers as children of immigrant families who translate and interpret for their parents, members of the family, teachers, neighbors, or other adults (McQuillan & Tse, 1995). In addition, these children also serve as mediators in a variety of
60 situations (DeMent & Buriel, 1999; Tse, 1996a). It is important to note here the distinction between translating and interpreting. Although translating and interpreting are often considered to be synonymous, or identical constructs, they are, in actuality, quite different. Trans-
65 lating is perhaps best associated with written work, where the translator is believed to possess exceptional understanding of multiple languages, thus having the ability and skill to translate documents, materials, and the like. Interpretation, on the other hand, is best asso-

70 ciated with verbal communication, where the interpreter is believed to possess exceptional understanding of potentially nuanced and circumscribed "meanings" that may be conveyed in ordinary social interactions (Westermeyer, 1989).

75 Language brokering is not merely bilingualism. Bialystok (2001) conceptualizes bilingualism as the ability to speak two or more languages. Others define it as absolute fluency in two languages (Bloomfield, 1933) or the ability to function in each language according to

80 given needs (Grosjean, 1989). Clearly, bilingualism deals with the ability to learn, to understand, and to speak two or more languages, whereas language brokering deals with, as noted earlier, the practices of translating and interpreting. Bilingual individuals

85 choose to learn a new language as part of their curriculum, whereas language brokers learn a language for their own and their family's survival. Thus, for these reasons, the literature on the area of bilingualism was not included in this review.

90 That said, it is also important to note here that Tse (1996b) was the first to review the literature on language brokering using 12 studies/articles. In her review, she focused on language brokering within the context of home-school communication. Tse proposed

95 that a potential reason teachers and immigrant parents may not have good communication is that children serve as the family's interpreter and/or mediator. She suggested that the information being sent from the home to school may not be coming from the parent but

100 the child. For example, the child may alter or select the information given by the parents to the teacher. Similarly, the information received from school may not be delivered accurately to parents, because the child may report selectively, reporting only information that he or

105 she believes to be relevant. Finally, Tse proposed that language brokers may express their stress in different ways at school. For instance, child language brokers may feel overwhelmed by the different responsibilities (i.e., translating and interpreting) that they have at

110 home, which in turn may affect their academic performance. Teachers and school administrators should make an attempt to be informed on how language brokers may experience stress differently from local, first language English-speaking students.

115 Little is known, at this point, about the process of language brokering and its effects on children and their families. It is imperative that social scientists, educators, and policy makers address this particular subgroup of children, especially considering the ongoing

120 changes in demographics within the United States. Hence, the purpose of this article is to integratively review the literature in this area. It will expand on Tse's (1996b) review, primarily by highlighting additional dimensions about the area of language brokering.

125 To help focus the article and to provide an organizing framework, the following research questions will be addressed: (a) What has been published on the topic of language brokering? (b) What are typical characteristics, or qualities, of the language broker? (c) How is a

130 child's cognitive development affected by language brokering? (d) Does language brokering influence children's academic performance? (e) How does language brokering affect the parent-child relationship? To answer these questions, a comprehensive, in-depth search

135 of the literature was conducted.

Method

Inclusion-Exclusion Criteria

Given that little research has been conducted in the area of language brokering, inclusion criteria were liberal, including journal articles, conference papers, unpublished manuscripts, newsletter reports, books, book

140 chapters, and dissertations. Studies that contained the words *language broker* or *language brokering* were considered. A separate search including the words *translator, interpreter, children,* and *adolescents* was also conducted. Resources that did not address issues

145 related to language brokers were excluded.

Literature Search

Upon entering the keywords *language broker* and *language brokering,* the *PsychInfo* and *ERIC* databases identified 38 matches. The outcome of this search led to 6 articles, 2 *ERIC* documents, 3 book chapters, and a

150 dissertation. The remaining 26 resources were excluded because they did not meet the above criteria. After back-checking each article, the *ERIC* documents, and the dissertation to identify other pertinent resources, 6 additional articles were identified. The second search

155 using the keywords *translator, interpreter, children,* and *adolescents* led to 19 matches, but none of them met the inclusion criteria.

As an added step, three preeminent language brokering researchers were contacted. These researchers

160 identified 3 additional journal articles and 2 unpublished manuscripts that met the inclusion criteria. Also during the peer-review process of this article, the editor of the journal provided a copy of a recent article about the area of language brokering. Thus, the total number

165 of resources used in this review was 24. Table 1 includes a listing and summary of each of them.

Results

What Has Been Published on the Topic of Language Brokering?

The literature in the area of language brokering is, generally speaking, scarce. Fifty-seven percent of the available research is published in peer-reviewed jour-

170 nals, 17% is published as book chapters, and 26% are conference papers, dissertations, or *ERIC* documents. Language brokering is a common phenomenon among children of immigrant parents (Orellana, 2003). For example, in a study by Tse (1995b), 100% of La-

175 tino/Hispanic children reported serving as language brokers for their parents and translated and interpreted in a variety of settings. Despite this common phe-

Table 1

List of Sources Included in Review

Authors	N	Methodology	Type	Purpose
Buriel, Perez, DeMent, Chavez, & Moran (1998)	122	qualitative	journal article	*To examine the relation of language brokering on biculturalism, self-efficacy, and academic performance. *This study focused on participants who spoke Spanish and English.

Summary of Major Findings

*Language brokering was more frequent among females. *Language brokering, language brokering feelings were associated with academic performance. *Academic self-efficacy was the strongest predictor of academic performance, followed by biculturalism, and total language brokering. *Places of brokering were the strongest predictor on performance.

| Chao (2002) | 307 | quantitative | conference paper | *To expand the research on the development of immigrant children by examining acculturation issues that are most central to their experiences as immigrants, that of language acculturation. *This study focused on participants who spoke Mandarin, Spanish, and English. |

Summary of Major Findings

*Translating is less likely to be performed by one child as family size increases, but it is less likely to be shared by all the siblings in the household. *Chinese parents are more likely to rely on one child for language brokering than are Mexican parents. *Translating is more frequent among the oldest and among those with higher levels of fluency in the native language and among children with prosocial behaviors. *Child's age was positively related to levels of translating in the past month. *Translation received in the past month was uncorrelated with any of the relationship variables.

| Cohen, Moran-Ellis, & Smaje (1999) | 38 | qualitative | journal article | *To explore the views of general practitioners about the appropriateness of children undertaking a task of interpretation between the general practitioners and an adult patient in primary care consultations. *This study focused on participants who spoke a variety of Asian (e.g., Mandarin), African languages (e.g., Swahili), and English. |

Summary of Major Findings

*Children were used as interpreters when professional interpreters were not available. *Children's interpretations were not available. *General practitioners felt children who serve as translators may not know the correct medical terminology when translating for their parents and/or general practitioner. *General practitioners stated that it was unsatisfactory to use children as translators, especially when discussing sensitive information (e.g., personal or intimate problems). *Children serving as translators could have an effect on the normal dynamics of the parent-child relationship. *Children may become extremely stressed when learning about parents' health and/or sexual activities.

| DeMent & Buriel (1999) | 13 | qualitative | unpublished manuscript | *To investigate in great depth the area of language brokering using college immigrants and children of immigrant parents who recall their experiences as language brokers. *This study focused on participants who spoke Mandarin, Vietnamese, Spanish, and English. |

Summary of Major Findings

*Children started brokering not very long after they arrived in the United States. They translated in different settings (e.g., making appointments with the doctor and paying bills). *Children reported that their parents stressed the importance of getting an education. *Children reported that they have a desire to help their parents. They also reported that, at times, they felt inadequate, frustrated, and upset because of brokering. *Children served as teachers. They introduced their parents to American holidays, culture, and values. *Language brokering was conceived as an obligation and as a form of not letting their parents down.

| Diaz-Lazaro (2002) | 159 | quantitative | dissertation | *To evaluate how language brokering, acculturation, and gender affect family authority structure, parental locus of control, and adolescents' perceptions of their solving abilities. *This study focused on participants who spoke Spanish and English. |

Summary of Major Findings

*There was no association between language brokering, family authority, and parental locus of control. *There was no association between language brokering and adolescents' problem-solving abilities. *There were no gender differences in language brokering. *There was no association between language brokering and adolescents' level of acculturation.

Note. In the original, this table contained a summary of all 24 studies. To save space, only the first five are shown.

nomenon in immigrant families, studies on language brokers or language brokering did not emerge in earnest in the literature until the mid-1990s. Early studies investigated the prevalence of language brokering among children of immigrant families. Instruments to measure this construct were also developed during this timeframe (Buriel, Perez, DeMent, Chavez, & Moran, 1998; Tse, 1996a). These studies revealed the following:

1. The majority of immigrant children and adolescents perform as language brokers (McQuillan & Tse, 1995; Orellana, 2003; Tse, 1995a, 1995b, 1996a).

2. Children may start brokering within 1 to 5 years of their arrival in the United States and may start brokering as young as 8 or 9 years of age (McQuillan & Tse, 1995; Tse, 1995a, 1996b).

3. Language brokers translate in a variety of settings, such as school, home, and the streets and they translate and interpret for their parents, other members of their family, and sometimes for school administrators (DeMent & Buriel, 1999; Gullingsrud, 1998; McQuillan & Tse, 1995; Orellana, Dorner, & Pulido, 2003; Shannon, 1990; Tse, 1995a, 1995b, 1996a; Valenzuela, 1999; Weisskirch, 2005; Weisskirch & Alva, 2002).

4. Documents that language brokers usually translate and interpret include notes and letters from school, bank/credit card statements, immigration forms, and job applications (DeMent & Buriel, 1999; McQuillan & Tse, 1995; Orellana, 2003; Tse, 1995a, 1995b; Valenzuela, 1999; Weisskirch, 2005; Weisskirch & Alva, 2002).

It is apparent that language brokers encounter a variety of situations where they are required to take the role of an adult. Given that these children are taking on such roles, one question that comes to mind is, "How do these children feel about their role as the family's translator and interpreter?" Studies on the feelings children have about language brokering report mixed results. Some of the research reveals that brokers see translating as something normal, something they do. These studies have also shown that children enjoy translating because it gives them feelings of pride and allows them to learn more about their first and second languages, as well as their culture (Orellana, 2003; Santiago, 2003; Shannon, 1990; Tse, 1995a, 1996b; Valdes, Chavez, & Angelelli, 2003; Walinchowski, 2001; Weisskirch, 2005).

Other studies have reported findings that contradict those mentioned above. These studies have reported that language brokers experience feelings of frustration, embarrassment, or pressure to translate accurately (DeMent & Buriel, 1999; Love, 2003; McQuillan & Tse, 1995; Ng, 1998; Tse, 1995a; Valenzuela, 1999; Weisskirch & Alva, 2002). Consequently, some researchers argue that using children as translators and

interpreters may affect the development of these children negatively. For example, Umaña-Taylor (2003) argues that language brokers take on adult roles during their adolescence and these experiences could have negative implications for their identity development. Others argue that language brokers do not find their experiences helpful or enjoyable, and for the majority of the time, they did not feel good about translating and interpreting (Weisskirch & Alva, 2002).

The literature presented in this section provides an introductory discussion of the different situations children experience when they serve as the family's translator and interpreter. It is evident that these children help their parents and other adults to understand a great variety of written documents and social interactions. Although these practices may be considered by some researchers as very positive or as a normative part of what these children are expected to do, others do not. It appears, then, that the area of language brokering is divided into two different camps. One camp believes that children serving as language brokers find the experience enjoyable and that it helps them learn more about their first and second languages. The other camp believes, in contrast, that children serving as language brokers find translating and interpreting stressful and a burden.

It is too early to decide which camp is correct, given that the majority of the studies presented in this section were more descriptive and did not include a large number of children of diverse backgrounds. For example, Orellana (2003) used survey data and case studies, but all of the participants were Spanish-speaking children. Another example is Weisskirch and Alva (2002), who based their results on a sample of 36 children of Latino/Hispanic descent.

What Are Typical Characteristics, or Qualities, of the Language Broker?

There are very few published studies that have attempted to clearly or fully describe the typical language broker. Thus, this section will aim to highlight characteristics of the language broker. Recent studies have used quantitative, qualitative, and mixed methods to answer this question. These studies reveal that children of immigrant families start their role as translator and interpreter shortly after their arrival in the United States (DeMent & Buriel, 1999; Valdes et al., 2003) and that they broker regardless of their place of birth (Tse, 1995a). The research shows (a) that these children usually start brokering between the ages of 8 and 12 (McQuillan & Tse, 1995; Tse, 1995a, 1995b, 1996a), (b) that they are usually the oldest child (Chao, 2002; Valdes et al., 2003), and (c) that brokers are predominantly female (Buriel et al., 1998; Love, 2003; McQuillan & Tse, 1995; Valenzuela, 1999; Weisskirch, 2005). These studies provide useful information on the characteristics of the children, yet there may be other qualities that language brokers have developed

290 that influence their parents to choose them for this important role. The few studies that have investigated such qualities suggest that these children tend to be fluent in English and Spanish, confident, extroverted, 295 good-natured, friendly, sociable, good listeners, able to provide great detail, and able to emphasize feelings and emotions when translating (Chao, 2002; DeMent & Buriel, 1999; Valdes et al., 2003; Valenzuela, 1999).

In sum, the research presented in this section highlights the characteristics of children who play the role 300 of their family's interpreter and translator. We may conclude, based on this research, that language brokers possess qualities that allow them to interact in a variety of settings with different types of people. Still, discrepancies and limitations exist in this literature. For exam305 ple, a number of studies argue that language brokering is a female-dominated activity, whereas other studies have not found gender differences (Diaz-Lazaro, 2002). Moreover, the few qualitative and mixed methods studies that have been conducted failed to include 310 more representative samples of children of immigrant families. The majority of the studies have been conducted with Latino/Hispanic children, and only a few studies have included Vietnamese and Chinese children, thus severely limiting the applicability of the 315 findings to the larger immigrant population in the United States.

How Is a Child's Cognitive Development Affected by Brokering?

Studies on translation have reported that children who speak two or more languages may translate and interpret information accurately (Harris & Sharewood, 320 1978). Language brokers tend to translate documents that require a high level of understanding, such as notes and letters from school, bank/credit card statements, job applications, and government and insurance forms (DeMent & Buriel, 1999; McQuillan & Tse, 1995). 325 There are researchers who argue that language brokers may, as a result, develop a more sophisticated vocabulary that could help them build their lexicons (Halgunseth, 2003). Furthermore, studies have shown that language brokers use higher cognitive abilities and prob330 lem-solving abilities to comprehend and interpret these types of documents (Walinchowski, 2001). Children not only translate documents but they also serve as mediators in conversations between their parents and first-language English speakers, such as at parent335 teacher conferences and when paying utility bills, making doctor's appointments, visiting hospitals, and making trips to the post office (DeMent & Buriel, 1999; Halgunseth, 2003; McQuillan & Tse, 1995; Tse, 1995a, 1996a). It is evident that language brokers act as trans340 lators and interpreters in a variety of settings—settings in which they must switch from being a child to assuming the role of the adult in order to translate and interpret for their parents or elders.

The research suggests that language brokers de345 velop linguistic abilities that monolingual children do not acquire, which may potentially help the child interact in a more mature and adult manner (Diaz-Lazaro, 2002; Shannon, 1990). The few qualitative studies that have been conducted report that language brokers feel 350 that translating and interpreting for their parents has allowed them to be more mature and independent, meet more people, and increase their proficiency in both languages (Halgunseth, 2003; Valdes et al., 2003). Given that language brokers are translating and inter355 preting a variety of documents in different settings, they may also develop higher decision-making strategies. These children not only develop higher cognitive abilities, but their decision-making may be considered more adultlike. Several researchers argue that language 360 brokers are considered the decision maker not only for their parents but also for the entire family (Diaz-Lazaro, 2002; McQuillan & Tse, 1995; Tse, 1995b; Valenzuela, 1999).

It is interesting that research has shown that lan365 guage brokers may be selective about the information they translate, especially for their parents. For example, a number of children who translated notes from school for their parents often omitted information that was negative (DeMent & Buriel, 1999). Although this find370 ing may call into question the accuracy of language brokers, we can only speculate that children are omitting this type of information because they do not want to hurt or cause shame to their parents. In certain communal cultures, children's poor behavior is often inter375 preted by parents as dishonorable (Comas-Diaz, 1993; Sue & Sue, 1990).

The literature presented in this section highlights how child language brokers may acquire higher cognitive and decision-making abilities due to their broker380 ing experiences. Although these studies highlight the benefits of brokering, they are still far from being widely accepted or definitive. There is simply not enough evidence to support the hypothesis that translating and interpreting enhances cognitive development 385 and decision-making abilities. More of these studies are needed to determine the nature of the relationship between language brokering and cognitive development and decision-making abilities.

Does Language Brokering Influence Children's Academic Performance?

It is a common belief in the United States that chil390 dren of immigrant families do not perform well in academia due to a lack of encouragement from parents (Evans & Anderson, 1973). Researchers who have studied the academic performance of children of immigrants have reported that individual and institutional 395 factors are the primary reasons for dropping out or performing poorly—not parents' lack of encouragement (Rumberger & Rodriguez, 2002). The literature in the area of language brokering and academic performance provides mixed results. Earlier studies suggest that language brokering is not significantly correlated with academic performance. For example, using a sample of 35 Latino/Hispanic students, Tse (1995a) reported that there was no association between academic performance and language brokering. Similarly, in other studies, children have stated that they did not associate their language brokering experiences with their academic performance. Furthermore, there are researchers who argue that language brokering may put children at risk for academic failure or may limit the child's academic and occupational opportunities because the family expects them to continue brokering (Umaña-Taylor, 2003).

Recently, mixed methods studies have been published with larger samples. These studies have started to look at the possible relationship between language brokering and academic performance. For example, Buriel et al. (1998) reported that language brokering was a strong predictor of academic performance. They also reported that language brokering scores and feelings about brokering were associated with academic self-efficacy. Similarly, in a study by Orellana (2003), children who have served as language brokers did significantly better on standardized tests of reading and math achievement. In another study by Walinchowski (2001), participants stated that although they felt frustrated about brokering, they used these experiences as tools for self-improvement.

In sum, the available literature informs us that there is no consensus on how language brokering experiences affect the academic performance of those who do it. Researchers are still debating about the positive or negative influences of language brokering on academic performance. The studies presented do provide important information that could be further investigated. A reliable approach for understanding this issue is to include mixed methodologies, as well as large and more diverse samples of children who are serving as language brokers.

How Does Language Brokering Affect the Parent–Child Relationship?

Research studies that have investigated the parent-child relationship of language brokers have been the sources of much controversy. Mental health professionals, social science scientists, legislators, policy makers, professionals in the medical field, and educators have all been discussing how children who serve as translators and interpreters may be potentially harmed or benefited by these experiences. Currently, there are two persistent perspectives on this issue. The first are those who are against children serving as translators and interpreters, stating that this type of experience negatively affects the normal dynamics of the parent-child relationship. Cohen, Moran-Ellis, and Smaje (1999) conducted a study with general practitioners whose patients requested to have their children

translate. In their study, the general practitioners reported being against using children in their consultations. The general practitioners strongly believed that having children serve as translators and interpreters when discussing their parents' health concerns could harm the parent-child relationship. Other researchers argue that having children translate and interpret for their parents led to unhealthy role reversals within the family, forcing the parents to become dependent on their children (Umaña-Taylor, 2003).

Earlier studies have shown that the experiences associated with language brokering help them develop a stronger bond to their parents. In a study by DeMent and Buriel (1999), (a) participants commented that brokering was a form of commitment to not disappoint their parents because they made a sacrifice in bringing the entire family to the United States, (b) other participants stated that they were concerned about finances and the health status of parents, (c) it was reported that parents developed a certain dependency on the language broker with regard to handling documents, and (d) the brokering experiences elicited feelings of compassion and helped them understand their parents' struggles. Language brokers are also considered active advocates of their parents' rights during complex situations (e.g., legal, financial). A qualitative study by Valenzuela (1999) reported that children inform their parents about their rights in the United States and educate them about the legal system. Some participants even helped their parents to hire a lawyer, if they believed that it was necessary.

More recent studies have revealed important information about how language brokers use their position of power to protect the welfare of their parents and other family members. Studies conducted by Orellana et al. (2003) and Valdes et al. (2003) reported that language brokers have stated that they use their position of power to protect their parents from embarrassment and humiliation. Some of the participants in their studies mentioned that they could not let employers, doctors, or other individuals embarrass their parents or other family members. These findings add new knowledge to this body of literature, where language brokers are now being considered the protectors or shields of the family.

In summary, there is no clear-cut answer to the question of whether language brokering has a positive or negative effect on the child-parent relationship. Furthermore, new research is suggesting how language brokers use their power to protect the well-being of the family. The research presented in this section provides promising, albeit somewhat limited, insights concerning the characteristics and role of language brokers in the family. However, more research is still needed. Past studies have not used participants of diverse backgrounds, which limits the generalizability of the results to larger groups of children. More studies are needed where more representative samples are used, as well as the inclusion of more sound, rigorous methodologies.

Discussion

In this article, information has been presented that describes the qualities of the language broker, the different situations language brokers experience, the types of documents they translate, the role language brokering plays in the child's cognitive development, the association between language brokering and academic success, and the role language brokering plays within the parent-child relationship. Taken together, results of this review suggest the following:

1. Language brokering is very common among children of immigrant parents (Orellana, 2003). Children start brokering at an early age (8 to 9 years), regardless of their place of birth or order of birth (McQuillan & Tse, 1995; Tse, 1995a, 1996b). Language brokering is often a female-dominated activity (Buriel et al., 1998; Love, 2003; McQuillan & Tse, 1995; Valenzuela, 1999; Weisskirch, 2005). The broker is not selected at random; parents base their selection on various qualities that language brokers possess (Chao, 2002; DeMent & Buriel, 1999; Valdes et al., 2003; Valenzuela, 1999).
2. Brokers may develop higher levels of cognitive ability, given the types of documents (e.g., bank/credit card statements) they translate and interpret for their parents. In addition, the situations where they translate or interpret (e.g., doctor's office, banks, government offices) highlight their adult-level cognitive capability (DeMent & Buriel, 1999; Halgunseth, 2003; McQuillan & Tse, 1995; Tse, 1995a, 1996a; Walinchowski, 2001).
3. Although earlier studies reported that there was not a strong relationship between language brokering and academic performance (McQuillan & Tse, 1995; Tse, 1995a), recent research has started to detect a positive relationship between these two constructs (Orellana, 2003).
4. There is insufficient evidence to conclude that language brokering has a positive or negative effect on the parent-child relationship. Scholars have not yet reached consensus on this issue. There are those, for example, who believe language brokering has negative consequences on the parent-child relationship and, likewise, there are those who believe it plays a positive role.

Based on the literature presented, it is safe to conclude that language brokers are unique children with qualities and skills that help them interact in two different worlds. On one hand, these children interact with other children their age through play and other types of activities. However, when necessary, language brokers assume their adultlike roles when they need to be the family's translator and interpreter. It is still unclear, though, whether children of immigrant families develop these qualities due to their brokering experiences or other environmental or biological factors.

Children who serve as translators and interpreters are active participants in a number of demanding situations. The literature suggests that language brokers develop higher cognitive abilities that allow them to be more knowledgeable of their first and second languages. Krashen (1985) stated that children who translate and interpret for their parents are being exposed to a variety of settings that, in the end, enhance their language acquisition. The literature reviewed demonstrates that language brokers translate immediately on arrival in the United States. Cummins (1989) affirmed that it takes 5 to 7 years for immigrant students to develop academic level accuracy. As mentioned, this is not the case for language brokers, because some broker within 1 to 5 years of their arrival in the United States. It appears, then, that language brokers must try to learn English at a much faster rate.

Although there is not a clear-cut relationship between language brokering and academic performance, researchers have argued that it is possible that the traditional educational assessment instruments used in school districts fail to capture the real abilities of language brokers. Oftentimes, the instruments used may be potentially biased, given the characteristics of the samples in which they were normed. Tse (1995b) acknowledged that school districts should develop appropriate and more relevant assessment instruments for children who are language brokers.

Language brokering serves as a bridge of communication and understanding between parents and children. In some instances, translating and interpreting may help a child feel more connected to his or her parents. Children may then be seen as their parents' "right hand," because they are required to make, or help make, decisions for the entire family. These activities allow the child to be more informed about different family concerns and to think and behave in a more adultlike manner. At the same time, this type of experience may have negative implications for the parent-child relationship, causing the parents to become dependent on the child, and the child to possibly feel overwhelmed by his or her role as the family's translator and interpreter.

As research in the area of language brokering grows, social scientists need to continue thinking critically about this topic. Some critical questions that remain unanswered include, Under what circumstances should children serve as interpreters and translators? The literature suggests that language brokering happens in various settings (e.g., home, school, government, and medical), yet it is unclear whether these are acceptable settings to have a child serve as a translator or interpreter. It is possible that parents prefer their child's assistance over that of a trained, adult interpreter because they feel more comfortable with them and trust them more. It is also possible that most service providers do not have the funds to hire trained interpreters and may believe that it is acceptable to have a family member translate. Another critical question is, Who should be responsible for making this decision? The parents? The service provider? The child? In addition, should it be legislated, so as to standardize the process for people? To begin answering these questions, more research is clearly needed.

Limitations

One limitation of this review is the number of resources included. Although 24 resources including journal articles, newsletter reports, conference papers, book chapters, *ERIC* documents, and dissertations are a fair amount of resources, more are needed to better understand the phenomenon of language brokering. It is imperative that further research be conducted to expand our knowledge base in this area. Another limitation is the type of studies used in this review. The majority of them were merely descriptive.

Implications for Theory

Language brokering is a relatively new area of study in the social sciences. This has caused those interested in it to use different theoretical frameworks to guide their work. Currently, there is no language brokering theory per se, but researchers have used three widely accepted theories to conduct their research. These theories include Acculturation theory, Family Systems theory, and contextual theories of cognitive development. These theoretical frameworks have guided the different research conducted with language brokers. We believe that a grounded theory approach is needed to develop a data-based theory that will better capture the experiences of language brokers and the nuances of the language brokering process.

Implications for Further Research

Language brokering is an open area that needs to be further explored. The majority of research studies on language brokering have been descriptive in nature. This may be interpreted as a call to researchers, educators, and policy makers to pay attention to this neglected area of research. Some recommendations for further research include the following: (a) scale development studies, (b) developmental studies, (c) studies of psychosocial variables associated with language brokering, (d) accuracy in translation, and (e) the characteristics of the language broker. No studies have evaluated the psychometric properties of the existing language brokering scales. This would be a good starting point, given that language brokering scales are already being used with children in different settings.

Developmental studies are needed given the lack of developmental data on language brokering. In this review, several of the studies were retrospective in nature, thus limiting our understanding of language brokering (Buriel et al., 1998; DeMent & Buriel, 1999; McQuillan & Tse, 1995). The results of such studies were based on participants' memories. A study by DeMent and Buriel (1999) suggests that language brokering happens in a developmental fashion. A number

of researchers have proposed that developmental studies could provide answers to the many questions that currently remain unanswered. Furthermore, new research using mixed methods has provided insightful information about the language brokering phenomenon (Orellana, 2003; Orellana et al., 2003). Thus, further research should consider adopting such methodologies.

Psychosocial variables need to be included in further research. For example, variables such as ethnic identity have been associated with native language use with ethnic minority adolescents (Heller, 1987; Phinney, Romero, Nava, & Huang, 2001). Recently, Weisskirch (2005) studied this relationship among Latino adolescents. In his study, he found that feelings about language brokering predicted ethnic identity, and combined subscales of language brokering, gender, and acculturation predicted ethnic identity. Other variables, such as language preference, immigration status, psychological distress, and self-esteem, are important constructs to consider when conducting research with these groups of children. Researching the interaction of these variables with language brokering will provide a better understanding of how children who serve as translators and interpreters are being affected by these experiences.

A critically important issue that has not yet been investigated concerns the accuracy and proficiency of the language broker. Language brokers are playing important roles in society, and they are transferring delicate information that, if done inaccurately or incorrectly, could harm the well-being of the family and those around them. Yet, to date, no studies have examined how proficient a child must be to translate or interpret for their parents. This is perhaps the greatest weakness, or limitation, of the extant research. Further research should, therefore, start to assess the accuracy and proficiency of these children and use this research to develop programs at the schools where children who serve in these roles are instructed in how to master these two important skills. First, research needs to develop methodologies that will allow us to investigate the accuracy and proficiency of language brokers. At this time, there is a deficiency in the availability of psychometrically sound instruments that may help measure these two skills. The need for such instruments is necessary, as we are not only dealing with children who come from different parts of the world but also children who will become part of mainstream U.S. society. These instruments need to consider worldview, family values, and acculturation. As the number of language minority students is increasing, schools are trying new methods to help them become bilingual. Until we have empirical evidence that informs us on the proficiency and accuracy of language brokers, we will not be able to clearly understand this phenomenon.

Language brokering is a common practice among children of immigrant families. The published studies

740 suggest that parents carefully select the child who will serve as the language broker, yet these studies fail to investigate the characteristics parents look for or what their process is for selecting the broker. It is recommended that more qualitative studies be conducted with immigrant parents to address this issue. It is also important to conduct developmental studies observing how language brokers evolve to discover the specific

745 qualities that best characterize the language broker.

Implications for Practice

Mental health researchers have argued that using children as translators and interpreters has negative consequences on the mental health of children (Umaña-Taylor, 2003; Weisskirch & Alva, 2002). This is a call

750 to those working in the mental health field to further investigate the implications of language brokering on children's mental health. Further research would also afford mental health professionals greater insight into the unique issues they face. It is also important that

755 mental health professionals be aware of the different roles children take and explore how language brokering experiences are affecting them.

Conclusion

This review presents the most current literature in the area of language brokering and introduces the

760 reader to some of the most salient issues in this area. It is evident that this line of research still has a long way to go. Many questions remain unanswered. Language brokering continues to be a form of adaptation and survival among immigrant families. Research clearly

765 needs to include language brokers from the full spectrum of immigrant families, as it is not a uniquely Latino phenomenon. This is a serious omission; children from all backgrounds engage in it. More research is needed to be able to answer the questions social scien-

770 tists, educators, and policy makers have with regard to children who serve as translators and interpreters. Research of this nature will help social scientists and policy makers develop better, more appropriate services for those who need them.

References

References marked with an asterisk (*N* = 24) indicate studies summarized in Table 1.

Baptise, D. (1987). Family therapy with Spanish heritage immigrant families in cultural transition. *Contemporary Family Therapy, 9,* 229–251.

Bialystok, E. (2001). *Bilingualism in development language, literacy, and cognition.* New York: Cambridge University Press.

Bloomfield, L. (1933). *Language.* New York: Holt.

*Buriel, R., Perez, W., DeMent, T. L., Chavez, D. V., & Moran, V. R. (1998). The relationship of language brokering to academic performance, biculturalism, and self-efficacy among Latino adolescents. *Hispanic Journal of Behavioral Sciences, 20(3),* 283–297.

*Chao, R. K. (April, 2002). The role of children's linguistic brokering among immigrant Chinese and Mexican families. In *Families of color: Developmental issues in contemporary sociohistorical contexts.* Symposium conducted at the biennial meeting of the Society for Research in Child Development, Minneapolis, Minnesota.

*Cohen, S., Moran-Ellis, J., & Smaje, C. (1999). Children as informal interpreters in GP consultations: Pragmatics and ideology. *Sociology of Health and Illness, 21(2),* 163–186.

Coleman, J. (2003, April 2). Bill would ban using children as interpreters. *The San Jose Mercury News,* p. 19A.

Comas-Diaz, L. (1993). Hispanic/Latino communities: Psychological implications. In D. R. Atkinson, G. Morten, & D. W. Sue (Eds.), *Counseling American minorities: A cross-cultural perspective* (4th ed., pp. 245–263). Madison, WI: Brown and Benchmark.

Cummins, J. (1989). *Empowering minority students.* Covina: California Association for Bilingual Education.

*DeMent, T., & Buriel, R. (1999, August). *Children as cultural brokers: Recollections of college students.* Paper presented at the SPSSI Conference on Immigrants and Immigration, Toronto, Canada.

*Diaz-Lazaro, C. M. (2002). *The effects of language brokering on perceptions of family authority structure, problem-solving abilities, and parental locus of control in Latino adolescents and their parents.* Unpublished doctoral dissertation, State University of New York at Buffalo.

Evans, F. B., & Anderson, J. G. (1973). The psychocultural origins of achievement and achievement motivation: The Mexican-American family. *Sociology of Education, 46,* 396–416.

Grosjean, F. (1989). Neurolinguistics, beware! The bilingual is not two monolinguals in one person. *Brain and Language, 36,* 3–15.

*Gullingsrud, M. (1998). I am the immigrant in my classroom. *Voices From the Middle, 6(1),* 3037.

*Halgunseth, L. (2003). Language brokering: Positive developmental outcomes. In M. Coleman & L. Ganong (Eds.), *Points and counterpoints: Controversial relationships and family issues in the 21st century: An anthology* (pp. 154–157). Los Angeles, CA: Roxbury.

Harris, B., & Sharewood, B. (1978). Translating as an innate skill. In D. Gerver & H. W. Sinaiko (Eds.), *Language interpretation and communication* (pp. 155–170). New York: Plenum.

Heller, M. (1987). The role of language in the formation of ethnic identity. In J. S. Phinney & M. Rotheram (Eds.), *Children's ethnic socialization* (pp. 180–200). Newbury Park, CA: Sage.

Krashen, S. (1985). *The input hypothesis: Issues and implications.* Torrance, CA: Laredo.

*Love, J. A. (2003, April). *Language brokering, autonomy, parent-child bonding, and depression.* Paper presented at the 2003 Conference of the Society on the Research of Child Development, Miami, Florida.

*McQuillan, J., & Tse, L. (1995). Child language brokering in linguistic minority communities: Effects on cultural interaction, cognition and literacy. *Language and Education, 9(3),* 195–215.

*Ng, J. (1998). From kitchen to classroom: Reflections of a language broker. *Voices From the Middle, 6(1),* 38–40.

*Orellana, M. F. (2003). Responsibilities of children in Latino immigrant homes. *New Directions for Youth Development, 100,* 25–39.

*Orellana, M. F., Dorner, L., & Pulido, L. (2003). Accessing assets: Immigrant youth's work as family translators or "para-phrasers." *Social Problems, 50(4),* 505–524.

Phinney, J. S., Romero, I., Nava, M., & Huang, D. (2001). The role of language, parents, and peers in ethnic identity among adolescents in immigrant families. *Journal of Youth and Adolescence, 30(2),* 135–153.

Rumbaut, R. G. (1994). The crucible within: Ethnic identity, self-esteem, and segmented assimilation among children of immigrants. *International Migration Review, 28,* 748–795.

Rumberger, R. W., & Rodriguez, G. M. (2002). Chicano dropouts: An update of research and policy issues. In R. Valencia (Ed.), *Chicano school failure and success past, present, and future* (2nd ed., pp. 114–146). New York: RoutledgeFalmer.

*Santiago, S. (2003). Language brokering: A personal experience. In M. Coleman & L. Ganong (Eds.), *Points and counterpoints: Controversial relationship and family issues in the 21st century: An anthology* (pp. 160–161). Los Angeles, CA: Roxbury.

*Shannon, S. M. (1990). English in the barrio: The quality of contact among immigrant children. *Hispanic Journal of Behavioral Sciences, 12(3),* 256–276.

Sue, D. W., & Sue, D. (1990). *Counseling the culturally different: Theory and practice* (2nd ed.). New York: Wiley.

*Tse, L. (1995a). Language brokering among Latino adolescents: Prevalence, attitudes, and school performance. *Hispanic Journal of Behavioral Sciences, 17(2),* 180–193.

*Tse, L. (1995b). When students translate for parents: Effects of language brokering. *CABE Newsletter, 17(4),* 16–17.

*Tse, L. (1996a). Language brokering in linguistic minority communities: The case of Chinese- and Vietnamese-American students. *Bilingual Research Journal, 20(3–4),* 485–498.

*Tse, L. (1996b). Who decides? The effects of language brokering on home-school communication. *Journal of Educational Issues of Language Minority Students, 16,* 225–234.

*Umaña-Taylor, A. J. (2003). Language brokering as a stressor for immigrant children and their families. In M. Coleman & L. Ganong (Eds.), *Points and counterpoints: Controversial relationship and family issues in the 21st century: An anthology* (pp. 157–159). Los Angeles, CA: Roxbury.

*Valdes, G., Chavez, C., & Angelelli, C. (2003). A performance team: Young interpreters and their parents. In G. Valdes (Ed.), *Expanding definitions of giftedness: The case of young interpreters from immigrant countries* (pp. 63–97). Mahwah, NJ: Lawrence Erlbaum.

*Valenzuela, A. (1999). Gender roles and settlement activities among children and their immigrant families. *American Behavioral Scientist, 42(4),* 720–742.

*Walinchowski, M. (2001). Language brokering: Laying the foundation for success and bilingualism. In R. Lara-Alecio (Chair), *Research in bilingual education.* Symposium conducted at the Annual Educational Research Exchange, College Station, Texas.

*Weisskirch, R. S. (2005). The relationship of language brokering to ethnic identity for Latino adolescents. *Hispanic Journal of Behavioral Sciences, 27(3),* 286–299.

*Weisskirch, R. S., & Alva, S. A. (2002). Language brokering and the acculturation of Latino children. *Hispanic Journal of Behavioral Sciences, 24(3),* 369–378.

Westermeyer, J. (1989). *Psychiatric care of immigrants: A clinical guide.* Washington, DC: American Psychiatric Press.

About the authors: *Alejandro Morales* is a doctoral student in counseling psychology at the University of Nebraska–Lincoln. He holds a bachelor's degree in psychology from California State University, Dominguez Hills, and a master's degree in counseling psychology from the University of Nebraska–Lincoln. His areas of research interest are language brokering, Latino ethnic/racial identity development, acculturation, Latino families, and Latino mental health. He enjoys reading Latin American literature, Harry Potter, and books about self-care and well-being and listening to Spanish rock. *William E. Hanson*, Ph.D., earned his doctorate in counseling psychology from Arizona State University and his master's from the University of Minnesota. He completed his predoctoral internship at the Duke/Durham VA Medical Center in 1996–1997. Between 1998 and 2005, he was an assistant professor in the Department of Educational Psychology at the University of Nebraska–Lincoln. Currently, he is a faculty member in the Department of Educational Studies at Purdue University, where he teaches in the APA accredited Counseling Psychology Program. He conducts and publishes research on the counseling process, in particular, the process of sharing psychological test results with clients; mixed methods; and problematic gambling among college students. For fun, he enjoys reading books by Carl Hiaasen, traveling, listening to live blues/jazz, and playing sports.

Authors' Note: An earlier version of this article was presented at the annual convention of the National Latina/o Psychological Association. Thanks to Drs. L. Mark Carrier and Silvia Santos for their many helpful editorial comments.

Address correspondence to: Alejandro Morales, Department of Educational Psychology, 114 TEAC, University of Nebraska–Lincoln, Lincoln, NE 68588-0345; E-mail: moralesl@bigred.unl.edu

Exercise for Review 2

Directions: Answer the following questions based on your opinions. While there are no right or wrong answers, be prepared to explain the bases for your answers in classroom discussions.

1. Did the reviewers convince you that the topic of the review is important? Explain.

2. Is the review an essay organized around topics (as opposed to a string of annotations)? Explain.

3. Is the number of headings and subheadings adequate? Explain.

4. Is the tone of the review neutral and nonemotional? Explain.

5. Overall, does the review provide a comprehensive, logically organized overview of the topic? Explain.

6. Is the conclusion/discussion at the end of the review appropriate in light of the material covered earlier? Explain.

7. Are the suggestions for future research, if any, appropriate in light of the material reviewed? Explain.

8. Are there any obvious weaknesses in this review? Explain.

9. Does this review have any special strengths? Explain.

10. What is your overall evaluation of this review on a scale from Excellent (10) to Very Poor (0)? Explain.

Model Review 3

Jamaican Child-Rearing Practices: The Role of Corporal Punishment

DELORES E. SMITH
University of Tennessee

GAIL MOSBY
University of Tennessee

ABSTRACT. The family is the most prominent social group that exists. It prepares its members for the various roles they will perform in society. Yet, the literature has unequivocally singled out the family as the most violent social group, with parental violence against children being the most prevalent type of family violence. While societies like the United States, Japan, and Sweden have taken a hard line on physical punishment and shifted to a gentler approach to discipline, harsh disciplining of children persists elsewhere. In the Caribbean, and Jamaica in particular, child-rearing and disciplinary practices that would warrant child abuse charges in other Western societies are rampant. This article examines the child-rearing techniques of Jamaican adults and their assumed effects on child outcomes. It also examines the plausibility of the assumption that the harsh physical punishment meted out to children is partially responsible for the current social problems of that island nation. We recommend approaches to tackle the broad goals of addressing familial and societal practices that compromise children's development and well being.

From *Adolescence, 38,* 369–381. Copyright © 2003 by Libra Publishers, Inc. Reprinted with permission.

Parents in all societies grapple with how to raise their children in a way that prepares them for the complexities of life (Yorburg, 2002) and equips them to one day become parents themselves (Hamner &
5 Turner, 2001). In order to accomplish this daunting task, parents rely on their own socialization into parenting, their intuitive sense of right and wrong, and their overall cultural beliefs (Hamner & Turner, 2001). The sanctions of these influences create a prerogative that
10 confers upon parents the responsibility to guide their children to become competent, responsible, and fully functioning members of society.

Culture guides parents' beliefs about child discipline, behavior management, and control. In Jamaica, a
15 small island nation of 2.5 million people, cultural beliefs have given rise to a parenting style that has been shown to negatively affect children's psychosocial outcomes, leading to serious concerns about the psychological adjustment of Jamaican children and adoles-
20 cents (Crawford-Brown, 1999; Leo-Rhynie, 1997).

According to ecological theory, the overlapping influences of the various cultural environments impact the individual's development and overall well-being (Bronfenbrenner, 1979). Although there is no research
25 specifically showing a causal link between problem behaviors and emotional well-being in Jamaica, the popular assumption is that the increase in antisocial behaviors in that society emanates from an impaired sense of self-worth and psychological maladjustment
30 among youth. From that assumption arises speculation about the source of that impairment and its concomitant problem behaviors. The most forceful conjecture centers on cultural socialization practices, particularly child rearing (Evans & Davies, 1997; Leo-Rhynie,
35 1997; Sharpe, 1997).

The purpose of this article is to examine the plausibility of speculations regarding harsh child-rearing practices and the psychosocial adjustment of Jamaican children and adolescents. It reviews the research litera-
40 ture on the effects of harsh physical punishment and offers recommendations for addressing the issue of excessive and inappropriate discipline. Recommendations are also offered for preventing and, perhaps, reversing the trend of antisocial and destructive behav-
45 iors that are thought to be linked to Jamaican child-rearing practices.

Jamaican Child-Rearing Practices

The dominant Caribbean parenting style is authoritarian, an approach consistently found to thwart optimal child socioemotional outcomes in Western cultures
50 (Baumrind, 1991). In keeping with this authoritarian style, Jamaican parenting has been characterized as highly repressive, severe, and abusive (Arnold, 1982; Leo-Rhynie, 1997; Sharpe, 1997) and the disciplining of children described as inconsistent and developmen-
55 tally inappropriate (Sloley, 1999). In fact, the sparse literature on Jamaican family processes has attested to the pervasiveness of corporal punishment and other violent disciplinary measures meted out to children by adults (Phillips, 1973; Evans & Davies, 1997; Walker,
60 Grantham-McGregor, Himes, Williams, & Duff, 1998). Flogging, the most common response of adults to perceived misbehavior in Jamaican children (Leo-Rhynie, 1997; Smith, 1989), has been vividly described. Arnold

(1982) has stated, "At times the 'beating,' as it is commonly called, can be severe and bears no relevance to the age of the child nor the stage of its development" (p. 141). The flogging of children "is carried out in such a way as to appear almost brutal. The hand, a stick, a belt, a shoe, or a tamarind switch are used to beat children to ensure compliance" (Leo-Rhynie, 1997, p. 44). Discipline "becomes severely enforced through 'shouting' and 'flogging' or 'beating.' Children are punished in this way for lying, stealing, disobedience, impoliteness, and not completing their chores. 'Playing in the house,' 'crying too much,' and 'not eating the meal provided' also constitute misdemeanors that warrant a 'beating'" (Barrow, 1996, p. 400).

The extent and prevalence of such harsh disciplinary measures have been examined empirically. Landmann, Grantham-McGregor, and Desai (1983) reported that 59% of the Jamaican mothers in their study indicated that they used a belt or stick to beat their children. Grant (cited in Leo-Rhynie, 1997) found that 84% of mothers of preschool children in his study admitted to beating their children. In Smith's (1989) study, 71% of rural parents and 55% of urban parents reported flogging as the most frequent response to perceived misbehavior in their children. To emphasize his point, Smith noted that spanking (a milder form of punishment) was virtually unknown, being practiced in only 3% of families. Walker et al. (1998) noted that 53% of the adolescent girls in their study reported that they had been physically punished by their parents during the previous year. In addition, children complained that adults, especially their parents, often publicly humiliated them.

Baptiste, Hardy, and Lewis (1997) reported that Caribbean immigrants in the United States tended to be overrepresented among parents charged with, and convicted of, child abuse and neglect. They noted that in therapy, these parents expressed anger and confusion about the punitive measures they faced in the United States for employing "generous doses of corporal punishment" (p. 296) and other harsh disciplinary methods against their children. Further, Baptiste, Hardy, and Lewis maintained that the sanctioning of corporal punishment in the culture of origin put these parents in serious conflict with the dominant culture, leading them to feel that their authority to discipline their children as they see fit had been eroded by the laws of the United States. These dynamics take a great mental toll on these families and often lead them to, uncharacteristically, seek professional counseling (Baptiste, Hardy, & Lewis, 1997).

The Jamaican practice of beating children is culturally sanctioned and extends to the larger society. Accordingly, "the sociocultural norm, 'the right to beat the child,' embraced by parents, teachers, and parent surrogates does lead to instances of abuse and neglect, and to repeated cases of abuse and the accompanying psychological damage" (Sharpe, 1997, p. 267). Evans and Davies (1997) pointed out that corporal punishment is, indeed, a convention in Jamaican schools—not only used as a means of discipline for misbehavior, it is very much a part of the pedagogical strategy. Further, numerous Jamaican newspaper stories and letters to the editor have attested to the pervasiveness of the severe corporal punishment meted out to children by teachers. For example, Clarke (2000), in a newspaper article titled "Please teacher don't beat me," related adults' recollections of extreme treatment from teachers and provided examples of the punishment meted out to schoolchildren in present-day Jamaica. One nine-year-old boy stated, "Sometimes my teacher beats me with a belt, sometimes a board.... Anytime I don't do my work, she hits me with the board, sometimes on my hand, sometimes on my head." An eleven-year-old girl related the story of her fourth-grade teacher, who beats students for coming to school or returning from lunch late and for being disobedient: "She uses a ruler, the long ones; some teachers use leather belts." Clarke also noted the case of a high school student who had to be hospitalized after being caned by a teacher.

Perhaps not surprisingly, many parents agree that children should be punished in school. Clarke noted one father's remarks: "I've never seen any statistics that show that flogging doesn't work. I send my boy to school for the teacher to take over; if she feels he should be whipped, then so be it; if he complains, he gets more at home." These dynamics have led Evans and Davies (1997) to express concern that Jamaican schools validated the use of the severe punishment that children received at home. They bemoaned the fact that "the school, charged with an important social and developmental role in society, does not act as a countervailing force to the family; rather, it reinforces a punitive, power-assertive, authoritarian approach to relationships and to resolving conflicts" (p. 19).

This kind of child maltreatment is not only socially endorsed, but sometimes also legally sanctioned. A Jamaican judge, in a family court hearing, advised a father that all the child needed to correct his behavior was "two good licks" (Sargent & Harris, 1992).

Communication Patterns

Authoritarian parenting is not conducive to open parent–child communication. Caribbean parents, and Jamaican parents in particular, as a rule do not engage in positive verbal interaction with children, neither do they offer warm and gentle guidance and direction. Evans and Davies (1997) contend that Caribbean parents lacked the propensity to have extended conversations or to reason with their children. Evans and Davies noted that parents often complained about their children talking too much or asking too many questions, ideas reinforced by the cultural belief that "children should be seen and not heard." Research has supported such views regarding parent–child communication. A study commissioned by the United Nations Children's Fund (UNICEF) cited poor parent–child communication, corporal punishment, and physical abuse as central to the serious social problems facing Jamaican society ("Unfriendly Parents in Jamaica," 2001; Sloley, 1999). Specifically, the study cited a serious lack of friendly communication between Jamaican parents and their children and highlighted the severe physical punishment and public humiliation meted out to children, dynamics that seriously hindered the development of positive socioemotional development. The study attributed the lack of positive communication to parents being handicapped by cultural practices that limit their ability to engage in cordial discussions with their children. The study noted: "Some of the factors central to [the country's social problems] are the lack of balanced communication between teenagers and parents, an unwillingness to engage in discussions with children, lack of information by parents, and a lack of understanding of adolescent behavior" ("Unfriendly Parents in Jamaica," 2001). According to Arnold (1982), "They need to learn to talk 'with' their children, rather than always 'to' or 'at' [them]" (p. 144). Clearly, many Jamaican parents lack the know-how of establishing trusting and cordial relationships with their children.

Origins of Harsh Parenting Practices

The etiology of such harsh disciplinary practices in the Caribbean has been pondered. Although many arguments have been forwarded, the most pervasive and often cited explanations point back to heritage, history, tradition, and socialization. Several authors have expressed the view that the extreme authoritarian style, along with the excessive discipline meted out to children, stems from the region's West African heritage combined with learned behavior, specifically from the brutality of slavery. These dynamics are bolstered by the religious sanction of "saving the rod and spoiling the child" (Arnold, 1982; Barrow, 1996; Leo-Rhynie, 1997).

The psychoanalytic concept of displacement has also been forwarded as a plausible explanation. Displacement involves shifting or redirecting anger or hostility from a threatening object to a less threatening target (Freud, 1965). It is often purported that harsh, stressful social and economic conditions create anger, frustration, and hostility in low-income parents. Parents in turn displace their anger and frustration on their children by administering unjustifiable physical punishment (Arnold, 1982; Sharpe, 1997), to the point that the beating of children has become ritualized (Arnold, 1982; Barrow, 1996). Although displacement theory seems fitting at the lower income levels (Arnold, 1982), it must be questioned in light of the fact that these extreme disciplinary practices are not confined to the poor but are pervasive at all levels of society (Leo-Rhynie, 1997). One might expect parents of better social standing to have the capacity to employ nonviolent forms of discipline, such as time-out, withholding privileges, or grounding. However, cultural values and beliefs supersede personal perspectives and provide the blueprint on how children ought to be reared (Barrow, 1996; Evans & Davies, 1997).

Effects of Harsh Disciplinary Practices

There is disagreement about the effects of physical punishment on children. While some researchers have noted a direct relationship between physical punishment and psychological maladjustment (Frias-Armenta, 2002; Swinford et al., 2000), others have contended that the outcomes are culture-dependent (e.g., Barrow, 1996). Still others, while not specifically refuting the relationship, have maintained that the mediating role of the child's perception of the punishment as rejection by the caretaker is substantial. A study of the effects of corporal punishment in one Caribbean locale found a modest, direct relationship between physical punishment and psychological adjustment. However, the indirect impact, mediated by the child's perception of rejection by the caregiver, was significantly stronger (Rohner, Kean, & Cournoyer, 1991).

More recent studies, conducted in a variety of settings and societies, have indicated that physical punishment, used even in moderation, has an adverse effect on psychosocial adjustment and behavior. Use of physical force against children has been found to predict impaired cognitive processes such as intelligence deficits and academic failure (Cicchetti & Toth, 1998), socioemotional dysfunction (Evans & Davies, 1997; Cicchetti & Toth, 1998), low empathy (Eisenberg & Fabes, 1998), hostile, aggressive, and oppositional tendencies, severe depression, conduct disorders in childhood (Frias-Armenta, 2002), and violence and criminality in adulthood (Swinford et al., 2000).

These outcomes not only have deleterious consequences for the individual but for families and society as well. In one study, 66% of the boys and 50% of the girls rated as highly aggressive were from home environments where physical punishment was the preferred disciplinary approach (Headley, 1994). Other studies have documented the long-term psychiatric and behavioral outcomes of physical maltreatment in childhood. Kamsner and McCabe (2000), in a review of the literature, found evidence of a strong link between physical maltreatment in childhood and later promiscuity, prostitution, teen pregnancy, and criminality. Specifically, male felons reported significantly higher rates of child physical abuse than their noninstitutionalized peers. The review also noted significant associations between child physical abuse and adult psychiatric illnesses such as anxiety disorders (panic disorder, social phobia), posttraumatic stress disorders, and depression. Further, Kamsner and McCabe, in their own investigation, found that child physical abuse was "the dominant abuse variable to contribute significantly to the prediction of trauma-related outcomes" (p. 1255). Sharpe

290 (1997), in addressing the issue of mental health and socialization in the Caribbean, focused on the problem of parental discipline and neglect. Based on clinical observations, she indicated that "conduct disorder and
295 childhood depression were common among victims of abuse and that the only cases of posttraumatic stress disorders seen in the clinic were in victims of abuse" (p. 268).

Heimer (1997) hypothesized that when adults use power-assertive and violent disciplinary methods, they
300 teach children that coercive force, aggression, and violence can be used to resolve conflicts and problems. Using longitudinal data, Heimer demonstrated that violent disciplinary measures against children translate into violent delinquency later in life; violence experi-
305 enced in childhood accounted for 39% of the variance in subsequent violence. Similarly, Paschall, Flewelling, and Ennett (1998) found that exposure to violence put children at increased risk for violent behavior. Craw-ford-Brown (1999), although not specifically studying
310 physical punishment, examined the impact of parenting on conduct disorders in Jamaican adolescents. She found a significant link between inadequate parenting and conduct disorders, with the child's perception of the parent as a negative role model as a contributing
315 factor. While Crawford-Brown's research did not indicate the expressed features of the negative role model construct, Rice (2000) contended that parents are positive models for their children when they restrain their expressions of anger and demonstrate that hitting and
320 other forms of violence are unacceptable. Conversely, parents become negative role models when they model aggression.

In general, research has confirmed that physical force as a means of punishment increases children's
325 vulnerability to psychosocial dysfunction. The reliance on physical punishment to control behavior inhibits children's development of internal controls, conformity to rules, and concern for the welfare of others. It also creates in children the propensity to misunderstand
330 how power is appropriated and wielded, and teaches them to become beaters themselves (Swinford, De-Maris, Cernkovich, & Giordano, 2000). However, some studies have shown a differential effect of physical punishment along gender lines. While physical pun-
335 ishment predicts externalizing behaviors, such as later violence, in males (Kamsner & McCabe, 2000), internalizing effects, such as depression, suicidal ideation, anxiety, and psychosis, are more prevalent for girls (Frias-Armenta, 2002). The Jamaican context does
340 seem to lend credence to gender differences in behavioral outcomes; the overwhelming majority of violent crimes occurring in Jamaica are committed by males (Robotham, 1999). However, there is controversy regarding the discipline meted out to each gender. Some
345 have noted that boys are flogged more often and more severely than girls, while girls are subjected to more verbal abuse (Leo-Rhynie, 1997). Others have main-

tained that mothers are more restrictive of their daughters, to protect them from sexual contact with boys and
350 potentially deleterious outcomes (Barrow, 1996; Evans & Davies, 1997; Phillips, 1973).

Discussion

Research has demonstrated that reliance on physical force as a means of discipline and punishment to control behavior leads to child maladjustment and de-
355 viancy in adolescence and beyond. The extant literature has also shown that the optimal environments for fostering healthy growth and development are a nurturing family and supportive community, both of which appear to be missing from the lives of many Jamaican
360 youth (Arnold, 1982; Leo-Rhynie, 1997; Phillips, 1973; Sloley, 1999). Consequently, the concern expressed by the Jamaican populace about the sense of worthlessness among young people may be warranted. Harsh disciplinary practices, typical of the Jamaican
365 culture, exact a heavy toll on children and evoke powerful and negative reactions in adolescents, with serious and far-reaching social implications. Indeed, poor socioemotional functioning has been found to be an important consequence, if not the cause, of problem
370 behavior (Kaplan & Lin, 2000). Furthermore, healthy psychosocial functioning acts as a deterrent to conduct disorders such as drug and alcohol use and abuse, delinquency, school dropout, precocious sexual activity, violence, and criminality (Harter, 1993; Kaplan & Lin,
375 2000).

The foregoing, then, calls into question the efficacy of traditional child-rearing practices in Jamaica. What might have been perceived as appropriate discipline is now criticized, publicly discredited, and deemed inap-
380 propriate by the media, researchers, and social science professionals, locally and abroad. It is clear, then, that harsh disciplinary practices beg for a reexamination in terms of their impact on child and adolescent outcomes. Both the public and policymakers must make
385 the protection of children from mistreatment a priority.

Recommendations

Undoubtedly, the traditional Jamaican parenting modus operandi conflicts with current knowledge. Prevailing socialization practices, guided by cultural beliefs and values, are contrary to modern thinking on
390 child rearing (Crawford-Brown, 1999) but there is obvious resistance to change (Leo-Rhynie, 1997). Therefore, consideration should be given to culturally palatable strategies to respond to the growing needs of children and families. Indeed, educating the populace
395 about the detrimental effects of certain practices on optimal child development would be a first step. The provision of relevant social services is also a necessity.

Parenting education. Parenting education programs have shown promise as both a prevention and interven-
400 tion tool in changing parental behavior and protecting children from physical abuse (Gomby, Culross, & Behrman, 1999). These programs not only provide

critical information to families about the developmental needs of their children, but also help families learn how to meet those needs. They may also educate families on how to find resources (e.g., training) in behavior and stress management techniques. However, at present, such resources are almost nonexistent in Jamaica (N. Gordon, personal communication, February 25, 2002).

Parenting education might be especially helpful to adolescent parents, considering the high rate of adolescent pregnancy in Jamaica (Wyatt, Durvasula, Guthrie, LeFranc, & Forge, 1999). Parents tend to imitate the disciplinary practices of their own childhood, thereby perpetuating a cycle of abuse and mistreatment, and their attendant psychological distress and negative behavioral outcomes (Frias-Armenta, 2002; Cicchetti & Toth, 1998). Young parents in particular may be ignorant of alternative methods of guidance and discipline. In a discussion of children's behavior management, Jamaican parents asked, "If you do not beat them [children], what do you do?" (Arnold, 1982, p. 143).

We, like Arnold (1982), suggest that parent education begin in schools, where children could, beginning at an early age, be taught the basic principles of growth, development, and effective parenting. Further up the educational ladder, it is imperative that the curriculum in teachers' colleges focus on the relevant theoretical and empirical information about the long-term effects and dangers of corporal punishment on child outcomes. Training in guidance techniques and age-appropriate discipline should also be a prominent feature of teacher-training pedagogy. To break the cycle of violence against children, teachers, like parents, must be taught alternatives to corporal punishment.

We also advocate the use of the media (e.g., radio and television) to educate the public by conveying practical and useful messages about best practices in child rearing. Media blitzes, similar to those employed in family planning advertisements and AIDS prevention and education, have great potential.

Counseling. The provision of counseling programs for parents and caregivers is a prudent strategy. Anxiety, anger, and emotional pain in parents' and caregivers' own lives often lead to child mistreatment (Arnold, 1982; Sharpe, 1997); therefore, providing counseling to help manage and alleviate persistent stress in families with children is appropriate and timely. Indeed, the severe physical punishment meted out to children might be, in part, an inappropriate displacement of adults' frustration (Sharpe, 1997). Bailey-Davidson (2001) noted that Jamaican children suffer from a wide range of psychiatric disorders and psychoses as a result of the parental abuse they suffer. Therefore, counseling and other programs to address the psychiatric needs of children, as well as families, are necessary.

Home visitation. The institution of home visitation programs is another option for policymakers to consider. Home visitation programs, using trained professionals, seek to create change in parents' attitudes, knowledge, and parenting behaviors "by providing parents with social support; practical assistance, often in the form of case management that links families with other services; and education about parenting and/or child development" (Gomby, Culross, & Behrman, 1999, p. 7). These programs, based on the premise that "parents who feel confident in their ability to be parents, who are less stressed, and who know a variety of ways to discipline their children will be warmer and more responsive to their children and less likely to resort to physical violence" (p. 10), have shown great promise in preventing and reducing child maltreatment.

Research. Sharpe (1997) maintained that the greatest challenge facing mental health professionals is "to map out ways in which to change those culturally influenced patterns of behavior toward children that endanger their mental health" (p. 270). Fortunately, some research on the mental health of Jamaican children (e.g., Crawford-Brown, 1999; Lambert, Lyubansky, & Achenbach, 1998) has begun to emerge, and has supported the findings of studies done in other cultures regarding the detrimental effects of certain parenting behaviors on child outcomes. However, much more is needed. For example, there is the need to better understand how Jamaican children's environments actually promote conditions of "alienation rather than connectedness and bondedness, distance in human relationships rather than deep and enduring intimacy, superficial rather than in-depth relationships, temporary rather than enduring solutions" (Burr & Christensen, 1992, p. 462). Although there is some research on the occurrence of physical punishment in the Jamaican culture, systematic examination of its effect on child outcomes is lacking. For example, some questions that beg empirical investigation include: Does the cultural sanctioning of corporal punishment protect children from the adverse socioemotional outcomes found in cultures where physical punishment is outlawed (e.g., the United States)? What is the role of socioeconomic status? For example, do children from families of lower socioeconomic status have better outcomes despite the occurrence of physical punishment? The role of child outcomes along gender lines should also be explored.

Conclusion

The development of social policies to prevent and reduce the adverse effects of the mistreatment of children is essential. Bailey-Davidson (2001) stressed the need for policymakers to focus on the prevention of violence to reduce the loss of human resources. Therefore, child mistreatment should become an issue of national importance. However, this will take the utmost commitment from both the government and private sector. Unfortunately, according to Crawford-Brown (1999), "the child welfare system in Jamaica can be described as archaic and ineffective, modeled on an English system of a bygone era" (p. 434). Modern social services employing best practices in mental health for families and children are desperately needed.

References

Arnold, E. (1982). The use of corporal punishment in child-rearing in the West Indies. *Child Abuse and Neglect, 6,* 141–145.

Bailey-Davidson, Y. (2001, March 28). Child abuse: A perpetual problem. *The Jamaican Gleaner Online.* Retrieved December 10, 2001, from http://www.jamaicagleaner.com/gleaner/20010328/health/health4.html.

Baptiste, D. A., Hardy, K. V., & Lewis, L. (1997). Clinical practice with Caribbean immigrant families in the United States: The intersection of emigration, immigration, culture, and race. In J. L. Rooparine & J. Brown (Eds.), *Caribbean families: Diversity among ethnic groups* (pp. 275–303). Greenwich, CT: Ablex.

Barrow, C. (1996). *Family in the Caribbean: Themes and perspectives.* Kingston, Jamaica: Ian Randle.

Baumrind, D. (1991). Parenting styles and adolescent development. In J. Brooks-Gunn, R. Lerner, & A. C. Peterson (Eds.), *The encyclopedia of adolescence* (pp. 746–758). New York: Garland.

Bronfenbrenner, U. (1979). *The ecology of human development.* Cambridge, MA: Harvard University Press.

Burr, W., & Christensen, C. (1992). Undesirable side effects of enhancing self-esteem. *Family Relations, 41,* 460–465.

Cicchetti, G., & Toth, S. L. (1998). Perspectives on research and practice in developmental psychopathology. In W. Damon (Series Ed.), I. E. Sigel, & K. A. Renninger (Vol. Eds.), *Handbook of child psychology: Vol. 4. Child psychology in practice* (5th ed., pp. 479–582). New York: Wiley.

Clarke, P. (2000, October 3). Please teacher don't beat me. *Jamaica Gleaner Online.* Retrieved May 3, 2002, from http://www.jamaicagleaner/gleaner/2000103/youth/youthl.html.

Crawford-Brown, C. (1997). The impact of parent–child socialization on the development of conduct disorder in Jamaican male adolescents. In J. L. Rooparine & J. Brown (Eds.), *Caribbean families: Diversity among ethnic groups* (pp. 205–222). Greenwich, CT: Ablex.

Crawford-Brown, C. (1999). The impact of parenting on conduct disorder in Jamaican male adolescents. *Adolescence, 34,* 417–436.

Eisenberg, N., & Fabes, R. A. (1998). Prosocial development. In W. Damon (Series Ed.) & Nancy Eisenberg (Vol. Ed.), *Handbook of child psychology: Vol. 3. Social, emotional, and personality development* (5th ed., pp. 463–552). New York: Wiley.

Evans, H., & Davies, R. (1997). Overview issues in childhood socialization in the Caribbean. In J. L. Rooparine & J. Brown (Eds.), *Caribbean families: Diversity among ethnic groups* (pp. 1–24). Greenwich, CT: Ablex.

Freud, S. (1965). *Normality and pathology in childhood.* New York: International Universities Press.

Frias-Armenta, M. (2002). Long-term effects of child punishment on Mexican women: A structural model. *Child Abuse and Neglect, 26,* 371–386.

Gomby, D. S., Culross, P. L., & Behrman, R. E. (1999). Home visiting: Recent program evaluations—Analysis and recommendations. *The Future of Children, 9,* 26.

Hamner, T. J., & Turner, P. H. (2001). *Parenting in contemporary society.* Boston: Allyn & Bacon.

Harter, S. (1993). Causes and consequences of low self-esteem in children and adolescents. In R. F. Baumeister (Ed.), *Self-esteem: The puzzle of low regard* (pp. 87–116). New York: Plenum.

Headley, B. (1994, August 14). The false promise of flogging. *The Sunday Gleaner,* p. 23A.

Heimer, K. (1997). Socioeconomic status, subcultural definitions, and violent delinquency. *Social Forces, 75,* 799–833.

Kamsner, S., & McCabe, M. P. (2000). The relationship between adult psychological adjustment and childhood sexual abuse, childhood physical abuse and family of origin characteristics. *Journal of Interpersonal Violence, 15,* 1243–1261.

Kaplan, H. B., & Lin, C. (2000). Deviant identity as a moderator of the relation between negative self-feelings and deviant behavior. *Journal of Early Adolescence, 20,* 150–177.

Lambert, C. L., Lyubansky, M., & Achenbach, T. (1998). Behavioral and emotional problems among the adolescents of Jamaica and the United States: Parent, teacher, and self-reports for ages 12 to 18. *Journal of Emotional and Behavioral Disorders, 6,* 180–187.

Landmann, J., Grantham-McGregor, S. M., & Desai, P. (1983). Child rearing practices in Kingston, Jamaica. *Child Care, Health and Development, 9,* 57–71.

Leo-Rhynie, E. A. (1997). Class, race, and gender issues in child rearing in the Caribbean. In J. L. Rooparine & J. Brown (Eds.), *Caribbean families: Diversity among ethnic groups* (pp. 25–56). Greenwich, CT: Ablex.

Paschall, M. J., Flewelling, R. L., & Ennett, S. T. (1998). Racial differences in violent behavior among adults: Moderating and confounding effects. *Journal of Research in Crime and Delinquency, 35,* 148–165.

Phillips, A. S. (1973). *Adolescence in Jamaica.* Kingston, Jamaica: Jamaica Publishing House.

Rice, F. P. (2000). *Human development: A life-span approach.* Upper Saddle River, NJ: Prentice Hall.

Robotham, D. R. (1999, August 15). Crime and public policy in Jamaica (1). *The Sunday Gleaner,* pp. 8A, 11A.

Rohner, R. P., Kean, K. J., & Cournoyer, D. E. (1991). Effects of physical punishment, perceived caretaker warmth, and cultural beliefs on the psychological adjustment of children in St. Kitts, West Indies. *Journal of Marriage and the Family, 53,* 681–693.

Sargent, C., & Harris, M. (1992). Gender ideology, childrearing, and child health in Jamaica. *American Ethnologist, 19,* 523–537.

Sharpe, J. (1997). Mental health issues and family socialization in the Caribbean. In J. L. Rooparine & J. Brown (Eds.), *Caribbean families: Diversity among ethnic groups.* Greenwich, CT: Ablex.

Sloley, M. (1999, November 17). Parenting deficiencies outlined. *The Jamaica Gleaner Online.* Retrieved April 2, 2002, from http://www.jamaicagleaner/1999117/news/n1.html.

Smith, M. G. (1962). *West Indian family structure.* Seattle: University of Washington Press.

Smith, M. G. (1989). *Poverty in Jamaica.* Kingston, Jamaica: University of the West Indies.

Swinford, S. P., DeMaris, A., Cernkovich, S. A., & Giordano, P. G. (2000). Harsh physical discipline in childhood and violence in later romantic involvements: The mediating role of problem behaviors. *Journal of Marriage and the Family, 62,* 508–519.

Unfriendly Parents in Jamaica. (2001). *Jamaica Gleaner Online.* Retrieved April 6, 2002, from http://www.jamaicagleaner200005/24/news2.html.

Walker, S. P., Grantham-McGregor, S. M., Himes, J. H., Williams, S., & Duff, E. M. (1998). School performance in adolescent Jamaican girls: Associations with health, social and behavioral characteristics, and risk factors for dropout. *Journal of Adolescence, 21,* 109–122.

Wyatt, G., Durvasula, R., Guthrie, D., LeFranc, & Forge, N. (1999). Correlates of first intercourse among women in Jamaica. *Archives of Sexual Behavior, 28,* 139–157.

Yorburg, B. (2002). *Family realities: A global view.* New Jersey: Prentice-Hall.

Address correspondence to: Delores E. Smith, Department of Child and Family Studies, The University of Tennessee, 115 Jessie Harris Building, 1215 West Cumberland Avenue, Knoxville, TN 37996. E-mail: delsmith@utk.edu

Exercise for Review 3

Directions: Answer the following questions based on your opinions. While there are no right or wrong answers, be prepared to explain the bases for your answers in classroom discussions.

1. Did the reviewers convince you that the topic of the review is important? Explain.

2. Is the review an essay organized around topics (as opposed to a string of annotations)? Explain.

3. Is the number of headings and subheadings adequate? Explain.

4. Is the tone of the review neutral and nonemotional? Explain.

5. Overall, does the review provide a comprehensive, logically organized overview of the topic? Explain.

6. Is the conclusion/discussion at the end of the review appropriate in light of the material covered earlier? Explain.

7. Are the suggestions for future research, if any, appropriate in light of the material reviewed? Explain.

8. Are there any obvious weaknesses in this review? Explain.

9. Does this review have any special strengths? Explain.

10. What is your overall evaluation of this review on a scale from Excellent (10) to Very Poor (0)? Explain.

Notes:

Model Review 4

Perceived Public Stigma and the Willingness to Seek Counseling: The Mediating Roles of Self-Stigma and Attitudes Toward Counseling

David L. Vogel
Iowa State University

Nathaniel G. Wade
Iowa State University

Ashley H. Hackler
Iowa State University

Editor's note: This review was written as an introduction to a
research report.

Many people who experience psychological and interpersonal concerns never pursue treatment (Corrigan,
2004). According to some estimates, within a given
year, only 11% of those experiencing a diagnosable
5 problem seek psychological services. In addition, fewer
than 2% of those who struggle with problems that do
not meet diagnosable criteria seek treatment (Andrews,
Issakidis, & Carter, 2001). As a result, it is important to
develop models that account for the reasons why peo-
10 ple do not seek services when experiencing a psychological or interpersonal problem to develop ways to
reach out to those in need.

The most often cited reason for why people do not
seek counseling and other mental health services is the
15 stigma associated with mental illness and seeking
treatment (Corrigan, 2004). Stigma can decrease the
likelihood that an individual will seek services even
when the potential consequences of not seeking counseling (e.g., increased suffering) are severe (Sibicky &
20 Dovidio, 1986). In fact, in April 2002, during the
launching of the New Freedom Commission on Mental
Health (http://www.mentalhealthcommission.gov), the
president declared that the stigma that surrounds mental illness is the major obstacle to Americans getting
25 the quality mental health care they deserve. This is
consistent with the 1999 surgeon general's report on
mental health (Satcher, 1999). The surgeon general's
report identified the fear of stigmatization as deterring
individuals from (a) acknowledging their illness, (b)
30 seeking help, and (c) remaining in treatment, thus creating unnecessary suffering. These commissions and
reports stress the importance of better understanding
the role of stigma in seeking care so that efforts to reduce stigma can be implemented.

Stigma Associated with Seeking Counseling

35 Stigma has been defined as a mark or flaw resulting
from a personal or physical characteristic that is
viewed as socially unacceptable (Blaine, 2000). The
"stigma associated with seeking mental health services,
therefore, is the perception that a person who seeks
40 psychological treatment is undesirable or socially unacceptable" (Vogel, Wade, & Haake, 2006, p. 325).
The existence of public stigma (i.e., negative views of
the person by others) surrounding mental illness and
the seeking of psychological services is clear. Past re-
45 search has found that the public often describes people
with a mental illness in negative terms (for a review,
see Angermeyer & Dietrich, 2006). For example, survey research has shown that the majority of community
respondents report negative attitudes toward people
50 with an identified disorder (Crisp, Gelder, Rix, Meltzer, & Rowlands, 2000) and tend to avoid and perceive
as dangerous those who are labeled as having been
previously hospitalized (Link, Cullen, Frank, &
Wozniak, 1987).

55 Whereas the stigma attached to being a mental
health patient may not be the same as the stigma associated with being a counseling client, researchers have
found that people tend to report more stigma surrounding counseling clients than nonclients. For example,
60 people labeled as having used counseling services have
been rated less favorably and treated more negatively
than those who were not labeled (Sibicky & Dovidio,
1986). In scenario-based research, individuals described as seeking assistance for depression were rated
65 as more emotionally unstable, less interesting, and less
confident than those described as seeking help for back
pain and than those described as not seeking help for
depression (Ben-Porath, 2002). As a result, it seems
that it is not just having a disorder but seeking psycho-
70 logical services that is stigmatized by the public.

Given the negative perceptions of those who seek
psychological services, it is not surprising that individuals hide their psychological concerns and avoid
treatment to limit the harmful consequences associated
75 with being stigmatized (Corrigan & Matthews, 2003).
Consistent with this, individuals are less likely to seek

help for issues that are viewed negatively by others (Overbeck, 1977). In addition, surveys of undergraduate students have found that those who endorse stigmas of the mentally ill are less likely to seek psychological help (Cooper, Corrigan, & Watson, 2003). Researchers have also found that perceptions of counseling stigma predict attitudes toward seeking counseling (Deane & Todd, 1996; Komiya, Good, & Sherrod, 2000; Vogel, Wester, Wei, & Boysen, 2005) as well as willingness to seek counseling (Rochlen, Mohr, & Hargrove, 1999). Survey research with community samples has also found that the fear of being viewed as crazy is a common barrier to seeking professional help (Nelson & Barbaro, 1985) and that participants who do not seek therapy are more likely to report stigma as a treatment barrier than those who do (Stefl & Prosperi, 1985). Furthermore, the stigma associated with mental illness has been linked to the early termination of treatment (Sirey et al., 2001). In all, there is clear support that awareness of the stigma associated with seeking treatment has a negative influence on people's attitudes toward seeking help and keeps many people from seeking help even when they have significant problems.

The Role of Self-Stigma

Despite the awareness of the relationship between perceived public stigma and the decision to seek treatment, the complex role that stigma plays in this decision-making process is not fully known. Corrigan (1998, 2004) asserted that there are two separate types of stigma affecting an individual's decision to seek treatment. The first, public stigma, is the perception held by others (i.e., by society) that an individual is socially unacceptable. The second, self-stigma, is the perception held by the individual that he or she is socially unacceptable, which can lead to a reduction in self-esteem or self-worth if the person seeks psychological help (Vogel et al., 2006). In other words, the negative images expressed by society toward those who seek psychological services may be internalized (Corrigan, 1998, 2004; Holmes & River, 1998) and lead people to perceive themselves as inferior, inadequate, or weak (Nadler & Fisher, 1986). As a result, people higher in self-stigma may decide to forego psychological services to maintain a positive image of themselves (Miller, 1985).

Whereas the direct relationship of perceived public stigma on one's willingness to seek psychological services is well established, the role of self-stigma has only recently been addressed. Related research, however, has shown that people can internalize negative perceptions when dealing with mental health issues (Link, 1987; Link & Phelan, 2001) and that being labeled mentally ill can lead to lower self-esteem (Link, Struening, Neese-Todd, Asmussen, & Phelan, 2001). In addition, modified labeling theory asserts that societal devaluation and discrimination toward the mentally ill could directly lead to negative consequences for peo-

ple's self-esteem if they are labeled, by themselves or others, as having a mental illness or as being in need of psychological care (Link, Cullen, Struening, Shrout, & Dohrenwend, 1989). Consistent with this, perceptions of stigma surrounding mental illness are related to lower self-esteem for those suffering from a mental illness (Link et al., 1987). Research has also shown that individuals are less likely to ask for help from nonprofessional sources, such as friends, if they fear embarrassment (Mayer & Timms, 1970) or if asking for help would lead them to feel inferior or incompetent (Nadler, 1991).

One study has directly measured the role of self-stigma in predicting psychological help-seeking attitudes and willingness to seek counseling (Vogel et al., 2006). This study showed that self-stigma was conceptually different from other, potentially related constructs, such as self-esteem and public stigma, suggesting that self-stigma is potentially unique in the conceptualization of help-seeking behavior. Supporting this, self-stigma uniquely predicted attitudes toward seeking psychological help and willingness to seek counseling above previously identified factors. It is interesting that the role of perceived public stigma in predicting attitudes toward and willingness to seek counseling was reduced when self-stigma was entered into the model. This suggests that self-stigma may mediate the relationship between perceived public stigma and attitudes toward seeking help as well as willingness to seek help. This mediating relationship makes sense, as public stigma's effect on one's decision to seek help may have as much or more to do with the internalization of societal messages about what it means to be mentally ill (Link et al., 1989) or to seek psychological services. The internalization can lead to shame and loss of self-esteem (Link, 1987), and the attempt to avoid those feelings may have the most direct effect on an individual's attitudes toward and willingness to seek counseling. This hypothesis, however, has not been empirically tested; only the direct effects of public and self-stigma on attitudes toward and willingness to seek counseling have been examined. As a result, we do not know the full relative effect of the different types of stigma on the decision to seek psychological help.

Sex Differences in Perceptions of Stigma

Studies consistently find that women are more likely to seek help for emotional issues (Moller-Leimkuhler, 2002) and possess more positive attitudes toward counseling than men (Fischer & Farina, 1995). One reason may be that men perceive greater stigma associated with seeking help. Society considers counseling to be a last resort, something to use only after other sources of support have failed (Angermeyer, Matschinger, & Riedel-Heller, 1999). Such attitudes may be particularly salient for men, who are expected to be stoic, controlled, and self-sufficient (Hammen & Peters, 1977). Consistent with this, adolescents are more willing to refer a girl to get help than a boy (Raviv, Sills, Raviv, & Wilansky, 2000). Thus, men may perceive that there is public stigma associated with their seeking help (Timlin-Scalera, Ponterotto, Blumberg, & Jackson, 2003) and believe that they would be stigmatized for discussing certain issues with a counselor (Martin, Wrisberg, Beitel, & Lounsbury, 1997). Similarly, the emphasis of the traditional male gender role on being independent and in control may lead to increased concerns about the loss of self-esteem associated with seeking help, as it may mean admitting to the inability to handle things on one's own (Addis & Mahalik, 2003). Therefore, if a man believed that he needed counseling, he might experience a greater sense of failure, which would make the act of asking for help particularly difficult. Consistent with this, men have been found to experience greater self-stigma than women regarding help-seeking in college settings (Vogel et al., 2006).

The Current Study

Although perceptions of public stigma may play an important role in the help-seeking process, it is difficult to alter, as it may require societal changes. However, interventions designed to reduce or alter the self-stigma associated with seeking help may encourage people to make use of counseling. Thus, a better understanding of how public and self-stigma relate to the help-seeking process can be used to boost service usage through outreach and educational programs. As a result, the goal of this research is to expand on the previous literature by using structural equation modeling (SEM) analyses to examine the hypothesis that the relationship between perceived public stigma and willingness to seek counseling will be indirectly mediated by self-stigma and attitudes toward seeking help.

References

Addis, M. E., & Mahalik, J. R. (2003). Men, masculinity, and the contexts of help-seeking. *American Psychologist, 58*, 5–14

Andrews, G., Issakidis, C., & Carter, G. (2001). Shortfall in mental health service utilization. *British Journal of Psychiatry, 179*, 417–425.

Angermeyer, M. C., & Dietrich, S. (2006). Public beliefs about and attitudes towards people with mental illness: A review of population studies. *Acta Psychiatrica Scandinavica, 113*, 163–179.

Angermeyer, M. C., Matschinger, H., & Riedel-Heller, S. G. (1999). Whom to ask for help in case of mental disorder? Preferences of the lay public. *Social Psychiatry and Psychiatric Epidemiology, 34*, 202–210.

Ben-Porath, D. D. (2002). Stigmatization of individuals who receive psychotherapy: An interaction between help-seeking behavior and the presence of depression. *Journal of Social & Clinical Psychology, 21*, 400–413.

Blaine, B. E. (2000). *The psychology of diversity: Perceiving and experiencing social difference.* Mountain View, CA: Mayfield Publishing.

Cooper, A. E., Corrigan, P. W., & Watson, A. C. (2003). Mental illness stigma and care seeking. *Journal of Nervous and Mental Disease, 191*, 339–341.

Corrigan, P. W. (1998). The impact of stigma on severe mental illness. *Cognitive and Behavioral Practice, 5*, 201–222.

Corrigan, P. (2004). How stigma interferes with mental health care. *American Psychologist, 59*, 614–625.

Corrigan, P. W., & Matthews, A. K. (2003). Stigma and disclosure: Implications for coming out of the closet. *Journal of Mental Health, 12*, 235–248.

Crisp, A. H., Gelder, M. G., Rix, S., Meltzer, H. I., & Rowlands, O. J. (2000). Stigmatization of people with mental illness. *British Journal of Psychiatry, 177*, 4–7.

Deane, F. P., & Todd, D. M. (1996). Attitudes and intentions to seek professional psychological help for personal problems or suicidal thinking. *Journal of College Student Psychotherapy, 10*, 45–59.

Fischer, E. H., & Farina, A. (1995). Attitudes toward seeking professional psychological help: A shortened form and considerations for research. *Journal of College Student Development, 36*, 368–373.

Hammen, C., & Peters, S. (1977). Interpersonal consequences of depression: Responses to men and women enacting a depressed role. *Journal of Abnormal Psychology, 87*, 322–332.

Holmes, E. P., & River, L. P. (1998). Individual strategies for coping with the stigma of severe mental illness. *Cognitive and Behavioral Practice, 5*, 231–239.

Komiya, N., Good, G. E., & Sherrod, N. B. (2000). Emotional openness as a predictor of college students' attitudes toward seeking psychological help. *Journal of Counseling Psychology, 47*, 138–143.

Link, B. (1987). Understanding labeling effects in the area of mental disorders: An assessment of the effects of expectations of rejection. *American Sociological Review, 52*, 96–112.

Link, B., Cullen, F., Frank, J., & Wozniak, J. (1987). The social rejection of former mental patients: Understanding why labels matter. *American Journal of Sociology, 92*, 1461–1500.

Link, B., Cullen, F., Struening, E., Shrout, P., & Dohrenwend, B. (1989). A modified labeling theory approach to mental disorders: An empirical assessment. *American Sociological Review, 54*, 400–423.

Link, B., & Phelan, J. (2001). Conceptualizing stigma. *Annual Review of Sociology, 27*, 363–385.

Link, B., Struening, E., Neese-Todd, S., Asmussen, S., & Phelan, J. (2001). Stigma as a barrier to recovery: The consequences of stigma for the self-esteem of people with mental illnesses. *Psychiatric Services, 52*, 1621–1626.

Martin, S. B., Wrisberg, C. A., Beitel, P. A., & Lounsbury, J. (1997). NCAA Division I athletes' attitudes toward seeking sport psychology consultation: The development of an objective instrument. *Sport Counselor, 11*, 201–218.

Mayer, J. E., & Timms, N. (1970). *The client speaks: Working class impressions of casework.* Oxford, England: Atherton Press.

Miller, W. R. (1985). Motivation for treatment: A review with special emphasis on alcoholism. *Psychological Bulletin, 98*, 84–107.

Moller-Leimkuhler, A. M. (2002). Barriers to help-seeking by men: A review of sociocultural and clinical literature with particular reference to depression. *Journal of Affective Disorders, 71*, 1–9.

Nadler, A. (1991). Help-seeking behavior: Psychological costs and instrumental benefits. In M. S. Clark (Ed.), *Prosocial behavior: Review of personality and social psychology* (Vol. 12, pp. 290–311). Thousand Oaks, CA: Sage.

Nadler, A., & Fisher, J. D. (1986). The role of threat to self-esteem and perceived control in recipient reaction to help: Theory development and empirical validation. In L. Berkowitz (Ed.), *Advances in experimental social psychology* (Vol. 19, pp. 81–122). San Diego, CA: Academic Press.

Nelson, G. D., & Barbaro, M. B. (1985). Fighting the stigma: A unique approach to marketing mental health. *Health Marketing Quarterly, 2*, 89–101.

Overbeck, A. L. (1977). Life stress antecedents to application for help at a mental health center: A clinical study of adaptation. *Smith College Studies in Social Work, 47*, 192–233.

Raviv, A., Sills, R., Raviv, A., & Wilansky, P. (2000). Adolescents' help-seeking behaviour: The difference between self- and other-referral. *Journal of Adolescence, 23*, 721–740.

Rochlen, A. B., Mohr, J. J., & Hargrove, B. K. (1999). Development of the Attitudes Toward Career Counseling scale. *Journal of Counseling Psychology, 46*, 196–206.

Satcher, D. (1999). *Mental health: A report of the surgeon general.* Retrieved December 5, 2005, from http://www.surgeongeneral.gov/library/mentalhealth /home.html

Sibicky, M., & Dovidio, J. F. (1986). Stigma of psychological therapy: Stereotypes, interpersonal reactions, and the self-fulfilling prophecy. *Journal of Counseling Psychology, 33*, 148–154.

Sirey, J., Bruce, M., Alexopoulos, G., Perlick, D., Raue, P., Friedman, S., & Meyers, B. (2001). Perceived stigma as a predictor of treatment discontinuation in young and older outpatients with depression. *American Journal of Psychiatry, 158*, 479–481.

Stefl, M. E., & Prosperi, D. C. (1985). Barriers to mental health service utilization. *Community Mental Health Journal, 21*, 167–178.

Timlin-Scalera, R. M., Ponterotto, J. G., Blumberg, F. C., & Jackson, M. A. (2003). A grounded theory study of help-seeking behaviors among White male high school students. *Journal of Counseling Psychology, 50*, 339–350.

Vogel, D. L., Wade, N. G., & Haake, S. (2006). Measuring the self-stigma associated with seeking psychological help. *Journal of Counseling Psychology, 53*, 325–337.

Vogel, D. L., & Wester, S. R. (2003). To seek help or not to seek help: The risks of self-disclosure. *Journal of Counseling Psychology, 50*, 351–361.

Exercise for Review 4

Directions: Answer the following questions based on your opinions. While there are no right or wrong answers, be prepared to explain the bases for your answers in classroom discussions.

1. Did the reviewers convince you that the topic of the review is important? Explain.

2. Is the review an essay organized around topics (as opposed to a string of annotations)? Explain.

3. Is the number of headings and subheadings adequate? Explain.

4. Is the tone of the review neutral and nonemotional? Explain.

5. Overall, does the review provide a comprehensive, logically organized overview of the topic? Explain.

6. Is the conclusion/discussion at the end of the review appropriate in light of the material covered earlier? Explain.

7. Are the suggestions for future research, if any, appropriate in light of the material reviewed? Explain.

8. Are there any obvious weaknesses in this review? Explain.

9. Does this review have any special strengths? Explain.

10. What is your overall evaluation of this review on a scale from Excellent (10) to Very Poor (0)? Explain.

Model Review 5

Linking Adolescent Family and Peer Relationships to the Quality of Young Adult Romantic Relationships: The Mediating Role of Conflict Tactics

LISA J. CROCKETT
University of Nebraska-Lincoln

BRANDY A. RANDALL
North Dakota State University

From *Journal of Social and Personal Relationships*, *23*, 761–780. Copyright © 2006 by SAGE Publications. Reprinted with permission.

Editor's note: This review was written as an introduction to a research report.

Over the last two decades, romantic relationships have emerged as a focal topic of study among scholars in a number of disciplines. Accompanying this shift has been a growing interest in the developmental antece-
5 dents of romantic relationships and the processes contributing to relationship quality. Compelling arguments have been made for the influential role of early parent–child and peer relationships in subsequent romantic relationships (Collins & Van Dulmen, 2006). However,
10 most of the empirical literature has focused on adolescent romantic relationships, with less attention to the early predictors of adult relationship quality. This lacuna is unfortunate, since early adulthood is thought to represent a critical time for the development of roman-
15 tic relationships. Theories of life-span development identify romantic intimacy (Erikson, 1963) and mate selection (Havighurst, 1972) as central tasks of early adulthood, and, consistent with this notion, young adults place a high priority on finding a long-term part-
20 ner (Cantor, Acker, & Cook-Flanagan, 1992). In the present study, we examined the associations between relationships with parents and peers in adolescence and the quality of young adults' romantic relationships.

Young Adult Romantic Relationships

Romantic relationships become increasingly com-
25 mon during adolescence and early adulthood. By age 15, most adolescents report having had a boyfriend or girlfriend sometime during the past three years (Feiring, 1996), and in the post high-school years most report an ongoing romantic relationship (Brown, 2004).
30 Moreover, romantic partners become increasingly important as a source of support from grade school to the college years (Furman & Buhrmester, 1992). The nature and quality of romantic relationships also appear to shift with age, in that they become more stable, ex-
35 clusive, and committed in late adolescence and early adulthood (Connolly & Goldberg, 1999).

Considerable research has addressed the concurrent or short-term predictors of satisfying adult relationships, especially marital partnerships, as well as factors
40 that may contribute to relationship distress and dissolution (e.g., Bradbury, Cohan, & Karney, 1998). These studies point to the importance of attitudes and behaviors in shaping relationship quality. However, few prospective studies have examined the developmental ori-
45 gins of satisfying romantic relationships in early adulthood. Collins and van Dulmen (2006) propose that experiences in early relationships with parents and peers are carried forward and influence the quality of early romantic relationships. Both parent–child and
50 peer relationships provide opportunities to learn expectations, skills, and behaviors that could carry over into subsequent romantic relationships, potentially affecting relationship quality.

Family Relationships and Adult Romantic Relationships

Families are considered a crucial training ground
55 for romantic relationships (Tallman, Burke, & Gecas, 1998). According to social learning theory, parents serve as important role models for their children. By observing their parents' marital relationship, children may learn specific behavior patterns (e.g., conflict
60 resolution strategies) and develop general expectations for appropriate behavior in romantic relationships (e.g., rules for expressing affection), as well as scripts for their own heterosexual relationships (Feldman, Gowen, & Fisher, 1998). In line with this notion, Martin (1990)
65 found that conflict between parents was associated with aggressive and avoidant patterns in parent–child conflict, patterns that were reproduced in the children's conflict with romantic partners. However, longitudinal studies have provided relatively little support for ef-

70 fects of observational learning on the quality of subsequent romantic relationships (Capaldi & Clark, 1998; Simons, Lin & Gordon, 1998). Instead, the subjective experience of participating in positive family relationships appears more central (Conger, Cui, Bryant, &
75 Elder, 2000).

Longitudinal research has documented a link between positive parent–child relations in adolescence and the quality of later romantic relationships. German youth who reported a reliable alliance with parents in
80 adolescence also reported greater feelings of connectedness and attraction to their romantic partners 6 years later (Seiffge-Krenke, Shulman, & Klessinger, 2001). In a U.S. sample, adolescents' reports of family interaction patterns predicted their happiness and distress in
85 romantic relationships as young adults (Feldman et al., 1998). Furthermore, adolescents' ratings of the quality of their relationships with parents have been associated with the perceived quality of their romantic and sexual relationships in emerging adulthood (Joyner & Campa,
90 2006). Using observer ratings of family interactions, Conger et al. (2000) found that adolescents' experiences of supportive, involved parenting were associated with their reported level of satisfaction and commitment in romantic relationships at age 20. Thus, ado-
95 lescents who experience positive family relationships appear to be advantaged in subsequent romantic attachments. These studies lead to the expectation that supportive family relationships in adolescence will predict better romantic relationships in early adulthood.

Peer Relationships and Romantic Relationships

100 Peer relationships are a second arena for learning about romantic relationships. Friendship theorists (Sullivan, 1953) have emphasized the role of close preadolescent friendships in the emerging capacity for intimacy; in turn, intimacy with same-sex friends may lay
105 the foundation for romantic intimacy (Connolly & Goldberg, 1999). Because peer relationships involve persons of similar age, social status, and competencies, they tend to be egalitarian and thus afford opportunities for cooperation, mutual altruism, and reciprocity that
110 are unlikely to be present in children's relationships with adults (Furman, 1999). Peer relationships also offer lessons in conflict resolution. Because peers are similar in status and power, mutual negotiation is needed to resolve conflicts. Furthermore, peer relation-
115 ships are voluntary and partners can opt out, so noncoercive strategies for resolving conflict are likely to predominate (Laursen, 1993). Adolescents tend to use negotiation strategies to manage conflict more than younger children do (von Salisch & Vogelgesang,
120 2005), and such skills may prove crucial in adult relationships, including romantic partnerships.

Consistent with the proposed link between peer relationships and romantic relationships, correlations have been reported between the quality of close friend-
125 ships and romantic relationships in adolescence (e.g.,

Connolly, Furman, & Konarski, 2000). However, the role of adolescent peer relationships in the more mature romantic relationships of adulthood has rarely been studied. In a sample of German youth, significant
130 bivariate associations emerged between adolescents' reported intimacy in close friendships and the level of connectedness and attraction they reported toward romantic partners in adulthood; however, this association was not seen in multivariate models that also included
135 parent–adolescent relationship quality (Seiffge-Krenke et al., 2001). Thus, although the linkage between adolescent peer and romantic relationships has been supported, the role of adolescent peer relationships in adult romantic relationships has not been established. One
140 goal of the present study was to assess the unique contributions of adolescent peer and family relationships and their relative importance as predictors of adult romantic relationship quality.

Gender Differences in Predictors of Romantic Relationship Quality

A second goal was to examine gender differences
145 in the predictive role of peer and family relationships. Research indicates that girls are more "relationship oriented" than boys and more invested in developing intimate relationships (see Block, 1983, for a review). Compared to boys, girls are more relationship focused
150 in their goals and anticipate greater distress when their relationships are threatened (Nelson & Crick, 1999). Girls also emphasize care and attachment in their relationships more than boys do (Shulman & Scharf, 2000), and women are thought to take greater responsi-
155 bility for the maintenance of adult romantic relationships (Wood, 2000). Thus, although both partners contribute to the quality of romantic relationships, women may be especially motivated to do so, and their relational competence may have a greater impact on the
160 relationship. If so, the negotiation skills and conflict tactics that women bring to the relationship may prove more influential than men's in determining adult relationship quality.

There is also empirical evidence that the quality of
165 peer and family relationships is differentially predictive of romantic relationship quality for women versus men. For example, family characteristics such as respect for privacy and flexible control more strongly predict women's than men's romantic attachment style and
170 happiness in love (Feldman et al., 1998). Moreover, girls' and boys' peer relationships emphasize different styles of relating and may afford different opportunities for developing relationship skills (Leaper, 1994). Studies of preadolescents indicate that boys' peer groups
175 are more hierarchical whereas girls' are more egalitarian, with a greater emphasis on joint decision making and interpersonal harmony (Maccoby, 1995). Thus, girls' peer relationships may provide more opportunities to learn practices such as turn taking and shared
180 decision making which could contribute to harmonious

romantic relationships. Based on these findings, we expected associations between the quality of adolescents' family and peer relationships and the quality of their adult romantic relationships to be stronger for females than males.

Conflict Tactics

A third goal of the present study was to examine conflict behaviors as possible mediators of the association between adolescent interpersonal relationships and young adult romantic relationships. Conflict is a central feature of close relationships, and conflict resolution skills have been linked empirically to adult relationship quality and satisfaction (Bradbury et al., 1998). Certain conflict management behaviors appear to be beneficial for healthy romantic relationships. In a study of couples followed over a 2-year period, higher marital satisfaction was associated with greater use of mutual discussion and less avoidance and coercion in resolving conflict (Noller & Feeney, 1998). Similarly, research with college students has shown that greater relationship satisfaction is associated with use of integrative conflict resolution strategies that allow both partners to meet their goals (Pistole, 1989). Thus, conflict behaviors in which both partners' perspectives are considered appear to be important for maintaining satisfying relationships. In contrast, attempts by partners to dominate each other and impose their will may be detrimental.

Conflict tactics may be learned through experiences with family members and peers. In a cross-sectional study, conflict resolution styles reported by late adolescents in their interactions with parents (e.g., attack, avoidance, or compromise) were associated with the styles they reported using with romantic partners (Reese-Weber & Bartle-Haring, 1998). In a prospective study, Conger et al. (2000) found that adolescents who experienced more nurturant-involved parenting subsequently showed greater warmth and less hostility in their interactions with a romantic partner. In turn, these affective displays predicted the quality of their adult romantic relationships. Similarly, peer relationships afford opportunities for learning conflict management, particularly noncoercive strategies (Laursen, 1993). Conflict tactics developed in adolescents' family and peer relationships could carry over into their adult romantic relationships and help explain associations between the quality of adolescent interpersonal relationships and adult romantic relationships.

In summary, most developmental research predicting the quality of young adults' romantic relationships has tended to focus on either family relationships or peer relationships, making it difficult to gauge their relative importance in predicting the quality of romantic relationships. Additionally, most studies have utilized concurrent or retrospective measures of adolescent relationships rather than examining the impact of these relationships prospectively. Finally, few prospective studies have examined specific processes through which early relationships influence the quality of adult romantic relationships. The present study addressed these gaps in the literature, using data from a sample of youth followed from adolescence into adulthood. Based on prior theory and research, peer and family relationships were each expected to show associations with adult relationship quality; the relative importance of these adolescent relationships in predicting adult relationship quality was also explored. Furthermore, we tested whether conflict behaviors mediated associations observed between the quality of adolescent interpersonal relationships and adult romantic relationships. Finally, we examined gender differences in the relations between adolescent peer and family relationships and young adult romantic relationships, anticipating somewhat stronger associations for females than males. We included controls for several demographic variables likely to be associated with romantic relationship quality, including age and adolescent family structure (Amato & Keith, 1991; Connolly & Goldberg, 1999; Shulman & Scharf, 2000).

References

Amato, P. R., & Keith, B. (1991). Parental divorce and adult well-being: A meta-analysis. *Journal of Marriage and the Family, 53,* 43–58.

Block, J. H., (1983). Differential premises arising from differential socialization of the sexes: Some conjectures. *Child Development, 54,* 1335–1354.

Bradbury, T. N., Cohan, C. L., & Karney, B. R. (1998). Optimizing longitudinal research for understanding and preventing marital dysfunction. In T. N. Bradbury (Ed.), *The developmental course of marital dysfunction* (pp. 279–311). New York: Cambridge University Press.

Brown, B. B. (2004). Adolescents' relationships with peers. In R. M. Lerner & L. Steinberg (Eds.), *Handbook of adolescent psychology* (pp. 363–394). New York: Wiley.

Cantor, N., Acker, M., & Cook-Flanagan, C. (1992). Conflict and preoccupation in the intimacy life task. *Journal of Personality and Social Psychology, 63,* 644–655.

Capaldi, D. M., & Clark, S. (1998). Prospective family predictors of aggression towards female partners for at-risk young men. *Developmental Psychology, 34,* 1175–1188.

Collins, W. A., & Van Dulmen, M. (2006). The course of true love(s): Origins and pathways in the development of romantic relationships. In A. Crouter & A. Booth (Eds.), *Romance and sex in emerging adulthood: Risks and opportunities* (pp. 63–86). Mahwah, NJ: Lawrence Erlbaum Associates.

Conger, R. D., Cui, M., Bryant, C. M., & Elder, G. H., Jr. (2000). Competence in early adult relationships: A developmental perspective on family influences. *Journal of Personality and Social Psychology, 79,* 224–237.

Connolly, J., Furman, W., & Konarski, R. (2000). The role of peers in the emergence of heterosexual romantic relationships in adolescence. *Child Development, 71,* 1395–1408.

Connolly, J., & Goldberg, A. (1999). Romantic relationships in adolescence: The role of friends and peers in their emergence and development. In B. B. Brown, C. C. Feiring, & W. Furman (Eds.), *Contemporary perspectives on adolescent romantic relationships* (pp. 266–290). Cambridge: Cambridge University Press.

Erikson, E. (1963). *Childhood and society.* New York: Norton.

Feiring, C. (1996). Concepts of romance in fifteen-year-old adolescents. *Journal of Research on Adolescence, 6,* 181–200.

Feldman, S. S., Gowen, L. K., & Fisher, L. (1998). Family relationships and gender as predictors of romantic intimacy in young adults: A longitudinal study. *Journal of Research on Adolescence, 8,* 263–286.

Furman, W. (1999). Friends and lovers: The role of peer relationships in adolescent romantic relationships. In W. A. Collins & L. B. Laursen (Eds.), *The Minnesota symposium on child psychology: Vol. 30. Relationships as developmental contents* (pp. 133–154). Mahwah, NJ: Lawrence Erlbaum Associates.

Furman, W., & Buhrmester, D. (1992). Age and sex differences in perceptions of networks of personal relationships. *Child Development, 63,* 103–115.

Havighurst, R. J. (1972). *Developmental tasks and education* (3rd ed.). New York: McKay.

Joyner, K., & Campa, M. (2006). How do adolescent relationships influence the quality of romantic relationships in young adulthood? In A. Crouter & A.

Booth (Eds.), *Romance and sex in emerging adulthood: Risks and opportunities* (pp. 93–101). Mahwah, NJ: Lawrence Erlbaum Associates.

Laursen, B. (1993). Conflict management among close peers. *New Directions for Child Development, 60,* 39–54.

Leaper, C. (1994). Exploring the consequences of gender segregation on social relationships. *New Directions for Child Development, 65,* 67–86.

Maccoby, E. E. (1995). The two sexes and their social systems. In P. Moen, G. H. Elder Jr., & K. Luescher (Eds.), *Examining lives in context: Perspectives on the ecology of human development* (pp. 347–364). Washington, DC: American Psychological Association.

Martin, B. (1990). The transmission of relationship difficulties from one generation to the next. *Journal of Youth and Adolescence, 19,* 181–199.

Nelson, D. A., & Crick, N. R. (1999). Rose-colored glasses: Examining the social information-processing of prosocial young adolescents. *Journal of Early Adolescence, 19,* 17–387.

Noller, R, & Feeney, J. A. (1998). Communication in early marriage: Responses to conflict, nonverbal accuracy, and conversational patterns. In T. N. Bradbury (Ed.), *The developmental course of marital dysfunction* (pp. 11–43). New York: Cambridge University Press.

Pistole, M. C. (1989). Attachment in adult romantic relationships: Style of conflict resolution and relationship satisfaction. *Journal of Personality and Social Psychology, 6,* 505–510.

Reese-Weber, M., & Bartle-Haring, S. (1998). Conflict resolution in family subsystems and adolescent romantic relationships. *Journal of Youth and Adolescence, 27,* 735–752.

Seiffge-Krenke, I., Shulman, S., & Klessinger, N. (2001). Adolescent precursors of romantic relationships in young adulthood. *Journal of Personality and Social Psychology, 18,* 327–346.

Shulman, S., & Scharf, M. (2000). Adolescent romantic behaviors and perceptions: Age- and gender-related differences and links with family and peer relationships. *Journal of Research on Adolescence, 10,* 99–118.

Simons, R. L., Lin, K., & Gordon, L. C. (1998). Socialization in the family of origin and male dating violence: A prospective study. *Journal of Marriage and the Family, 60,* 467–478.

Sullivan, H. S. (1953). *The interpersonal theory of psychiatry.* New York: Norton.

Tallman, I., Burke, P. J., & Gecas, V. (1998). Socialization into marital roles: Testing a contextual, development model of marital functioning. In T. N. Bradbury (Ed.), *The developmental course of marital dysfunction* (pp. 312–342). New York: Cambridge University Press.

von Salisch, M., & Vogelgesang, J. (2005). Anger regulation among friends: Assessment and development from childhood to adolescence. *Journal of Social and Personal Relationships, 22,* 837–855.

Wood, J. T. (2000). Gender and personal relationships. In C. Hendrick & S. S. Hendrick (Eds.), *Close relationships: A sourcebook* (pp. 301–313). Thousand Oaks, CA: SAGE Publications.

Authors' note: This research was funded by grant APR 000933-01 from the Office of Adolescent Pregnancy Programs to Judith R. Vicary, and grant AA 09678-01 from NIAAA to the first author. We gratefully acknowledge the contributions of the participating schools and the project staff of the Rural Adolescent Development Study and the Rural Young Adult Transitions Study.

Address correspondence to: Lisa J. Crockett, Department of Psychology, 319 Burnett Hall, University of Nebraska-Lincoln, Lincoln, NE 68588-0308, USA. E-mail: ecrockettl@unl.edu

Exercise for Review 5

Directions: Answer the following questions based on your opinions. While there are no right or wrong answers, be prepared to explain the bases for your answers in classroom discussions.

1. Did the reviewers convince you that the topic of the review is important? Explain.

2. Is the review an essay organized around topics (as opposed to a string of annotations)? Explain.

3. Is the number of headings and subheadings adequate? Explain.

4. Is the tone of the review neutral and nonemotional? Explain.

5. Overall, does the review provide a comprehensive, logically organized overview of the topic? Explain.

6. Is the conclusion/discussion at the end of the review appropriate in light of the material covered earlier? Explain.

7. Are the suggestions for future research, if any, appropriate in light of the material reviewed? Explain.

8. Are there any obvious weaknesses in this review? Explain.

9. Does this review have any special strengths? Explain.

10. What is your overall evaluation of this review on a scale from Excellent (10) to Very Poor (0)? Explain.

Model Review 6

The Changing Influences of Self-Worth and Peer Deviance on Drinking Problems in Urban American Indian Adolescents

SANDRA M. RADIN
University of Washington

CLAYTON NEIGHBORS
University of Washington

PATRICIA SILK WALKER
Oregon Health and Science University

R. DALE WALKER
Oregon Health and Science University

G. ALAN MARLATT
University of Washington

MARY LARIMER
University of Washington

From *Psychology of Addictive Behaviors*, 20, 161–170. Copyright © 2006 by the American Psychological Association. Reprinted with permission.

Editor's note: This review was written as an introduction to a research report.

In the general population and across American Indian communities, low self-esteem and peer influence are commonly believed to contribute to a young person's alcohol use. Empirical studies have not, however, unequivocally demonstrated these relations. Of the two possible risk factors, peers have been shown to be more important and more consistently implicated in adolescent substance use, although the magnitude and mechanisms of the relation are not well understood. Comparatively, self-esteem has been less consistently shown to be an important risk factor in adolescent substance use. Considering that the mixed findings in both literatures may be due to self-esteem and peer influences jointly affecting risk for substance use, consideration of either variable alone may provide an incomplete picture of their influence. The current study explores a mediational relation between these variables, operationalized as "*self-worth*" and "*peer deviance*," and their effects on alcohol-related problems in a sample of urban-dwelling, American Indian adolescents. With data collected annually over 7 years, we detected changes in the relations between these variables over time. We discuss these changes in terms of developmental transitions during adolescence and changing functions of self-esteem.

Introduction to the Issue

Our nation's drug use as a whole is a great concern; however, compared with the general population, American Indian youths manifest higher rates of usage, especially of alcohol; tend to begin experimentation earlier; and experience more dire consequences related to use (Beauvais, 1992; Novins, Beals, & Mitchell, 2001; Oetting et al., 1983). American Indian people are more likely to report poor health compared with other racial/ethnic groups (Denny, Holtzman, & Cobb, 2003), the average life expectancy for American Indians is lower than for the general population, and rates of accidental death are higher (Moncher, Holden, & Trimble, 1990; U.S. Indian Health Service, 1997). Furthermore, it is evident that substance use poses serious problems in academic performance, delinquency, socialization, and overall well-being among members of this population, and American Indian youths are considered at higher risk than other youths for developing substance use problems (Novins et al., 2001).

Role of Peer Influence in Substance Use

Although most studies of adolescent substance use, including studies of peers as risks, have been conducted with majority population samples, many researchers emphasize that risk and protective factors for alcohol abuse affect Native and non-Native youths similarly (Oetting & Beauvais, 1987). Likewise, results from a national household probability study of over 4,000 adolescents aged 12 to 17 years showed no differences between Native and Caucasian youths in race-based risk for substance abuse or dependence.

Research with youths from the general population clearly supports a connection between peer influence and substance use (Curran, Stice, & Chassin, 1997; Dishion & Owen, 2002; Kaplan, 1995). Clayton, Leukefeld, Donohew, Bardo, and Harrington (1995) noted that the correlation between self-reported delinquency and number of delinquent friends is one of the strongest and most consistently reported findings in the literature. Similarly, Oetting and Beauvais (1987) identified peer influence as the single dominant variable in whether adolescents chose to use drugs. Dielman, Campanelli, Shope, and Butchart (1987) likewise found significant influences of peers on adolescents' drug use. In fact, Dielman et al.'s "susceptibility to peer pressure" index correlated more highly with ado-

70 lescent substance use, misuse, and intentions to use than did other variables, such as self-esteem or locus of control.

Researchers have also proposed possible explanations to account for the relation between peer influence 75 and substance use. Many studies have implicated affiliation with drug-using peers or peer selection as the linking mechanism. Investigators have suggested that adolescents may be introduced to drugs by "delinquent" friends and then selectively befriend drug-using 80 peers (Clayton et al., 1995). Oetting and Beauvais (1987) proposed that although there are a number of underlying psychosocial factors that may create the potential for involvement with drugs, actual use takes place in the context of a "*peer cluster*," which may be a 85 dyad or a small group of close friends in which the sharing of ideas, similar attitudes and beliefs about drugs, and social opportunities and access to drugs influence drug use. Consistent with peer cluster theory, Beauvais, Oetting, Wolf, and Edwards (1989) found 90 higher rates of drug use for Indian youths compared with the general population and stated that small groups of peers had the strongest influence on a youth's decision to use or not use drugs. Because there is more limited access to a diverse group of peers on 95 reservations and in close-knit Indian communities, peers may have greater influence than in the general population.

Prospective studies have also provided important information about the relation between peers and ado- 100 lescent substance use. Kaplan, Martin, and Robbins (1984) demonstrated that involvement in a drug-using peer network directly increased susceptibility to peer influence and indirectly affected initiation and continued use of drugs over their 3-year study. Similarly, 105 Ary, Tildesley, Hops, and Andrews (1993) found strong effects for both peer modeling and peer attitude across 1 year. Because of the psychosocial and developmental changes that occur during adolescence, longitudinal studies of substance use behavior may be par- 110 ticularly useful.

Finally, all of these studies have contributed important and interesting ideas to the peer influence literature and implicate peers in adolescent substance use. However, all do not agree about the strength of the relation, 115 nor do they agree on the mechanisms through which peers influence substance use. Thus, it may be useful to look at peer variables in a context with other risk variables, such as self-esteem.

Role of Self-Esteem in Adolescent Substance Use

Self-esteem is generally viewed as an evaluation of 120 one's self that entails a judgment of personal worth, approval, or disapproval (Demo & Savin-Williams, 1992; Rosenberg, 1965). For some time there has been a common belief that low self-esteem contributes to youth alcohol or other drug use; however, the research 125 to date has provided mixed support. Some studies have

failed to find a relation between self-esteem and substance use (Jessor, Donovan, & Costa, 1991; McBride, Joe, & Simpson, 1991; Thompson, 1989). Indeed, Schroeder, Laflin, and Weis (1993) stated that no mat- 130 ter what definition of self-esteem had been used across studies, "no sizable relationship between SE [self-esteem] and drug use has been found" (p. 659). In contrast, other studies have supported an association between low self-esteem and adolescent substance use 135 (Dielman, Shope, Butchart, Campanelli, & Caspar, 1989; Stacy, Newcomb, & Bentler, 1992). Low self-esteem has also been prospectively linked to later substance use (Kumpulainen & Roine, 2002; Stein, Newcomb, & Bentler, 1987).

140 Discrepancies in self-esteem findings may be due to a number of factors. There is disagreement about the definition of self-esteem and about standard measures with which to assess the construct. Cross-sectional studies do not allow for the determination of cause and 145 effect, nor do they enable one to assess the long-term effects of self-esteem on behavior. Most measures of self-esteem tap "global self-esteem," and there are so many different factors that it is challenging to isolate one or a few. Finally, important aspects of self-esteem 150 change as we mature. Thus, effects in some studies may not be found in others.

Furthermore, many researchers consider self-esteem a stable trait that predicts future behavior (Harter, 1998; Rosenberg, 1965); however, others em- 155 phasize the statelike nature of self-esteem (Leary & Baumeister, 2000). If levels of self-esteem fluctuate over time and in different daily situations, a person may be more susceptible to peer influence during different stages of life as well as across varying daily 160 situations. Trzesniewski, Donnellan, and Robins (2003) demonstrated that self-esteem stability increased from adolescence to early adulthood and decreased from middle adulthood to old age. Other researchers view self-esteem as reactive to social evaluation and con- 165 tinually changing in response to external feedback (Leary & Baumeister, 2000) and characterize self-esteem as a "barometer" of transient self-worth relative to others. Such fluctuations and changes in self-esteem suggest varying susceptibility to peer influences, par- 170 ticularly for young adolescents. Additionally, because of developmental shifts, one may consider peer associations separately for different adolescent stages (Savin-Williams & Berndt, 1990) or, more realistically, as a continuously changing influence.

Linking Peer Influence and Self-Esteem in Adolescent Substance Use

175 Considering the predominant lay and clinical viewpoint that self-esteem is important in adolescent substance use outcomes suggests that dismissing it as a variable of interest is premature. Peer influences have received stronger support, but even here, the strength 180 of peer influence as a risk factor and the nature of its

relation with substance use are unclear. It is possible that the mixed findings in both literatures are due to the fact that self-esteem and peer influences jointly affect risk for substance abuse and that consideration of either variable alone provides an incomplete picture of their influence.

Some researchers have proposed comprehensive explanations for the peer-self-esteem relation, including *"self-derogation"* or *"self-enhancement"* theory (Kaplan, Martin, & Robbins, 1982; Kaplan et al., 1984) and the sociometer model (Leary, Schreindorfer, & Haupt, 1995). By incorporating self-esteem, peer deviance, and detachment from conventional society, these models rely on intrapersonal characteristics, social learning theory (Bandura, 1976), and commitment and attachment theories (Petraitis, Flay, & Miller, 1995) to explain the influences of low self-esteem on substance use outcomes.

Leary et al. (1995) described a *"sociometer"* model whereby self-esteem functions as a psychological gauge or indicator that allows individuals to monitor others' reactions to them and thus to modify their behavior in response to avoid social rejection. The researchers also suggested that the link between perceived rejection and self-esteem might indicate that the dysfunctional concomitants of low self-esteem (e.g., substance use) are effects of social exclusion, not of low self-esteem. Some dysfunctional behaviors associated with low self-esteem may be maladaptive attempts to increase acceptance by others.

Self-derogation/self-enhancement theory proposes that generalized self-esteem is central to understanding experimental substance use (Kaplan, 1995; Kaplan et al., 1982, 1984). According to this model, if adolescents consistently receive negative evaluations from conventional others or feel deficient in desirable social attributes, they may experience low self-esteem and frequent self-derogation, which can lead to alienation from conventional role models. Motivated to rebel against conventional standards and believing that they can bolster their self-worth by engaging in unconventional behavior, youths may become involved with deviant peers. Thus, low self-esteem contributes to substance use in an indirect fashion through association with deviant peers.

In addition to examining peer and self-esteem variables together, recent studies have begun to explore adolescent developmental processes, such as separation from family and individuation (i.e., becoming more independent and self-directed without parental control), to help explain the strong relation between peers and alcohol use and explore possible influences of self-esteem (Baer & Bray, 1999; Bell, Forthun, & Sun, 2000; Bray, Adams, Getz, & McQueen, 2003). Study outcomes suggest that characteristic emotional reactivity and susceptibility to contextual influences, such as peers, contribute to adolescent problem behaviors, including alcohol use. In the context of low self-esteem,

teens may become "codependent" or relate to others in a way that is characterized by focus outside the self and an attempt to derive acceptance and esteem through relationships (Beattie, 1989). Teens in this context may base their worth on their ability to meet others' needs or expectations (Beattie, 1989). Given the increasing importance of peer relationships during adolescence and peer influences on teen alcohol use (Brown, 1990), the risk of being more sensitive to the influences of peers (Jessor & Jessor, 1977), and fluctuations in self-esteem (Trzesniewski et al., 2003), adolescents' use of alcohol may be differentially influenced across early, middle, and late adolescence.

Current Study

The current study is an attempt to sort out the influences of peers and self-esteem across adolescence, when important developmental transitions are taking place among various psychosocial domains. Initiation and escalation of heavy drinking during this time may set the stage for problems in adulthood (Schulenberg & Maggs, 2002).

As a logical progression from earlier work and theory, we hypothesize that younger versus older teens will be differentially influenced by their peers in terms of alcohol use, and we suggest two functions of self-esteem related to adolescents' alcohol use. First, the way youths feel about themselves reflects the way they believe others feel about them. If they believe that others do not value them because they have not succeeded in conventionally valued pursuits, they have low self-esteem and feel bad about themselves, and they seek others who they believe are similar or offer alternative opportunities to indirectly enhance self-esteem. Second, when youths feel bad about themselves, they want to feel better and therefore use substances to achieve this (Oetting, Swaim, Edwards, & Beauvais, 1989). For the purposes of this study, we more narrowly defined peer influence as peer deviance, we operationalized self-esteem as self-worth, and we specified alcohol-related problems as the substance use outcome variable. We hypothesized that peer deviance would mediate the effects of self-worth on alcohol-related problems in earlier adolescence but that as adolescents entered adulthood, self-esteem would be more directly related to alcohol problems.

References

Ary, D. V., Tildesley, E., Hops, H., & Andrews, J. (1993). The influence of parent, sibling, and peer modeling and attitudes on adolescent use of alcohol. *International Journal of the Addictions, 28*, 853–880.

Baer, P. E., & Bray, J. H. (1999). Adolescent individuation and alcohol usage. *Journal of Studies on Alcohol, 13*, 52–62.

Bandura, A. (1976). *Social learning theory.* Morristown, NJ: General Learning Press.

Beattie, M. (1989). *Beyond codependency, and getting better all the time.* New York: Harper & Row.

Beauvais, F. (1992). Trends in Indian adolescent drug and alcohol use. *American Indian Alaska Native Mental Health Research, 5*, 1–12.

Beauvais, F., Oetting, E. R., Wolf, W., & Edwards, R. W. (1989). American Indian youth and drugs, 1976–87: A continuing problem. *Public Health Briefs, 79*, 634–636.

Bell, N. J., Forthun, L. F., & Sun, S. W. (2000). Attachment, adolescent competencies, and substance use: Developmental considerations in the study of risk behaviors. *Substance Use & Misuse, 35,* 1177–1206.

Bray, J. H., Adams, G. J., Getz, J. G., & McQueen, A. (2003). Individuation, peers, and adolescent alcohol use: A latent growth analysis. *Journal of Consulting and Clinical Psychology, 71,* 553–564.

Brown, B. B. (1990). Peer groups and peer cultures. In S. S. Feldman & G. R. Elliott (Eds.), *At the threshold: The developing adolescent* (pp.171–196). Cambridge, MA:

Clayton, R. R., Leukefeld, C. G., Donohew, L., Bardo, M., & Harrington, N. G. (1995). Risk and protective factors: A brief review. *Drugs and Society, 8,* 7–14.

Curran, P. J., Stice, E., & Chassin, L. (1997). The relation between adolescent alcohol use and peer alcohol use: A longitudinal random coefficients model. *Journal of Consulting and Clinical Psychology, 65,* 130–140.

Demo, D. H., & Savin-Williams, R. C. (1992). Self-concept stability and change during adolescence. In R. P. Lipka & T. M. Brinthaupt (Eds.), *Self-perspectives across the life span* (pp. 116–148). Albany: State University of New York Press.

Denny, C. H., Holtzman, D., & Cobb, N. (2003). Surveillance for health behaviors of American Indian and Alaska Natives: Findings from the behavioral risk factor surveillance system, 1997-2000. *Morbidity and Mortality Weekly Report, 52* SS-7, 1–13.

Dielman, T. E., Campanelli, P. C., Shope, J. T., & Butchart, A. T. (1987). Susceptibility to peer pressure, self-esteem, and health locus of control as correlates of adolescent substance abuse. *Health Education Quarterly, 14,* 207–221.

Dielman, T. E., Shope, J. T., Butchart, A. T., Campanelli, P. C., & Caspar, R. A. (1989). A covariance structural model test of antecedents of adolescent alcohol misuse and a prevention effort. *Journal of Drug Education, 19,* 337–361.

Dishion, T. J., & Owen, L. D. (2002). A longitudinal analysis of friendships and substance use: Bidirectional influence from adolescence to adulthood. *Developmental Psychology, 38,* 480–491.

Harter, S. (1998). The development of self-representations. In W. Damon & N. Eisenberg (Eds.), *Handbook of child psychology* (pp. 553–617). New York: Wiley.

Jessor, R., Donovan, J. E., & Costa, F. M. (1991). *Beyond adolescence: Problem behavior and young adult development.* Cambridge, England: Cambridge University Press.

Jessor, R., & Jessor, S. L. (1977). *Problem behavior and psychosocial development: A longitudinal study of youth.* New York: Academic Press.

Kaplan, H. B. (1995). Drugs, crime, and other deviant adaptations: Longitudinal studies. In H. B. Kaplan (Ed.), *Drugs, crime, and other deviant adaptations: Longitudinal studies* (pp. 3–46). New York: Plenum Press.

Kaplan, H. B., Martin, S. S., & Robbins, C. (1982). Application of a general theory of deviant behavior: Self-derogation and adolescent drug use. *Journal of Health and Social Behavior, 23,* 274–294.

Kaplan, H. B., Martin, S. S., & Robbins, C. (1984). Pathways to adolescent drug use: Self-derogation, peer influence, weakening of social controls, and early substance use. *Journal of Health and Social Behavior, 25,* 270–289.

Kumpulainen, K., & Roine, S. (2002). Depressive symptoms at the age of 12 years and future heavy alcohol use. *Addictive Behaviors, 27,* 425–436.

Leary, M. R., & Baumeister, R. F. (2000). The nature and function of self-esteem: Sociometer theory. In M. P. Zanna (Ed.), *Advances in experimental social psychology* (pp. 1–62). San Diego, CA: Academic Press.

Leary, M. R., Schreindorfer, L. S., & Haupt, A. L. (1995). The role of low self-esteem in emotional and behavioral problems: Why is low self-esteem dysfunctional? *Journal of Social and Clinical Psychology, 14,* 297–314.

McBride, A. A., Joe, G. W., & Simpson, D. D. (1991). Prediction of long-term alcohol use, drug use and criminality among inhalant users. *Hispanic Journal of Behavioral Sciences, 13,* 315–323.

Moncher, M. S., Holden, G. W., & Trimble, J. E. (1990). Substance abuse among Native-American youth. *Journal of Consulting and Clinical Psychology, 58,* 408–415.

Novins, D. K., Beals, J., & Mitchell, C. M. (2001). Sequences of substance use among American Indian adolescents. *Journal of the American Academy of Child & Adolescent Psychiatry, 40,* 1168–1174.

Oetting, E. R., & Beauvais, F. (1987). Peer cluster theory, socialization characteristics and adolescent drug use: A path analysis. *Journal of Counseling Psychology, 34,* 205–213.

Oetting, E. R., Beauvais, F., Edwards, R., Waters, M. R., Velarde, J., & Goldstein, G. (1983). *Drug use among Native American youth.* Fort Collins: Colorado State University.

Oetting, E. R., Swaim, R. C., Edwards, R. W., & Beauvais, F. (1989). Indian and Anglo adolescent alcohol use and emotional distress: Path models. *American Journal of Drug and Alcohol Abuse, 15,* 153–172.

Petraitis, J., Flay, B. R., & Miller, T. Q. (1995). Reviewing theories of adolescent substance use: Organizing pieces in the puzzle. *Psychological Bulletin, 117,* 67–86.

Rosenberg, M. (1965). *Society and the adolescent self-image.* Princeton, NJ: Princeton University Press.

Savin-Williams, R. C., & Berndt, T. J. (1990). Friendship and peer relations. In S. S. R. Elliott (Eds.), *At the threshold: The developing adolescent* (pp. 277–307). Cambridge, MA: Harvard University Press.

Schroeder, D., Laflin, M., & Weis, D. (1993). Is there a relationship between self-esteem and drug use? Methodological and statistical limitations of the research. *Journal of Drug Issues, 23,* 645–664.

Schulenberg, J. E., & Maggs, J. L. (2002). A developmental perspective on alcohol use and heavy drinking during adolescence and the transition to young adulthood. *Journal of Studies on Alcohol, 14,* 54–70.

Stacy, A. W., Newcomb, M. D., & Bentler, P. M. (1992). Interactive and higher-order effects of social influences on drug use. *Journal of Health and Social Behavior, 33,* 226–241.

Stein, J. A., Newcomb, M. D., & Bentler, P. M. (1987). Personality and drug use: Reciprocal effects across four years. *Personality and Individual Differences, 8,* 419–430.

Thompson, K. M. (1989). Effects of early alcohol use on adolescents' relations with peers and self-esteem: Patterns over time. *Adolescence, 24,* 837–849.

Trzesniewski, K. H., Donnellan, M. B., & Robins, R. W. (2003). Stability of self-esteem across the life span. *Journal of Personality and Social Psychology, 84,* 205–220.

U.S. Indian Health Service. (1997). *Regional differences in Indian health.* Rockville, MD: Author.

Authors' note: This research was supported in part by National Institute for Alcohol Abuse and Alcoholism Grants R01AA07103 and T32AA07455.

Address correspondence to: Sandra M. Radin, Addictive Behaviors Research Center, University of Washington, Seattle, WA 98195-1525. E-mail: sradin@u.washington.edu

Exercise for Article 6

Directions: Answer the following questions based on your opinions. While there are no right or wrong answers, be prepared to explain the bases for your answers in classroom discussions.

1. Did the reviewers convince you that the topic of the review is important? Explain.

2. Is the review an essay organized around topics (as opposed to a string of annotations)? Explain.

3. Is the number of headings and subheadings adequate? Explain.

4. Is the tone of the review neutral and nonemotional? Explain.

5. Overall, does the review provide a comprehensive, logically organized overview of the topic? Explain.

6. Is the conclusion/discussion at the end of the review appropriate in light of the material covered earlier? Explain.

7. Are the suggestions for future research, if any, appropriate in light of the material reviewed? Explain.

8. Are there any obvious weaknesses in this review? Explain.

9. Does this review have any special strengths? Explain.

10. What is your overall evaluation of this review on a scale from Excellent (10) to Very Poor (0)? Explain.

Notes:

Model Review 7

Treating Depression During Pregnancy and the Postpartum: A Preliminary Meta-Analysis

SARAH E. BLEDSOE
Columbia University

NANCY K. GROTE
University of Pittsburgh

ABSTRACT. This meta-analysis evaluates treatment effects for nonpsychotic major depression during pregnancy and postpartum comparing interventions by type and timing. *Methods*: Studies for decreasing depressive severity during pregnancy and postpartum applying treatment trials and standardized measures were included. Standardized mean differences were calculated for continuous variable outcome data. *Results*: Thirteen interventions reported positive effect sizes, one reported marginally positive effect size, one reported no effect, and the remaining reported marginally negative effect size. By type of treatment, medication with cognitive behavioral therapy (CBT 3.871, $p < .001$) and medication alone (3.048, $p < .001$) reported largest effect size, followed by group therapy (CBT, educational, and transactional analysis; 2.045, $p < .001$), interpersonal psychotherapy (1.260, $p < .001$), CBT (.642, $p < .001$), psychodynamic (.526, $p = .014$), counseling (.418, $p = .014$), and educational (.100, $p = .457$). Postpartum implementation produced larger effect size (.837, $p < .001$) than implementation during pregnancy (.377, $p = .002$). When medication interventions are excluded, postpartum effect size is .704 ($p < .001$). Conclusions: Preliminary findings suggest medication, alone or with CBT; group therapy with CBT, educational, and transactional analysis components; interpersonal psychotherapy; and CBT produce largest effect sizes in this population among interventions tested.

From *Research on Social Work Practice*, *16*, 109–120. Copyright © 2006 by Sage Publications. Reprinted with permission.

Depression during pregnancy and the postpartum is a widespread, serious health problem for women and infants. Approximately 10% of women develop nonpsychotic maternal postpartum depression following delivery (Cooper, Campbell, Day, Kennerley, & Bond, 1988; Cooper, Murray, Wilson, & Romaniuk, 2003; Cox, Holden, & Sagovsky, 1993; O'Hara & Swain, 1996). A recent study of depression during pregnancy and the postpartum has documented that in a cohort of 1,400 women, 13.5% met criteria for major depression at 32 weeks of pregnancy and 9.1% met criteria at 8 weeks postpartum (Evans, Heron, Francomb, Oke, & Golding, 2001). Similar rates of major and minor depression were found in middle-income women and predominantly Latina women (Yonkers et al., 2001) during pregnancy: 9% to 10% (Gotlib, Whiffen, Wallace, & Mount, 1991; O'Hara, Neunaber, & Zeboski, 1984). Higher rates (26%), however, have been identified in low-income, urban, African American and Caucasian women (Hobfoll, Ritter, Lavin, Hulszier, & Cameron, 1995).

Nonpsychotic postpartum depression has harmful, lasting effects on infant and child well-being (Moore, Cohn, & Campbell, 2001; Murray & Cooper, 1997), on the mothers' and fathers' subsequent mental health (Areias, Kumar, Barros, & Figueiredo, 1996; Kumar & Robson, 1984), and on the quality of the couple's relationship (Campbell, Cohn, Flanagan, Popper, & Meyers, 1992; O'Hara, 1994). Additionally, depression during pregnancy has been demonstrated repeatedly to be the most powerful predictor of postpartum depression (O'Hara & Swain, 1996). Evidence also suggests that depression during pregnancy results in adverse outcomes for mother and fetus or infant well-being. Higher levels of anxiety and stress are associated with maternal depression and predict dysregulation of hypothalamic-pituitary-adrenal axis in the fetus (Sandman et al., 1994), low birth weight, and prematurity (Wadwha, Sandman, Porto, Dunkel-Schetter, & Garite, 1993). Furthermore, infants of mothers depressed during pregnancy exhibit substandard neuromotor performance (Lundy et al., 1999) and dysregulation in behavior, physiology, and biochemistry (Field, 2000).

Although women are not more vulnerable to depression during pregnancy and the postpartum than at any other points across the life span (Gotlib, Whiffin, Mount, Milne, & Cordy, 1989; Kumar & Robinson, 1984; O'Hara, Zekoski, Philipps, & Wright, 1990), this period may be critical because of the risk posed to the fetus or infant as well as the mother and other family members. Furthermore, pregnant women may be unusually open to interventions directed at improving their own mental health before the birth of their child (Cowan & Cowan, 2000), and pregnancy is known to be an opportune time for suggesting health interventions (Institute of Medicine, 1996). It is imperative that doctors, clinicians, and social workers be provided with evidence regarding the treatment of depression during pregnancy and the postpartum on which to base best-

60 practice decisions. Higher rates of depression during pregnancy and the postpartum among low-income, urban women may create a special relevance for social work practitioners. Treatment that reduces maternal depression may offer protective advantages, not only 65 for the woman herself but also for the fetus, infant, and other family members (Kaplan, Bachorowski, Smoski, & Hudenko, 2002; Orr, James, & Prince, 2002; Sanderson et. al, 2002; Susman, Trickett, Iannotti, Hollenbeck, & Zahn-Waxler, 1985; Zuravin, 1989).

70 The following interventions for nonpsychotic major depression are included in this review based on their use in treatment trials: (1) medication in combination with cognitive behavioral therapy (CBT); (2) medication; (3) group therapy with cognitive behavioral, edu-75 cational, and transactional analysis components; (4) interpersonal psychotherapy (IPT); (5) CBT; (6) psychodynamic therapy; (7) counseling; and (8) educational interventions. IPT, used in four studies, is a time-limited, manualized treatment for depression focused 80 on interpersonal problems related to the onset of the current episode of depression (Klerman, Weissman, Rounsaville, & Chevron, 1984). All four studies using this approach modified IPT to address the particular needs of women with major depression during preg-85 nancy or postpartum (Grote, Swartz, Bledsoe, & Frank, 2004; O'Hara, Stuart, Gorman, & Wenzel, 2000; Spinelli, 1997; Spinelli & Endicott, 2003). CBT was used in three studies. CBT is a manualized form of psychotherapy focused on enhancing cognitive skills, 90 evaluating and modifying dysfunctional thoughts, encouraging self-reinforcement, generating positive coping statements, developing problem-solving abilities, and improving social skills (Appleby, Warner, Whitton, & Faragher, 1997; Beck, Rush, Shaw, & Emery, 95 1979; Chabrol et al., 2002; Cooper et al., 2003; D'Zurilla, 1986). One study used a psychodynamic approach focused on the early attachment experiences, mother's representation of the infant, and the mother-infant relationship (Cooper et al., 2003; Cramer et al., 100 1990; Stern, 1995). Two studies provided counseling interventions where women were given an opportunity to raise any personal or infant-care concerns (Cooper et al., 2003; Holden, Sagovsky, & Cox, 1989). A group intervention with a cognitive behavioral component, an 105 educational component, and a transactional analysis component was employed by Lane, Roufeil, Williams, and Tweedie (2001). Two studies used educational interventions to address major depression during pregnancy and the postpartum. These interventions were 110 tailored to the educational needs of pregnant and postpartum women and focused on topics such as parenting education and perinatal depression (Hayes, Muller, & Bradley, 2001; Spinelli, 2003). Two studies used antidepressant medications (fluoxetine and fluvoxamine) to 115 treat postpartum depression (Appleby et al., 1997; Suri, Burt, Altshuler, Zuckerbrow-Miller, & Fair, 2001).

One study included an intervention that combined medication with CBT (Appleby et al., 1997).

The primary aim of this review is to evaluate the ef-120 fects of current treatment interventions for nonpsychotic major depression during pregnancy and the postpartum. A second aim is to compare the relative effect sizes of the different types of interventions for nonpsychotic major depression during pregnancy and 125 the postpartum to determine which treatments appear to be most effective. A third and final aim is to evaluate the effect of the timing (during pregnancy or postpartum) of the interventions targeting nonpsychotic major depression. In examining and synthesizing the avail-130 able evidence relevant to these specific aims, this review contributes to the literature available to social work practitioners and other professional clinicians working with pregnant or postpartum women who desire to make evidence-based, best-practice decisions.

Criteria for Considering Studies for This Review
Types of Studies, Participants, Interventions, and Outcome Measures

135 All treatment trials that evaluated interventions directed at treating women with nonpsychotic major depression during pregnancy and the postpartum that used either a randomized controlled trial or a pretest, posttest (without comparison or control group) were 140 sought for the purposes of this review. Because of the limited number of trials focusing on depression during pregnancy and postpartum, the decision was made to include both randomized controlled trials and nonrandomized studies (but limited to those with a pretest, 145 posttest design) in this meta-analysis. Only studies with participants who were women diagnosed with nonpsychotic major depression during pregnancy or the postpartum were selected for inclusion in this review. The review was further limited to studies using interven-150 tions designed to treat nonpsychotic major depression during pregnancy or the postpartum. A standardized measure of depressive symptomatology was the main outcome measure.

Search Strategy for Identification of Studies

Electronic searching, reference searching, and per-155 sonal contact were used to identify studies for inclusion in this review. Relevant treatment trials were identified by searching the following electronic databases using the following terms: *depression, treatment* or *clinical trials* or *trials,* and *postpartum* or *pregnancy* or *postna-160 tal.* Terms such as *interpersonal psychotherapy* or *IPT, education, cognitive behavioral* or *CBT, group* (cognitive behavioral, educational, and transactional analysis components), and *medication* were used to ensure that additional trials were not overlooked. This search was 165 also limited to studies published in the past 15 years to increase relevance to current clinical practice (Weissman & Sanderson, 2002). Four databases were used in electronic searching: Cochrane Central Register of Controlled Trials, Medline, Psychlit, and Social Work

170 Abstracts. The reference lists of all papers selected were inspected for further relevant studies. Additionally, personal contact resulted in the inclusion of one article that has been recently published.

Methods of the Review

Selection of Studies

175 The entire search was performed by two reviewers. All studies were evaluated according to the above criteria. Studies not meeting the above criteria were discarded and only those studies that met the criteria of being treatment studies for nonpsychotic depression during pregnancy or the postpartum were retained. Au-
180 thorship was not concealed at the point of data collection.

Quality Assessment

Studies were given a quality rating of high, medium, or low based on the following criteria: presence of randomization, presence of a control group, number
185 of participants, and year of publication. The rating scale was entered into the analysis as a grouping variable.

Data Extraction and Management

All data were extracted by one reviewer. Studies that met the inclusion criteria regarding the targeted
190 outcome (reduction of depressive symptomatology) were reported as detailed in the *Type of Outcome* section. Reported analyses include only participants who completed the intervention. We report the attrition rate for each study in Appendix A. Although some studies
195 provide follow-up data, follow-up data were not included in the meta-analysis.

Comprehensive Meta-Analysis software (Borenstein & Rothstein, 1999) was used to assess continuous outcome data with a 95% confidence interval. Data were
200 reported as presented in the original studies with no exceptions. Analysis of interventions by type of treatment is also presented. Type of treatment data were retrieved from the published studies. Timing of intervention implementation is also presented. Studies were
205 divided into two categories based on the reported start time of intervention: (a) pregnancy (for interventions implemented before the birth of the child) and (b) postpartum (for interventions implemented after the birth of the child). For more detail, see Appendix A.

Description of Studies

Included, Excluded, and Ongoing Studies

210 Eleven studies describing 16 intervention trials met inclusion criteria for the review (see Appendix A for more details about the studies). Eight identified studies were excluded from the review (see Appendix B). Three studies were prevention studies, and all partici-
215 pants did not meet criteria for major depression at prevention implementation. One study did not focus specifically on women during pregnancy and the postpartum. Data reported specifically on women during preg-

nancy and the postpartum could not be separated from
220 the study sample based on information in the study publication. Two studies did not focus on depression as the outcome measure. One study was excluded because the type of intervention—early, middle, or late-night sleep deprivation—was not easily compared to the in-
225 terventions included in this analysis. One study was excluded because it had a sample size of one (see Appendix B). One ongoing study was identified. This study was a randomized, controlled treatment trial testing IPT in a low-income population of pregnant
230 women. Because outcome data were not available at the time of this review, the study is not included. However, it has been identified for inclusion in future reviews.

Interventions

All interventions were designed to treat nonpsy-
235 chotic depression during pregnancy and the postpartum. The treatments are classified as follows for further analysis: IPT, CBT, psychodynamic therapy, counseling, educational, group therapy with cognitive behavioral, educational, and transactional analysis compo-
240 nents, medication, and medication in combination with CBT.

Outcome Scales

Depressive symptomatology was measured using one of the following standardized inventories or standardized interviews (see Appendix A for the measures
245 used in each study). Rating scales used to measure clinical outcomes are the Edinburgh Postnatal Depression Scale (EPDS; Cox, Holden, & Sagovsky, 1987), Hamilton Rating Scale for Depression (Hamilton, 1960), and Profile of Mood States (McNair, Lorr, &
250 Droppleman, 1981). Because the EPDS was designed to differentiate the symptoms of depression from the somatic symptoms of pregnancy (Cox et al., 1987), we chose it as the primary outcome measure for the meta-analysis. For studies that did not include the EPDS as a
255 measure of depressive symptomatology, we chose the Hamilton Rating Scale for Depression that was used in one study, and the Profile of Mood States, which was the only measure of depressive symptoms used in another study.

Methodological Quality

260 A relatively simple method was used to determine the quality of studies. Studies were given a quality rating of high, medium, or low based on the following criteria: presence of randomization, presence of a control group, number of participants, and year of publica-
265 tion. Randomization in each of the trials was assessed using the following scale: 1 = *randomized, 2 = not randomized.* Studies were ranked on the presence or absence of a control group using the following scale: 1 = *control group present, 2 = no control group.* All
270 studies falling into the second category used a pretest/posttest design to measure depressive symptoma-

tology before and after intervention. Studies were ranked based on the number of participants using the following scale: 1 = *more than 30 participants*, 2 = *less than 30 participants*. Interventions of 30 or more scored more favorably because of the likelihood of greater generalization for trials including 30 or more participants. Studies were ranked based on year of publication using the following scale: 1 = *less than 10 years from date of publication*, 2 = *10 to 15 years from date of publication*. The cutoff for year of publication was chosen based on relevance to current clinical practice as there has been an increase in evidence for the efficacy of interventions in mental health based on controlled clinical trials in the past decade (Weissman & Sanderson, 2002).

Studies were given the following quality rankings based on the above criteria.

High: Appleby et al., 1997; Cooper et al., 2003; Hayes et al., 2001; O'Hara et al., 2000; and Spinelli et al., 2003.

Medium: Chabrol et al., 2002; Grote et al., 2004; Holden et al., 1989; Lane et al., 2001; and Spinelli, 1997.

Low: Suri et al., 2001.

Results

The first objective of this review was to evaluate the effects of current evidence-based treatments for nonpsychotic major depression during pregnancy and the postpartum (see Table 1). Eleven studies provided 16 treatment trials with a total of 922 participants contributing to this analysis. The overall effect size of all interventions in the analysis was .673 ($p < .001$). Of the 16 interventions compared, 14 interventions from the 11 studies included in the review had a positive effect size. Of the 16 interventions, 8 had effect sizes between 1.193 and 4.718 ($p < .020$). Five had effect sizes between .434 and .955 ($p < .047$). None of the final 3 interventions (counseling-Cooper et al., 2003; educational-Hays et al., 2001; CBT-Appleby et al., 1997) showed any significant effect size.

The second objective was to compare the relative effectiveness of treatments for nonpsychotic major depression during pregnancy and the postpartum. For this analysis, studies were grouped according to type of treatment intervention (see Table 2). From the 16 treatment trials, treatments were categorized into eight intervention types. Of the eight intervention types compared, four had positive effect sizes between 1.260 and 3.871 ($p < .001$). Of the 8 intervention types, three had effect sizes between .418 and .642 ($p < .014$). The final intervention type (educational) did not show any significant effect size. The results in Table 3 are shown by treatment intervention and ranked from highest to lowest by effect size.

The third objective was to evaluate the effect of the timing of the implementation (during pregnancy or postpartum) of interventions targeting nonpsychotic major depression (see Table 3). For this analysis, interventions were grouped according to the timing of the implementation of the intervention. Of the 16 interventions, 11 were implemented after diagnosis of nonpsychotic major depression during the postpartum period. For this group, $N = 618$ and effect size = .837 ($p < .001$). The remaining 5 interventions were implemented during pregnancy after the diagnosis of nonpsychotic major depression. For this group, $N = 304$ and effect size = .377 ($p = .002$). To determine whether inclusion of medication in postpartum interventions was responsible for the difference in effect size between interventions begun during pregnancy and those initiated postpartum, a second analysis was run. In this analysis, the 3 interventions using medication to treat depression postpartum were removed from the analysis. When treatments using medication were eliminated, the postpartum effect size decreased from .837 to .703, $p < .001$ ($N = 256$).

Discussion and Applications to Research and Practice

According to Thomas Insel (2004), director of the National Institute of Mental Health, social workers are doing the majority of frontline work treating individuals with mental illnesses. Citing a 1998 SAMSA report, the current psychotherapy workforce is dominated by social work consisting of 192,814 social workers, 73,014 psychologists, 33,486 psychiatrists, and 17,318 psychiatric nurses (Insel, 2004). Given this information, it seems necessary that social workers be informed regarding intervention evidence in the treatment of mental illnesses such as depression during pregnancy and postpartum, specifically in a population where medication may not be an option for treatment. Therefore, the findings of this review are specifically relevant to social workers.

With respect to the primary aim of this review, the results of the first analysis provide an overview of the effects of current treatments for nonpsychotic major depression during pregnancy and the postpartum included in this review. With the exception of CBT, there is a marked split between the individual treatment interventions when arranged hierarchically by effect size. Interventions using medication, medication in combination with CBT, IPT, and group therapy with cognitive behavioral, educational, and transactional analysis components had the largest effect sizes (> .95), whereas interventions using counseling, educational, and psychodynamic approaches had smaller effect sizes (< .75) or no effect. It is important to note that in this analysis, several of the evaluated treatment types (medication in combination with CBT, group therapy, and psychodynamic therapy) were represented by only one treatment intervention trial. The remaining interventions in this analysis were represented by two, three, or four trials. As research evolves in the treat-

Table 1
Meta-Analysis: All Interventions Ranked by Effect Size

		Timing of Intervention	Number of Participants	Effect Size	*p* Value
	Medication +				
Appleby, Warner, Whitton, and Faragher (1997)	CBT	Postpartum	30	3.871	< 0.001
Appleby et al. (1997)	Medication	Postpartum	33	4.781	< 0.001
Grote, Swartz, Bledsoe, and Frank (2004)	IPT-B	Pregnancy	18	2.178	< 0.001
Chabrol et al. (2002)	CBT	Postpartum	48	2.109	< 0.001
Lane, Roufeil, Williams, and Tweedie (2001)	Group[a]	Postpartum	30	2.046	< 0.001
Spinelli (1997)	IPT	Pregnancy	26	1.598	< 0.001
Suri, Burt, Altshuler, Zuckerbrow-Miller, and Fair (2001)	Medication	Postpartum	12	1.473	0.020
O'Hara, Stuart, Gorman, and Wenzel (2000)	IPT	Postpartum	99	1.193	< 0.001
Spinelli and Endicott (2003)	IPT	Pregnancy	38	0.955	0.005
Holden, Sagovsky, and Cox (1989)	Counseling	Postpartum	50	0.747	0.010
Spinelli and Endicott (2003)	Education	Pregnancy	34	0.693	0.047
Cooper, Murray, Wilson, and Romanuik (2003)	Psychodynamic	Postpartum	95	0.526	0.011
Cooper et al. (2003)	CBT	Postpartum	92	0.434	0.039
Cooper et al. (2003)	Counseling	Postpartum	97	0.259	0.202
Hayes, Muller, and Bradley (2001)	Education	Pregnancy	188	0.000	1.000
Appleby et al. (1997)	CBT	Postpartum	92	-0.099	0.777
Total			922	0.673	< 0.001

Note. CBT = cognitive behavioral therapy; IPT-B = brief interpersonal psychotherapy; IPT = interpersonal psychotherapy.
[a]Group therapy with cognitive behavioral, educational, and transactional analysis components.

Table 2
Meta-Analysis: All Interventions Grouped by Intervention Type

Type of Intervention	Number of Intervention Trials	Number of Participants	Effect Size	*p* Value
Medication + CBT	1	30	3.871	< .001
Medication	2	45	3.048	< .001
Group[a]	1	30	2.046	< .001
IPT	4	181	1.260	< .001
CBT	3	172	0.642	< .001
Psychodynamic	1	95	0.526	.014
Counseling	2	147	0.418	.014
Educational	2	222	0.100	.457

Note: CBT = cognitive behavioral therapy; IPT = interpersonal psychotherapy.
[a]Group therapy with cognitive behavioral, educational, and transactional analysis components.

Table 3
Meta-Analysis: All Interventions Grouped by Timing of Implementation of Intervention

Timing of Intervention	Number of Intervention Trials	Number of Participants	Effect Size	*p* Value
Postpartum				
Analysis 1	11	618	.837	< .001
Analysis 2	8	256	.703	< .001
Pregnancy	5	304	.377	.002

ment of major depression during pregnancy and the postpartum, additional, updated meta-analyses will be needed. Additionally, extraneous variables may be contributing to the effect sizes detected in the analyses.

Regarding the second aim of this review, when we grouped the treatment interventions by type of treatment to determine their relative effectiveness, the results are similar to those reported above. Medication in combination with CBT has the largest effect size (3.871, $p < .001$) followed by medication alone (3.048, $p < .001$); group therapy with cognitive behavioral,

educational, and transactional analysis components (2.046, $p < .001$); and IPT (1.260, $p < .001$). The combined effect size of CBT (.642, $p < .001$) is followed by psychodynamic therapy (.526, $p = .014$), counseling (.418, $p = .014$), and educational interventions (.100, $p = .457$).

With respect to those treatments with the largest effect sizes (medication and CBT, medication alone, group therapy with cognitive behavioral, educational and transactional analysis components, and IPT), findings are similar to those of the National Institute of

Mental Health Treatment of Depression Collaborative Research Program (NIMHTDCRP; Elkin et al., 1989) suggesting that the treatment of major depression in women during pregnancy and the postpartum and the treatment of depression at other times in the life cycle may be similar. There are two exceptions, however. The first is the large effect size (2.046, $p < .001$) found for the treatment intervention using group therapy with cognitive behavioral, educational, and transactional analysis components. Although the NIMHTDCRP did not examine the use of group treatment for depression, studies support the use of group therapy, especially in postnatal populations, because of its ability to address both psychosocial problems and cognitive behavioral deficits (Meager & Miligram, 1996). In light of the results of the NIMHTDCRP suggesting the efficacy of medication, medication and psychotherapy (CBT or IPT), and CBT and IPT alone for the treatment of major depression, the fact that CBT had varied effect sizes in this analysis is surprising. Although this could suggest that CBT may not be as effective in the treatment of major depression during pregnancy and the postpartum, there is an alternate explanation. Because of the limited scope of this analysis, the reviewers were only able to examine one of the targeted outcomes for each included study. The reviewers chose to use the EPDS, if available, because this scale was designed to assess depressive symptomatology during pregnancy and the postpartum period (Cox et al., 1987). CBT is focused strongly on the cognitive symptoms of depression (Beck et al., 1979). If the measurement of the targeted outcome had been a scale more sensitive to the cognitive symptoms of depression, such as the Beck Depression Inventory (Beck, Steer, & Garbin, 1988), the analysis might have yielded different results.

The third and final aim of this review was to evaluate the effect sizes of interventions based on the timing of implementation. Whereas those interventions implemented postpartum had a slightly larger effect size (.837, $p < .001$) than those implemented during pregnancy (.377, $p = .002$), this may be due to an alternative explanation. Medication interventions were implemented only during postpartum. When interventions using medication are omitted from analysis, the effect size of interventions implemented postpartum decreases (from .837 to .703, $p < .001$). This indicates that although part of the difference in timing effect size can be attributed to medication interventions (with large effect sizes) being used in the postpartum period and not during pregnancy, differences cannot be explained in their entirety. Further investigation is needed to examine these differences.

The scope of this review is limited by the fact that we did not assess all of the reliable and valid measures of depressive symptomatology that most of the reported treatment intervention studies used. Future research should conduct further meta-analyses using other available measures of depression.

The mixing of randomized and nonrandomized studies may be a limitation, but this is necessitated by the fact that currently, there are a limited number of adequate studies on depression during pregnancy and postpartum that can be selected. As the field develops, future meta-analyses on randomized and nonrandomized studies should be run separately. This review also includes treatment trials with small numbers of participants and meta-analyses are less robust with small trials. Thus, the results should be interpreted with caution. In addition, the overall quality of trials was variable. Publication bias is suggested by the paucity of negative or no effect trials found for this analysis. However, it is possible that the small number of negative or no effect trials denotes the effectiveness of treatment interventions reported in the literature to date. Additional trials and larger numbers of participants in a future meta-analysis would be required to address these issues. Furthermore, the review was only able to rank the methodological quality of studies using a simple method. Additionally, reported results were limited to the main outcome, depressive symptomatology. Future studies should examine other important variables of interest such as occupational and social functioning, social support, and cost-effectiveness of interventions.

Nonpsychotic major depression during pregnancy and the postpartum are a widespread health threat to mother, infants, and families. This review has described the effects of treatments for depression during pregnancy and has begun to identify those treatments that are most effective in this population. Although further research and analyses are needed to validate the results of this review, preliminary findings suggest that medication, alone or in combination with CBT; group therapy with cognitive behavioral, educational, and transactional analysis components; interpersonal therapy; and CBT produce the largest effect sizes in this population. However, doctors may be reluctant to prescribe medication during pregnancy and the postpartum (for mothers who choose to breastfeed) because absolute safety cannot be assured, although some selective serotonin reuptake inhibitors and other antidepressant medications have demonstrated relative safety during this period (Wisner, Gelenberg, Leonard, Zarin, & Frank, 1999). Additionally, many women may be unwilling to take medication during pregnancy and the postpartum (Oren et al., 2002). This situation creates an urgent need to develop other effective, nonpharmacological treatment alternatives to antidepressant medication. This review has begun the process of identifying these alternative treatments with findings supporting group therapy with cognitive behavioral, educational, and transactional analysis components; IPT; and CBT, respectively.

Although this review has attempted to evaluate the effects of current treatment interventions for nonpsychotic major depression during pregnancy and the

520 postpartum, additional research is needed to validate the findings in this report. In light of the fact that medication—alone and in combination with CBT—was found to have the largest effect size, research should continue to address the safety of pharmacological 525 treatment for major depression during pregnancy and the postpartum. Additional research is also needed to develop and improve existing nonpharmacological treatment of perinatal depression as many women prefer alternatives to medication for the treatment of major 530 depression while pregnant and breastfeeding. Culturally relevant treatments should also be explored in research on depression during pregnancy and the postpartum as low-income and ethnic minority women have higher rates of depression during this point in the life 535 cycle (Hobfoll et al., 1995).

References

References marked with an asterisk indicate studies included in the meta-analysis.

*Appleby, L., Warner, R., Whitton, A., & Faragher, B. (1997). A controlled study of fluoxetine and cognitive-behavioural counseling in the treatment of postnatal depression. *British Medical Journal, 314,* 932–936.

Areias, M., Kumar, R., Barros, H., & Figueiredo, E. (1996). Correlates of postnatal depression in mothers and fathers. *British Journal of Psychiatry, 169,* 36–41.

Beck, A. T., Rush, J. A., Shaw, B. F., & Emery, G. (1979). *Cognitive therapy for depression.* New York: Guilford.

Beck, A. T., Steer, R., & Garbin, M. (1988). Psychometric properties of the Beck Depression Inventory: Twenty-five years of evaluation. *Clinical Psychology Review, 8,* 77–100.

Borenstein, M., & Rothstein, H. (1999). *Comprehensive meta-analysis: A computer program for research synthesis.* Englewood, NJ: Biostat. Retrieved from www.MetaAnalysis.com

Bosquet, M., & Egeland, B. (2001). Associations among maternal depressive symptomatology, state of mind and parent and child behaviors: Implications for attachment-based interventions. *Attachment & Human Development, 3,* 173–99.

Campbell, S. B., Cohn, J. F., Flanagan, C., Popper, S., & Meyers, T. (1992). Course and correlates of postpartum depression during the transition to parenthood. *Development and Psychopathology, 4,* 29–47.

*Chabrol, H., Teissedre, F., Saint-Jean, M., Teisseyre, N., Roge, B., & Mullet, E. (2002). Prevention and treatment of postpartum depression: A controlled randomized study on women at risk. *Psychological Medicine, 32,* 1039–1047.

Cooper, P. J., Campbell, E. A., Day, A., Kennerley, H., & Bond, A. (1988). Non-psychotic psychiatric disorder after childbirth: A prospective study of prevalence, incidence, course, and nature. *British Journal of Psychiatry, 152,* 799–806.

*Cooper, P. J., Murray, L., Wilson, A., & Romaniuk, H. (2003). Controlled trial of the short- and long-term effect of psychological treatment of postpartum depression. 1. Impact on maternal mood. *British Journal of Psychiatry, 182,* 412–419.

Cowan, C., & Cowan, P. (2000). *When partners become parents: The big life change for couples.* Mahwah, NJ: Lawrence Erlbaum.

Cox, J. L., Holden, J., & Sagovsky, R. (1987). Detection of postnatal depression: Development of the Edinburgh postnatal depression scale. *British Journal of Psychiatry, 198,* 213–220.

Cox, J. L., Murray, D., & Chapman, G. (1993). A controlled study of the onset, duration and prevalence of postnatal depression. *British Journal of Psychiatry, 163,* 27–31.

Cramer, B., Robert-Tissot, C., Stern, D., Serpa-Rusconi, S., De Muralt, G. B., Palacio-Espasa, F., et al. (1990). Outcome evaluation in brief mother-infant psychotherapy: A preliminary report. *Infant Mental Health Journal, 11,* 278–300.

D'Zurilla, T. J. (1986). *Problem-solving therapy: A social competence approach to clinical intervention.* New York: Springer.

Elkin, I., Shea, T., Watkins, J. T., Imber, S. D., Sotsky, S. M., Collins, J. F., et al. (1989). National Institute of Mental Health Treatment of Depression Collaborative Research Program: General effectiveness of treatments. *Archives of General Psychiatry, 46,* 971–982.

Evans, J., Heron, J., Francomb, H., Oke, S., & Golding, J. (2001). Cohort study of depressed mood during pregnancy and after childbirth. *British Medical Journal, 323,* 257–260.

Field, T. (2000). Infants of depressed mothers. In S. Johnson & A. Hayes (Eds.), *Stress, coping, and depression* (pp. 3–22). Mahwah, NJ: Lawrence Erlbaum.

Gotlib, I., Whiffen, V., Wallace, P., & Mount, J. (1991). Prospective investigation of postpartum depression: Factors involved in onset and recovery. *Journal of Abnormal Psychology, 100,* 122–132.

Gotlib, I. H., Wiffen, V. E., Mount, J. H., Milne, K., & Cordy, N. I. (1989). Prevalence rates and demographic characteristics associated with depression in pregnancy and the postpartum. *Journal of Consulting & Clinical Psychology, 57,* 269–274.

*Grote, N. K., Swartz, H. A., Bledsoe, S. E., & Frank, E. (2004). Treating depression in low-income pregnant patients: The role of brief interpersonal psychotherapy. *Research on Social Work Practice, 14,* 397–406.

Hamilton, M. (1960). A rating scale for depression. *Journal of Neurology, Neurosurgery and Psychiatry, 23,* 56–62.

*Hayes, B. A., Muller, R., & Bradley, B. S. (2001). Perinatal depression: A randomized controlled trial of an antenatal education intervention for primaparas. *Birth, 28,* 28–35.

Hobfoll, S., Ritter, C., Lavin, J., Hulszier, M., & Cameron, R. (1995). Depression prevalence and incidence among inner-city pregnant and postpartum women. *Journal of Consulting and Clinical Psychology, 63,* 445–453.

*Holden, J. M., Sagovsky, R., & Cox, J. L. (1989). Counseling in a general practice setting: Controlled study of health visitor intervention in treatment of postnatal depression. *British Medical Journal, 298,* 223–226.

Insel, T. (2004, January 16). *Science to service: Mental health care after the decade of the brain.* Presentation given at Society for Social Work Research Annual Conference, New Orleans, LA.

Institute of Medicine. (1996). *Fetal alcohol syndrome: Diagnosis, epidemiology, prevention, and treatment.* Washington, DC: National Academy Press.

Kaplan, P. S., Bachorowski, J., Smoski, M. J., & Hudenko, W. J. (2002). Infants of depressed mothers, although competent learners, fail to learn in response to their own mothers' infant-directed speech. *Psychological Science, 13,* 268–271.

Klerman, G. L., Weissman, M. M., Rounsaville, B. H., & Chevron, E. S. (1984). *Interpersonal psychotherapy for depression.* New York: Basic Books.

Kumar, R., & Robson, M. (1984). A prospective study of emotional disorders in childbearing women. *British Journal of Psychiatry, 144,* 35–47.

*Lane, B., Roufeil, L. M., Williams, S., & Tweedie, R. (2001). It's just different in the country: Postnatal depression and group therapy in a rural setting. *Social Work in Healthcare, 34,* 333–348.

Lewis-Hall, F. C., Wilson, M. G., Tepner, R. C., & Koke, S. C. (1997). Fluoxetine vs. tricyclic antidepressants in women with major depressive disorder. *Journal of Women's Health, 6,* 337–343.

Lundy, B., Jones, N., Field, T., Nearing, G., Davalos, M., Pietro, P. A., et al. (1999). Prenatal depression effects on neonates. *Infant Behavior and Development, 22,* 119–129.

McNair, D. M., Lorr, M., & Droppleman, L. (1981). *Manual: Profile of mood states.* San Diego, CA: Education and Industrial Testing Service.

Meager, I., & Milgrom, J. (1996). Group treatment for postpartum depression: A pilot study. *Australian and New Zealand Journal of Psychiatry, 30,* 852–860.

Moore, G., Cohn, J., & Campbell, S. (2001). Infant affective responses to mother's still face at 6 months differentially predict externalizing and internalizing behaviors at 18 months. *Developmental Psychology, 37,* 706–714.

Murray, L., & Cooper, P. (1997). The role of infant and maternal factors in postpartum depression, mother-infant interactions, and infant outcome. In L. Murray & P. J. Cooper (Eds.), *Postpartum depression and child development* (pp. 201–220). New York: Guilford.

Nahas, Z., Bohning, D. E., Molloy, M. A., Oustz, J. A., Risch, S. C., & George, M. S. (1999). Safety and feasibility of repetitive trans-cranial magnetic stimulation in the treatment of anxious depression in pregnancy: A case report. *Journal of Clinical Psychiatry, 60,* 50–52.

O'Hara, M. (1994). *Postpartum depression: Causes and consequences.* New York: Springer-Verlag.

O'Hara, M., Neunaber, D., & Zekoski, E. (1984). Prospective study of postpartum depression: Prevalence, course, and predictive factors. *Journal of Abnormal Psychology, 93,* 158–171.

O'Hara, M. H., & Swain, A. M. (1996). Rates and risks of postpartum depression—A meta-analysis. *International Review of Psychiatry, 8,* 37–54.

O'Hara, M. H., Zekoski, E. M., Philipps, L. H., & Wright, E. J. (1990). Controlled prospective study of postpartum mood disorders: Comparison of childbearing and nonchildbearing women. *Journal of Abnormal Psychology, 99,* 3–15.

*O'Hara, M. W., Stuart, S., Gorman, L. L., & Wenzel, A. (2000). Efficacy of interpersonal psychotherapy for postpartum depression. *Archives of General Psychiatry, 57,* 1039–1045.

Oren, D. A., Wisner, K. L., Spinelli, M., Epperson, C. N., Peindl, K. S., Terman, J. S., et al. (2002). An open trial of morning light therapy for treatment of antepartum depression. *American Journal of Psychiatry, 159,* 666–669.

Orr, S. T., James, S. A., & Prince, C. B. (2002). Maternal prenatal depressive symptoms and spontaneous preterm births among African American women in Baltimore, Maryland. *American Journal of Epidemiology, 156,* 797–802.

Parry, B. L., Curran, M. L., Stuenkel, C. A., Yokimozo, M., Tam, L., Powell, K. A., et al. (2000). Can critically timed sleep deprivation be useful in pregnancy and postpartum depression? *Journal of Affective Disorders, 60,* 201–212.

Reid, M., Glazener, C., Murray, G. D., & Taylor, G. S. (2002). A two-centered pragmatic randomized controlled trial of two interventions for postnatal support. *BJOG: An International Journal of Obstetrics & Gynecology, 109,* 1164–1170.

Sanderson, C. A., Cowden, B., Hall, D. M. B., Taylor, E. M., Carpenter, R. G., & Cox, J. L. (2002). Is postnatal depression a risk factor for sudden infant death? *British Journal of General Practice, 52,* 636–640.

Sandman, C., Wadwha, P. D., Dunkel-Schetter, C., Chicz-Demet, A., Belman, J., Porto, et al. (1994). Psychobiological influence of stress and HPA regulation on the human fetus and birth outcomes. *Annals of the New York Academy of Science, 739,* 198–210.

*Spinelli, M. G. (1997). Interpersonal psychotherapy for depressed antepartum women: A pilot study. *American Journal of Psychiatry, 154,* 1028–1030.

*Spinelli, M. G., & Endicott, J. (2003). Controlled clinical trial of interpersonal psychotherapy versus parenting education program for depressed pregnant women. *American Journal of Psychiatry, 160,* 555–562.

Stern, D. (1995). *The motherhood constellation.* New York: Basic Books.

*Suri, R., Burt, V. K., Altshuler, L. L., Zuckerbrow-Miller, J., & Fair, L. (2001). Fluvoxamine for postpartum depression. *American Journal of Psychiatry, 10,* 1739–1740.

Susman, E. J., Trickett, P. K., Iannotti, R. J., Hollenbeck, B. E., & Zahn-Waxler, C. (1985). Child-rearing patterns in depressed, abusive, and normal mothers. *American Journal of Orthopsychiatry, 55,* 237–251.

Wadwha, P. D., Sandman, C., Porto, M., Dunkel-Schetter, C., & Garite, T. (1993). The association between prenatal stress and infant birth weight and gestational age at birth: A prospective investigative investigation. *American Journal of Obstetrics and Gynecology, 169,* 858–865.

Weissman, M. M., & Sanderson, W. C. (2001). Promises and problems in modern psychotherapy: The need for increased training in evidence-based treatments. In M. Hager (Ed.), *Modern psychiatry: Challenges in educating health professionals to meet new needs* (pp. 132–165). New York: Josiah Macy, Jr., Foundation.

Wisner, K. L., Gelenberg, A. J., Leonard, H., Zarin, D., & Frank, E. (1999). Pharmacologic treatment of depression during pregnancy. *Journal of the American Medical Association, 282,* 1264–1269.

Wisner, K. L., Perel, J. M., Peindl, K. S., Hanusa, B. H., Findling, R. L., & Rapport, D. (2001). Prevention of recurrent postpartum depression: A randomized clinical trial. *Journal of Clinical Psychiatry, 62,* 82–86.

Yonkers, K., Ramin, S., Rush, J., Navarrete, C., Carmody, T., March, D., et al. (2001). Onset and persistence of postpartum depression in an inner-city maternal health clinic system. *American Journal of Psychiatry, 158,* 1856–1863.

Zlotnick, C., Johnson, S. L., Miller, I. W., Pearlstein, T., & Howard, M. (2001). Postpartum depression in women receiving public assistance: Pilot study of an interpersonal-therapy-oriented group intervention. *American Journal of Psychiatry, 158,* 638–640.

Zuravin, S. J. (1989). Severity of maternal depression and three types of mother-to-child aggression. *American Journal of Orthopsychiatry, 59,* 377–389.

Authors' Note: This work was supported by the National Institute of Mental Health Grant 5T32MH014623-24 (S. E. Bledsoe) and National Institute of Mental Health Grant K23 MH67595 (N. K. Grote). The authors would like to thank Jennifer Bellamy and Edward Mullen for their assistance with this project.

Address correspondence to: Sarah E. Bledsoe, MSW, Columbia University School of Social Work, c/o Doctoral Program, 1255 Amsterdam Avenue, New York, NY 10027. E-mail: seb2108@columbia.edu

Appendix A
Characteristics of Included Studies

Study	Study design	Participants	Interventions	Outcomes	Site	Timing	Study quality
Appleby et al. (1997)	Randomized, controlled treatment trial	87 women satisfying criteria for depressive illness 6 to 8 weeks postpartum completed the study; 30% attrition rate	Fluoxetine plus one counseling session (Medication), Placebo plus one counseling session (Control), Fluoxetine plus six sessions of CBT therapy (Medication + CBT), six sessions of CBT	Revised Clinical Interview Schedule, EPDS, and the Hamilton Rating Scale for Depression at 1, 4, and 12 weeks posttreatment	South Manchester	Postpartum	High
Chabrol et al. (2002)	Randomized, controlled treatment trial	48 women meeting criteria for major depression at 4 to 6 weeks postpartum; 0% attrition rate	CBT for 5 to 8 weeks provided in the participant's home	EPDS, Hamilton Rating Scale for Depression, and Beck Depression Inventory posttreatment at 10 to 12 weeks postpartum	Toulouse and Narbonne, France	Postpartum	High
Cooper et al. (2003)	Randomized, controlled treatment trial	193 women meeting criteria for postpartum depression in the early postpartum period completed the study; 17% attrition rate	Routine primary care (Control), nondirective counseling (Counseling), CBT, or psychodynamic therapy (Psychodynamic); counseling, CBT, and Psychodynamic interventions delivered weekly from 8 to 18 weeks postpartum in the participant's home	EPDS, Structured Clinical Interview for DSM-III-R immediately posttreatment at 4.5 postpartum and at 9, 18, and 60 months postpartum	Cambridge	Postpartum	High
Grote et al. (2004)	Open trial treatment study using pretest and posttest design	9 women meeting criteria of major and minor depression during pregnancy completed the study; 78% of women were African American or Latina, 22% were Caucasian; all women were financially disadvantaged	Brief Interpersonal Psychotherapy for Depression—8 weekly sessions of acute treatment during pregnancy, monthly maintenance sessions up to 6 months postpartum delivered in clinic or by telephone	Diagnostic Interview Schedule, EPDS, Beck Depression Inventory, Hamilton Rating Scale for Depression, Beck Anxiety Inventory immediately following 8 session intervention and at 2 and 6 months postpartum	Pittsburgh, Pennsylvania	Pregnancy	Medium
Hayes et al. (2001)	Randomized, controlled treatment trial	188 primaparous women meeting criteria for major depression during pregnancy completed the study; 8.7% attrition rate; 94% were Caucasian	Educational intervention (Education) from Week 28 to 36 of pregnancy; Delivered at antenatal clinic or in the participant's home	Profile of Mood States at 8 to 12 and 16 to 24 weeks postpartum	Townsville, Melbourne and Adelaide, Australia	Pregnancy	High
Holden et al. (1989)	Randomized, controlled treatment trial	50 women identified as depressed by screening at 6 weeks postpartum and by psychiatric interview at 13 weeks postpartum completed the study; 9% attrition rate	Counseling for postnatal depression (Counseling) for 8 weeks in the participant's home	Goldberg's Standardized Psychiatric Interview and EPDS posttreatment	Edinburgh and Livingston	Postpartum	Medium
Lane et al. (2001)	Open treatment trial using a pretest and posttest design	18 rural women diagnosed with postpartum depression at 13 weeks postpartum completed the study; 22% attrition rate	Group therapy with cognitive behavioral, educational, and transactional analysis components for postnatal depression (Group) for 10 weeks	EPDS posttreatment	New South Wales, Australia	Postpartum	Medium
O'Hara et al. (2000)	Randomized, controlled treatment trial	99 postpartum women meeting DSM-IV criteria for major depression completed the study; 18% attrition rate	IPT for 12 weekly sessions	Hamilton Rating Scale for Depression, Structured Clinical Interview for DSM-IV Axis 1 Disorders, and Beck Depression Inventory at 4, 8, and 12 weeks in treatment	Polk, Johnson, Linn, and Scott Counties, Iowa	Postpartum	High
Spinelli (1997)	Open treatment trial using a pretest and posttest design	9 pregnant women who met DSM-III-R criteria for major depression; 31% attrition rate; 54% of participants were Latina, 15% were Black, and 31% were Caucasian	16 weeks of IPT for antepartum depression	Structured Clinical Interview for DSM-IV Axis Disorders, Clinical Global Impression, Hamilton Rating Scale for Depression, Beck Depression Inventory, and EPDS posttreatment	New York City	Pregnancy	Medium

Continued →

Study	Study design	Participants	Interventions	Outcomes	Site	Timing	Study quality
Spinelli et al. (2003)	Randomized, controlled, bilingual treatment trial	38 pregnant women who met DSM-IV criteria for major depression; 24% attrition rate; 66% were Latina, 29% were Caucasian, and 5% were African American; 53% had total annual household incomes under $25,000	IPT for antenatal depression, didactic parenting education (Education); 16 weekly sessions	Structured Clinical Interview for *DSM-IV* Axis 1 Disorders, Clinical Global Impression, Hamilton Rating Scale for Depression, Beck Depression Inventory, and EPDS posttreatment		Pregnancy	High
Suri et al. (2001)	Open treatment trial	6 women diagnosed with major depression within 8 weeks postpartum completed the study; 17% attrition rate	Treatment with Fluvoxamine (50mg to start, titrated to 150 mg by Week 2) for 8 weeks (Medication)	Hamilton Rating Scale for Depression and the EPDS weekly	Los Angeles, California	Postpartum	Low

CBT = cognitive behavioral therapy; *DSM-III-R = Diagnostic and Statistical Manual of Mental Disorders*, 3rd edition, revised; *DSM-IV = Diagnostic and Statistical Manual of Mental Disorders*, 4th edition; IPT = interpersonal psychotherapy; EPDS = Edinburgh Postnatal Depression Scale.

Appendix B
Characteristics of Excluded Studies

Study	*Reason for Exclusion*
Bosquet and Egeland (2001)	Study did not focus on depression as a main outcome
Lewis-Hall, Wilson, Tepner, and Koke (1997)	Study was not specifically focused on women during pregnancy and the postpartum; data on this subgroup could not be separated from the study sample
Morrell, Spiby, Stewart, Walters, and Morgan (2000)	Study did not focus on depression as a main outcome
Nahas et al. (1999)	$N = 1$
Parry et al. (2000)	Intervention not comparable to interventions included in the analysis
Reid, Glazener, Murray, and Taylor (2002)	This was a prevention study, not a treatment study
Wisner et al. (2001)	This was a prevention study, not a treatment study
Zlotnick, Johnson, Miller, Pearlstein, and Howard (2001)	This was a prevention study, not a treatment study

Exercise for Review 7

Directions: Answer the following questions based on your opinions. While there are no right or wrong answers, be prepared to explain the bases for your answers in classroom discussions.

1. Did the reviewers convince you that the topic of the review is important? Explain.

2. Is the review an essay organized around topics (as opposed to a string of annotations)? Explain.

3. Is the number of headings and subheadings adequate? Explain.

4. Is the tone of the review neutral and nonemotional? Explain.

5. Overall, does the review provide a comprehensive, logically organized overview of the topic? Explain.

6. Is the conclusion/discussion at the end of the review appropriate in light of the material covered earlier? Explain.

7. Are the suggestions for future research, if any, appropriate in light of the material reviewed? Explain.

8. Are there any obvious weaknesses in this review? Explain.

9. Does this review have any special strengths? Explain.

10. What is your overall evaluation of this review on a scale from Excellent (10) to Very Poor (0)? Explain.

Notes:

Model Review 8

Cognitive Bibliotherapy for Depression: A Meta-Analysis

ROBERT J. GREGORY
Wheaton College

SALLY SCHWER CANNING
Wheaton College

TRACY W. LEE
Wheaton College

JOAN C. WISE
Wheaton College

ABSTRACT. Do you want to use bibliotherapy with clients but wonder about the size and mechanism of effectiveness? The authors report a meta-analysis of 29 outcome studies of cognitive forms of bibliotherapy for depression. Seventeen studies with stronger research designs (pretest-posttest waiting list control group) yielded a respectable effect size of 0.77, considered the best estimate of effect size from this study. This result compares favorably with outcomes from individual psychotherapy. In light of the substantial positive effects associated with bibliotherapy for depression, the authors discuss clinically relevant questions related to the use of cognitive bibliotherapy. These include why practitioners might consider the use of this technique, which individuals can benefit from this approach, and how professionals can structure care.

From *Professional Psychology: Research and Practice, 35*, 275–280. Copyright © 2004 by the American Psychological Association. Reprinted with permission.

Many practitioners use bibliotherapy as an adjunct to individual or group therapy. A form of self-administered treatment in which structured materials provide a means of self-improvement or help to alleviate distress, bibliotherapy is reportedly used by psychologists with a variety of objectives in mind, most frequently to increase awareness, reinforce specific in-session concepts or strategies, and enhance lifestyle changes (Campbell & Smith, 2003). Advocates of this approach point to several advantages: ease of use, inexpensive nature, and potential to provide services to individuals who would otherwise be assigned to waiting lists, or who would have little or no access to traditional care, or who would have resources for only a restricted course of treatment (Williams, 2001).

The treatment of depression is one area in which practitioners reportedly use bibliotherapy with considerable frequency (Starker, 1988a, 1988b). Most often, the materials used are cognitive, behavioral, or cognitive-behavioral in nature; in other words, forms of bibliotherapy in which the reading materials are based on the principles of cognitive or behavior therapy (e.g., Burns, 1980; Lewinsohn, Munoz, Youngren, & Zeiss, 1986). These materials incorporate the foundational elements of a cognitive conceptualization of depression

and provide exercises designed to help the reader overcome negative feelings associated with depression (e.g., sadness, loneliness, guilt, inferiority). For example, the 10-part program outlined by Burns (1993) includes the following elements: self-assessment for depression, anxiety, and relationship satisfaction; didactic instruction on the core principle that you "feel the way you think" and, furthermore, that bad feelings often arise from distorted thinking; exercises on identifying and disputing distorted thinking; instruction and practice on additional techniques such as cost-benefit analysis and examining the evidence; practice with more advanced cognitive techniques including the acceptance paradox; practice in identifying and modifying self-defeating beliefs; cost-benefit analysis of beliefs about self-esteem; identification and correction of perfectionism; analysis of procrastination and prescriptive help with it; and ongoing practice with all of the above ingredients.

In the last 30 years, a few dozen empirical studies have been published testing the value of cognitive bibliotherapy on depression alone. So just how effective is cognitive bibliotherapy as a treatment for depression? Researchers have begun to use meta-analysis to answer this question. In meta-analysis, diverse studies are combined quantitatively by means of a common metric known as the effect size, which is the difference in means at posttest between experimental and control groups, divided by the pooled standard deviation. By convention, effect sizes of around 0.20 are considered "small," those of about 0.50 in magnitude are viewed as "moderate," and effect sizes in the vicinity of 0.80 or higher are deemed "large" (Durlak, 1995). Meta-analysis also allows for examining the impact of moderator variables (e.g., length of bibliotherapy treatment) on the obtained effect size.

Meta-analytic reviews of bibliotherapy began to appear in 1990, with at least six published to date (Cuijpers, 1997, 1998; Gould & Clum, 1993; Marrs, 1995; Scogin, Bynum, Stephens, & Calhoon, 1990; Scogin & McElreath, 1994). For the most part, these reviews have been broad based. Some have examined bibliotherapy across a wide variety of problem areas such as anxiety, weight loss, and assertion (e.g., Marrs, 1995);

70 others have included bibliotherapy alongside diverse forms of psychosocial intervention such as group therapy for depression (e.g., Scogin & McElreath, 1994).

Two recent reviews have focused on bibliotherapy tailored to persons who experience depression. The
75 results yielded by these meta-analyses were quite positive. Specifically, Cuijpers (1997) reported a mean effect size of 0.82 for six diverse studies that compared cognitive bibliotherapy clients with wait list control clients. In a separate analysis of 10 studies using a par-
80 ticular manualized bibliotherapy intervention, Cuijpers (1998) found a mean effect size of 0.65 for depressed clients in comparison with wait list controls.

As the amount of literature in this area has continued to grow, the methodological quality of individual
85 studies has improved and the technical methods of meta-analysis itself have been refined. These developments are important because the confidence that consumers can have in the results of meta-analysis is linked to the number and quality of studies reviewed.
90 Additionally, the increase in the number of studies provides the opportunity to ask more detailed questions about cognitive bibliotherapy by investigating moderator variables influencing effect sizes.

The purpose of the current review, therefore, is to
95 access a wider base of studies than previous reviews, including many recent reports, in order to obtain a more robust estimate of the overall effect size for the cognitive bibliotherapy of depression. Another purpose is to conduct several preliminary investigations of the
100 impact of certain moderator variables on the outcome of cognitive bibliotherapy for depression. The following questions guided our analysis:

Is cognitive bibliotherapy for depression effective in general? It was hypothesized that it would be mod-
105 erately effective, but not as effective as individual psychotherapy for depression. As our comparison benchmark, we used the mean effect size of 0.83 (for therapy vs. wait list control subjects) reported by Gloaguen, Cottraux, Cucherat, and Blackburn (1998) in their
110 comprehensive review of controlled outcome research on individual cognitive therapy for depression.

Does cognitive bibliotherapy work better when supplemented by group psychoeducation or when used as a self-administered treatment? It was hypothesized
115 that bibliotherapy effectiveness would be stronger in a group format because of the facilitative and motivating support provided by this setting. Specifically, clients working in a group format have access to the psychologist-facilitator (and to other group members as
120 well) as a means of profiting from the principles of cognitive therapy, whereas clients working in a self-administered format must interpret, understand, and apply the principles of cognitive therapy largely on their own.
125 Does the length of treatment influence the effectiveness of bibliotherapy? We hypothesized a positive correlation, that is, we predicted that program length would be positively correlated with degree of effectiveness. This hypothesis was based on the concept of
130 dose-response relationship in which longer treatment duration is associated with greater improvement (e.g., Seligman, 1995).

Is cognitive bibliotherapy more effective for one age group than another? On the basis of previous find-
135 ings (e.g., Dobson, 1989), we hypothesized that younger participants would show greater benefit from bibliotherapy than older participants.

The Cognitive Bibliotherapy Meta-Analysis Project
Study Details

Experts on meta-analysis have published elaborate and sophisticated methods for pursuing this kind of
140 research (e.g., Durlak, 1995; Hedges & Olkin, 1985). As a consequence, a full description of the procedures used in this study would constitute a lengthy and distracting detour. We have opted instead to describe the essential methods as succinctly as possible, using ta-
145 bles to summarize key features. A more detailed presentation of specific methodologies is available from Robert J. Gregory.

Using standard procedures for journal literature search, we looked for studies of cognitive bibliotherapy
150 published from 1967 through 1999. Cognitive bibliotherapy was defined as the use of written or computerized materials that teach principles of cognitive-behavioral therapy for the purpose of reducing a client's level of depression. Brief contacts or group ses-
155 sions could be used to introduce these materials, but in order to qualify as bibliotherapy, clients also had to read and apply the materials on their own time. Studies were included only if they met certain reasonable inclusion criteria (Table 1). Although we did not select
160 studies based on the manner in which they screened for other disorders, in fact, virtually all cognitive bibliotherapy studies reviewed here did screen prospective clients for psychotic features, suicidal tendencies, drug problems, personality disorders, and serious health
165 problems (e.g., anorexia, cancer, and HIV infection). In addition, virtually all of the studies used rigorous diagnostic procedures to ensure that prospective clients were experiencing a significant depressive disorder, (e.g., a clinical diagnosis of major depressive disorder
170 or meeting research diagnostic criteria for a depressive disorder).

In the end, we found 27 studies, including 21 refereed journal articles, 1 book chapter, and 5 doctoral dissertations. Two of the studies included two separate
175 bibliotherapy treatment groups (Scogin, Jamison, & Gochneaur, 1989; Thompson, Gallagher, Nies, & Epstein, 1983). We considered each of these to be separate studies. Thus, we analyzed a grand total of 29 studies. For each study, we coded sample sizes, means
180 and standard deviations for outcome variables, and

Table 1
Inclusion Criteria for Cognitive Bibliotherapy Studies.

- Intervention corresponded to the definition given in the text
- Clients were adolescent or adult outpatients
- Sample size was at least 5 participants
- Intervention target included depression
- Results included posttest data from treatment and wait list control clients, or
- Pretest and posttest data were available from a single treatment group
- Bibliotherapy was a structured program described in a workbook
- Results were reported in English
- Results were amenable to the methods of meta-analysis

Table 2
Variables and Data Coded for Each Study.

- Sample sizes of treatment and wait list control groups
- Means and standard deviations for outcome variables(s) at posttest (two groups), or
- Means and standard deviations for outcome variables(s) at pretest and posttest (one group)
- Cognitive bibliotherapy delivery method (two options):
  Self-administered approach (clients read materials on their own)
  Group-administered approach (clients meet in groups, read materials on own)
- Length of treatment program in weeks
- Age group (three options):
  Adolescent (ages 13–19 years)
  Adult (ages 20–59 years)
  Elderly (age 60 years and above)

Table 3
Descriptive Summary of Effect Size Results.

Defining parameter	No. of studies	Effect size	95% CI
All studies	29	0.99	0.87–1.10
Design			
Between-groups	7	0.77	0.61–0.94
Within-subjects	12	1.20	1.02–1.38
Delivery method			
Group-administered	14	0.99	0.83–1.15
Self-administered	15	0.98	0.83–1.14
Age group			
Adolescent (ages 13–19 years)	5	1.32	0.90–1.73
Adult (ages 20–59 years)	15	1.18	1.03–1.33
Elderly (age 60 years and above)	9	0.57	0.37–0.77

Note. CI = confidence interval

several other variables relevant to the hypotheses of this study (Table 2). Each study was coded for relevant variables by two of five raters (two PhD clinicians and three advanced graduate students), with initial agreement of 94%. Discrepancies were resolved by means of conference with Robert J. Gregory.

Using the DSTAT software program (Version 1.11), we computed unbiased effect sizes (d, per Hedges & Olkin, 1985) for all dependent variables included in this meta-analysis (Johnson, 1995). For 17 of the 29 studies, the effect sizes were computed on posttest scores using means and standard deviations of depression measures for treatment versus control participants (between-groups design). In all but one case, the control group consisted of randomly assigned wait list control participants. One study (Organista, Munoz,

& Gonzalez, 1994) used a nonequivalent control group of early dropouts for comparison. For the remaining 12 of the 29 studies, the effect sizes were based on the pretest and posttest means and standard deviations for a single treatment group (within-subjects design). For studies using more than one depression measure, the effect size consisted of the average of the effect sizes across the multiple outcome measures.

Results

A descriptive summary of the findings is reported in Table 3. The overall weighted effect size for the 29 studies was 0.99 (with a 95% confidence interval of 0.87 to 1.10). Of course, this large effect size was highly significant ($p < .00001$). However, this result included a mixture of studies with traditional designs (e.g., treatment group vs. wait list control group) as well as studies with less robust designs (e.g., single-group pretest vs. posttest), so the resulting effect size was considered potentially inflated. In fact, the 17 studies with traditional designs (between groups) yielded a smaller weighted effect size of 0.77, whereas the 12 studies with less robust designs (within subjects) yielded a larger effect size of 1.20, a difference that was highly significant (Q_B = 12.88, p <.0005). The effect size of 0.77 (with a 95% confidence interval of 0.61 to 0.94) for the 17 between-groups studies is considered the best estimate of bibliotherapy effect size from this meta-analysis and is a healthy effect size that compares favorably with data from studies of individual psychotherapy. For example, Lipsey and Wilson (1993) reported effect sizes for cognitive or cognitive and behavioral therapies ranging from 0.15 to 0.99. Robinson, Berman, and Neimeyer (1990) reported an average effect size of 0.84 for controlled studies of individual therapy for depression. Gloaguen et al. (1998) found an average effect size of 0.83 for controlled studies of cognitive therapy for depression. We used this latter value as our benchmark and compared the results of our study against it. Our average effect size of 0.77 (with a 95% confidence interval of 0.61 to 0.94) was not significantly different from this comparison value.

We also examined whether a group-administered format (14 studies) produced a greater effect size than a self-administered format (15 studies) for cognitive bibliotherapy. The weighted effect sizes for these two approaches were essentially identical (0.989 and 0.983, respectively). Of course, this difference was not significant (Q_B =.003, p =.96). An analysis of covariance controlling for type of design (within vs. between) confirmed the same result.

We also analyzed whether length of treatment influenced the effectiveness of bibliotherapy by correlating these two variables. The average treatment length was 7.4 weeks, with a standard deviation of 3.1 weeks. The simple correlation between length of treatment and effect size (weighted by sample size) was a trivial .057, which was not significant (p =.38, one-tailed test). The most likely explanation for this lack of significance was the restriction of range on length of therapy. Most of the studies lasted between 6 and 10 weeks—and only three studies were longer than this. In other words, there were too few studies with longer durations to reveal whether length of therapy was related to effect size. Dobson (1989) also reported a similar finding in his meta-analysis of cognitive therapy for depression.

Finally, we also examined whether the age of the participants impacted the effect size. We used a simple categorical test available with the DSTAT software. The resulting analysis indicated huge and significant differences in averaged weighted effect sizes for the three age groups (Q_B = 25.57, p <.0001). In particular, the five studies with teenagers yielded an average effect size of 1.32 (95% confidence interval of 0.90 to 1.73), the 15 studies with adults yielded an average effect size of 1.18 (95% confidence interval of 1.03 to 1.33), and the 9 studies with older individuals yielded an average effect size of only 0.57 (95% confidence interval of 0.37 to 0.77). On the basis of the 95% confidence intervals for each effect size, it is evident that the effect size for the elderly sample was significantly different from the effect sizes for both the adult sample and the teenage sample, whereas the latter two samples did not differ from one another. These results, while intriguing, are merely suggestive of real group differences, given the relatively small number of studies in some of the groups. In addition, further analyses uncovered important preexisting differences in the three age groups. In particular, we found that older adults reported substantially lower levels of depression at pretest than younger adults and adolescents. For example, in studies using the Beck Depression Inventory as a pretest, the average pretest score for older adults was 13.34 (6 studies), compared with pretest means of 22.85 for adults (14 studies) and 23.09 for adolescents (3 studies). Put simply, the older adults had less room for improvement because they were substantially less depressed at the beginning of the bibliotherapy studies. Most likely, if the three age groups had started at the same levels of depression, the differences in effect sizes would have been smaller or nonexistent.

Implications for Clinical Practice

Our finding that studies of cognitive bibliotherapy yield outcomes that compare favorably with studies of psychotherapy lends credibility to bibliotherapy as an option in the treatment of depression. Although additional carefully designed research is needed and our findings cannot be considered conclusive, practitioners appear to be justified in considering the use of cognitive bibliotherapy for depression. In so doing, a number of important questions for practitioners immediately arise, several of which we identify and discuss here. Although these questions cannot be fully and finally answered given the current state of the literature, practitioners must do their best to consider the knowledge at hand and make decisions in light of current findings.

Why Consider Cognitive Bibliotherapy?

Linking cognitive bibliotherapy with positive outcomes is essential to establishing the value of this modality as a clinical intervention for depression. Still, proponents have identified a number of additional advantages of this treatment format. Bibliotherapy has the potential to be highly accessible to a wide variety of populations (Williams, 2001). It can provide an immediate, inexpensive, noninvasive route to treatment without the threat of stigmatization that may accompany the seeking of mental health treatment (Cuijpers, 1997). Underserved groups, individuals on waiting lists, or people who would otherwise rule out traditional therapy may be potentially reached through this

325 modality, making it a model for the ideal of "giving psychology away" (Miller, 1969, p. 1063). Bibliotherapy has been characterized as empowering for recipients, potentially enhancing the sense of both responsibility in treatment and control over their condition 330 (Floyd, 2003; Mains & Scogin, 2003; Scogin, 2003). Practitioners using bibliotherapy to augment other treatments may appreciate the reinforcement and additional experiences outside the treatment room that can be provided through this format (Scogin, 2003). The 335 objective of this approach is often to accelerate the change process, shortening length of treatment.

Who May Benefit from Cognitive Bibliotherapy for Depression?

No established guidelines currently exist regarding the use of bibliotherapy for depression or any other problem type. However, a review of the literature re-340 veals some findings and patterns that may be instructive to practitioners. First, most studies and anecdotal reports apply cognitive bibliotherapy to individuals with mild to moderate depression (Cuijpers, 1997). Considering the very serious risks associated with se-345 vere depression including suicide, restricting the use of a treatment with minimal professional involvement to those with lower levels of depression makes sense. In addition, bibliotherapy requires sustained attention and motivation, yet these are the very skills that may be 350 significantly impaired by a serious depression. Consequently, cognitive bibliotherapy may be more appropriate with less severely depressed individuals (Campbell & Smith, 2003; Floyd, 2003).

Second, research studies supporting the effective-355 ness of cognitive bibliotherapy have typically been carried out using participants who are depressed, but who are free of other clinically significant problems (Mains & Scogin, 2003). Actual clinical practice, however, includes many individuals with comorbid condi-360 tions. It is unclear whether bibliotherapy would be useful in the treatment of adults with, say, depression and anxiety, or adolescents with depression and attention-deficit/hyperactivity disorder. Using cognitive bibliotherapy under these conditions does not appear well 365 justified by the current state of our knowledge.

Third is the general admonition that bibliotherapy should be offered when there is a good enough fit among a variety of client characteristics and the modality. Little empirical research is available to guide us 370 confidently in this respect. Our examination of the relationship of age of recipient to outcomes can only be taken as suggestive, because of the relatively few studies examined. These preliminary results are consistent, however, with the notion that bibliotherapy can be ef-375 fectively used with adolescents, adults, and older adults alike. Additional research is needed to further establish and elaborate the relationship of age to outcomes.

Practitioners would do well to consider a number of additional client characteristics in their selection of this 380 treatment. Some of these characteristics include the cultural relevance and acceptability of bibliotherapy content and format to the potential recipient (Campbell & Smith, 2003); the client's pretreatment expectations of therapy, especially their expectations for the rela-385 tionship with the therapist and their potential for feeling discounted or rejected by receiving a recommendation for bibliotherapy (Floyd, 2003); a client's reading level (Campbell & Smith, 2003) or disabilities (Silverberg, 2003); as well as history with, and perceptions of, 390 the kinds of school-like tasks that characterize this type of treatment (Floyd, 2003).

Campbell and Smith (2003) made an especially interesting, although presently uninvestigated, recommendation. They suggested assessing potential biblio-395 therapy clients' readiness for change as a means of assessing relevance of the technique, but also in order to tailor the type of content selected for clients referred to bibliotherapy (see their article for an expanded discussion). Future research could investigate the useful-400 ness of this approach.

How Should Care Be Structured?

Ostensibly, anyone can walk into a bookstore, leave with a copy of *Feeling Good* (Burns, 1980), go home, undergo the treatment, and get better without the knowledge or involvement of a professional. As might 405 be expected, however, published accounts and discussions of bibliotherapy typically reflect a "reduced" or "minimal therapist contact" model or one that characterizes bibliotherapy as "adjunctive" or "integrated" with other professional services. One particularly 410 promising formulation is the "stepped-care" model (Mains & Scogin, 2003), in which bibliotherapy can be offered as the first, least invasive line of care for individuals with mild to moderate depression, but in which other treatments are offered should the former ap-415 proach prove ineffective or insufficient.

In an adjunctive or integrative approach, then, what are the roles for a mental health practitioner in relation to bibliotherapy? Again, there is an absence of well-designed investigations to guide us, so we offer the 420 following observations and suggestions from the current literature. One valuable role for the psychologist is to diagnose and screen clients for their appropriateness for this kind of treatment, taking into account the variables identified above (Campbell & Smith, 2003; Cui-425 jpers, 1997). Recommended strategies for assessing depression in various populations may be found elsewhere, but diagnostic interviews as well as validated self-report measures such as the Beck Depression Inventory (Beck, Steer, & Brown, 1996) may be useful as 430 part of a comprehensive assessment in determining the individual's level of depression. Patients who appear severely depressed or who present with other problems or contraindications to this treatment may be referred instead for other services, such as individual cognitive 435 therapy or psychopharmacological evaluation.

Next, clinicians can play an important role in negotiating and orienting a person to bibliotherapy. As with any skillful negotiation regarding treatment options, advantages and disadvantages of this modality must be clearly described and discussed with patients (Mains & Scogin, 2003), and a clear enough picture of the content and process of treatment must be given to enable participants to form realistic and positive expectations of the treatment. Care must be taken to avoid conveying the impression that patients are being shunted off into an inferior form of treatment or are somehow not being taken seriously or cared for by the professional (Campbell & Smith, 2003).

A third valuable service provided by the professional is their expertise in selecting materials that are well researched and have support for their effectiveness (Mains & Scogin, 2003), such as the two often-referenced materials *Feeling Good* (Burns, 1980) and *Control Your Depression* (Lewinsohn et al., 1986). Additional considerations in the choice of materials include cultural relevance, availability, and do-ability with respect to the scope and nature of assignments, and the goodness of fit of the client with the type of media used (book, audio, computer, etc. [Silverberg, 2003]). Our investigation of two other format considerations (group-administered vs. self-administered and length of treatment) did not yield significant differences, therefore we offer no firm recommendations with respect to these variables as means of maximizing treatment outcomes. Practitioners will need to follow the research in this area and take other factors into account such as patient volume, third-party constraints and opportunities, as well as patient preferences to make these format decisions.

Another area for decision making, but one for which there is conflicting direction, is the degree to which the professional should be in contact with bibliotherapy participants during the course of treatment. Although claims have been made that treatments involving therapists are superior to those that are self-administered (Mains & Scogin, 2003), other research, including two previous meta-analyses (Marrs, 1995; Scogin, Jamison, & Davis, 1990), contradicts that assertion. Additional studies and meta-analyses are needed to further dissect the impact of therapist contact on bibliotherapy outcomes. In the meantime, a variety of roles within the course of treatment have been outlined for practitioners. Williams (2001), for example, advocated for the use of review sessions or brief, periodic meetings with the client, during which concepts and skills can be clarified, application to the particular client can be facilitated, and support and accountability can be provided. Also within the review sessions, Williams suggested addressing common obstacles to the success of self-administered treatments, such as the client having problems finding time to do the intervention, understanding what is expected, or perceiving positive results.

The practitioner who remains in some sort of contact with his or her bibliotherapy client, whether through periodic visits or phone contacts, is in a position to monitor progress or possible deterioration. Regardless of the modality of treatment, psychologists maintain responsibility for the well-being of their clients and should make provisions for tracking the impact of treatment on the client as well as for instances in which bibliotherapy participants worsen, exhibit untoward side effects, or display other symptoms requiring supplementary treatment. Finally, bibliotherapy that has proceeded with some therapist involvement provides the opportunity for follow-up and prophylaxis that may help promote longer-term freedom from depression.

References

References marked with an asterisk indicate studies included in the meta-analysis.

*Ackerson, J., Scogin, F., McKendree-Smith, N., & Lyman, R. D. (1998). Cognitive bibliotherapy for mild and moderate adolescent depressive symptomatology. *Journal of Consulting and Clinical Psychology*, 66, 685–690.

*Antonuccio, D., Akins, W., Chatham, P., Monagin, J., Tearnan, B., & Ziegler, B. (1984). An exploratory study: The psychoeducational group treatment of drug-refractory unipolar depression. *Journal of Behavioral Therapy and Experimental Psychiatry*, 15, 309–313.

Beck, A. T., Steer, R. A., & Brown, G. K. (1996). *Manual for the Beck Depression Inventory—II*. San Antonio, TX: Psychological Corporation.

*Bowman, D., Scogin, F., & Lyrene, B. (1995). The efficacy of self-examination therapy and cognitive bibliotherapy in the treatment of mild to moderate depression. *Psychotherapy Research*, 5, 131–140.

*Breckenridge, J., Zeiss, A., & Thompson, L. (1987). The Life Satisfaction Course: An intervention for the elderly. In R. F. Munoz (Ed.), *Depression prevention: Research directions* (pp. 185–196). Washington, DC: Hemisphere Publications.

*Brown, R. A., & Lewinsohn, P. M. (1984). A psychoeducational approach to the treatment of depression: Comparison of group, individual, and minimal contact procedures. *Journal of Consulting and Clinical Psychology*, 52, 774–783.

Burns, D. D. (1980). *Feeling good*. New York: Avon.

Burns, D. D. (1993). *Ten days to self-esteem*. New York: Morrow.

Campbell, L. F., & Smith, T. P. (2003). Integrating self-help books into psychotherapy. *Journal of Clinical Psychology/In Session*, 59(2), 177–186.

*Clarke, G. N. (1985). *A psychoeducational approach to the treatment of depressed adolescents*. Unpublished doctoral dissertation, University of Oregon.

Cuijpers, P. (1997). Bibliotherapy in unipolar depression: A meta-analysis. *Journal of Behavior Therapy and Experimental Psychiatry*, 28, 139–147.

Cuijpers, P. (1998). A psychoeducational approach to the treatment of depression: A meta-analysis of Lewinsohn's "Coping with Depression" course. *Behavior Therapy*, 29, 521–533.

Dobson, K. S. (1989). A meta-analysis of the efficacy of cognitive therapy for depression. *Journal of Consulting and Clinical Psychology*, 57, 414–419.

Durlak, J. A. (1993). Understanding meta-analysis. In L. Grimm & P. Yarnold (Eds.), *Reading and understanding multivariate statistics* (pp. 319–352). Washington, DC: American Psychological Association.

*Floyd, M. R. (1998). *Cognitive therapy for depression: A comparison of individual psychotherapy and bibliotherapy for depressed older adults*. Unpublished doctoral dissertation, University of Alabama.

Floyd, M. R. (2003). Bibliotherapy as an adjunct to psychotherapy for depression in older adults. *Journal of Clinical Psychology/In Session*, 59(2), 187–195.

Gloaguen, V., Cottraux, J., Cucherat, M., & Blackburn, I. (1998). A meta-analysis of the effects of cognitive therapy in depressed patients. *Journal of Affective Disorders*, 49, 59–72.

Gould, R. A., & Clum, G. A. (1993). A meta-analysis of self-help treatment approaches. *Clinical Psychology Review*, 13, 169–186.

*Grant, G., Salcedo, V., Hynan, L., Frisch, M., & Puster, K. (1995). Effectiveness of quality of life therapy for depression. *Psychological Reports*, 76, 1203–1208.

Hedges, L. V., & Olkin, I. (1985). *Statistical methods for meta-analysis*. New York: Academic Press.

*Hoberman, H. M., Lewinsohn, P., & Tilson, M. (1988). Group treatment of depression: Individual predictors of outcome. *Journal of Consulting and Clinical Psychology*, 56, 393–398.

*Jamison, C., & Scogin, F. (1995). The outcome of cognitive bibliotherapy with depressed adults. *Journal of Consulting and Clinical Psychology, 63,* 644–650.

Johnson, B. T. (1995). DSTAT 1.11: Software for the meta-analytic review of research literatures [Computer software]. Hillsdale, NJ: Erlbaum.

*Landreville, P. (1997). Effects of cognitive bibliotherapy for depressed older adults with a disability. *Clinical Gerontologist, 17*(4), 35–55.

*Langford, R. A. (1987). *Social skills versus self-monitoring as psychoeducational treatment approaches for conduct disordered-depressed adolescents.* Unpublished doctoral dissertation, University of Oregon.

*Lewinsohn, P. M., Clarke, G., Hops, H., Andrews, J. (1990). Cognitive-behavioral treatment for depressed adolescents. *Behavior Therapy, 21,* 385–401.

Lewinsohn, P. M., Munoz, R., Youngren, M., & Zeiss, A. (1986). *Control your depression.* Englewood Cliffs, NJ: Prentice-Hall.

Lipsey, M. W., & Wilson, D. B. (1993). The efficacy of psychological, educational, and behavioral treatment: Confirmation from meta-analysis. *American Psychologist, 48,* 1181–1209.

*Mahalik, J. R., & Kivlighan, D. (1988). Self-help treatment for depression: Who succeeds? *Journal of Counseling Psychology, 35,* 237–242.

Mains, J. A., & Scogin, F. R. (2003). The effectiveness of self-administered treatments: A practice-friendly review of the research. *Journal of Clinical Psychology/In Session, 59,* 237–246.

Marrs, R. W. (1995). A meta-analysis of bibliotherapy studies. *American Journal of Community Psychology, 23,* 843–870.

Miller, G. A. (1969). Psychology as a means of promoting human welfare. *American Psychologist, 24,* 1063–1075.

*Organista, K., Munoz, R., & Gonzalez, G. (1994). Cognitive-behavioral therapy for depression in low-income and minority medical outpatients: Description of a program and exploratory analyses. *Cognitive Therapy and Research, 18,* 241–259.

*Pitkow, A. B. (1980). *Effects of rational emotive therapy, rational emotive bibliotherapy, and psychodynamically oriented psychotherapy on adjustment in adult clinical outpatients.* Unpublished doctoral dissertation, Hofstra University.

*Richards, P. S., Owen, L., & Stein, S. (1993). A religiously oriented group counseling intervention for self-defeating perfectionism: A pilot study. *Counseling and Values, 37,* 96–104.

Robinson, L. A., Berman, J. S., & Neimeyer, R. A. (1990). Psychotherapy for the treatment of depression: A comprehensive review of controlled outcome research. *Psychological Bulletin, 108,* 30–49.

*Rokke, P., Tomhave, J., & Jocic, Z. (1999). The role of client choice and target selection in self-management therapy for depression in older adults. *Psychology and Aging, 14,* 155–169.

*Schmidt, M. M., & Miller, W. (1983). Amount of therapist contact and outcome in a multidimensional depression treatment program. *Acta Psychiatrica Scandinavica, 67,* 319–332.

Scogin, F. R. (2003). Introduction: Integrating self-help into psychotherapy. *Journal of Clinical Psychology/In Session, 59,* 175–176.

Scogin, F. R., Bynum, J., Stephens, G., & Calhoon, S. (1990). Efficacy of self-administered treatment programs: Meta-analytic review. *Professional Psychology, 21,* 42–47.

*Scogin, F. R., Hamblin, D., & Beutler, L. (1987). Bibliotherapy for depressed older adults: A self-help alternative. *The Gerontologist, 27,* 383–387.

*Scogin, F. R., Jamison, C., & Davis, N. (1990). Two-year follow-up of bibliotherapy for depression in older adults. *Journal of Consulting and Clinical Psychology, 58,* 665–667.

*Scogin, F. R., Jamison, C., & Gochneaur, K. (1989). Comparative efficacy of cognitive and behavioral bibliotherapy for mildly and moderately depressed older adults. *Journal of Consulting and Clinical Psychology, 57,* 403–407.

Scogin, F. R., & McElreath, L. (1994). Efficacy of psychosocial treatments for geriatric depression: A quantitative review. *Journal of Consulting and Clinical Psychology, 62,* 69–74.

Seligman, M. (1995). The effectiveness of psychotherapy: The Consumer Reports study. *American Psychologist, 50,* 965–974.

*Selmi, P. M., Klein, M. H., Greist, J. H., Sorrell, S. P., & Erdman, H. P. (1990). Computer-administered cognitive-behavioral therapy for depression. *American Journal of Psychiatry, 147,* 51–56.

Silverberg, L. I. (2003). Bibliotherapy: The therapeutic use of didactic and literary texts in treatment, diagnosis, prevention, and training. *Journal of the American Osteopathic Association, 103*(3), 131–135.

Starker, S. (1988a). Do-it-yourself therapy: The prescription of self-help books by psychologists. *Psychotherapy, 25,* 142–146.

Starker, S. (1988b). Psychologists and self-help books: Attitudes and prescriptive practices of clinicians. *American Journal of Psychotherapy, 42,* 448–455.

*Steinmetz, J., Lewinsohn, P., & Antonuccio, D. (1983). Prediction of individual outcome in a group intervention for depression. *Journal of Consulting and Clinical Psychology, 51,* 331–337.

*Teri, L., & Lewinsohn, P. (1986). Individual and group treatment of unipolar depression: Comparison of treatment outcome and identification of predictors of successful treatment outcome. *Behavior Therapy, 17,* 215–228.

*Thompson, L. W., Gallagher, D., Nies, G., & Epstein, D. (1983). Evaluation of the effectiveness of professionals and nonprofessionals as instructors of "Coping with Depression" classes for elders. *The Gerontologist, 23,* 390–396.

Williams, C. (2001). Use of written cognitive-behavioral therapy self-help materials to treat depression. *Advances in Psychiatric Treatment, 7,* 233–240.

*Wollersheim, J. P., & Wilson, G. L. (1991). Group treatment of unipolar depression: A comparison of coping, supportive, bibliotherapy, and delayed treatment groups. *Professional Psychology: Research and Practice, 22,* 496–502.

About the authors: *Robert J. Gregory* received his PhD in adult clinical psychology from the University of Minnesota. He is professor and director of the PsyD program at Wheaton College. *Sally Schwer Canning* received her PhD in professional–scientific psychology from the University of Pennsylvania. She is associate professor of psychology at Wheaton College. *Tracy W. Lee* serves as the program administrator for the PsyD program at Wheaton College, where she also received her PhD. *Joan C. Wise* received her PhD from Wheaton College. She is employed in a group practice in Palos Heights, Illinois.

Address correspondence to: Robert J. Gregory, Department of Psychology, Wheaton College Wheaton, IL 60187 E-mail: robert.j.gregory@wheaton.edu

Exercise for Review 8

Directions: Answer the following questions based on your opinions. While there are no right or wrong answers, be prepared to explain the bases for your answers in classroom discussions.

1. Did the reviewers convince you that the topic of the review is important? Explain.

2. Is the review an essay organized around topics (as opposed to a string of annotations)? Explain.

3. Is the number of headings and subheadings adequate? Explain.

4. Is the tone of the review neutral and nonemotional? Explain.

5. Overall, does the review provide a comprehensive, logically organized overview of the topic? Explain.

6. Is the conclusion/discussion at the end of the review appropriate in light of the material covered earlier? Explain.

7. Are the suggestions for future research, if any, appropriate in light of the material reviewed? Explain.

8. Are there any obvious weaknesses in this review? Explain.

9. Does this review have any special strengths? Explain.

10. What is your overall evaluation of this review on a scale from Excellent (10) to Very Poor (0)? Explain.

Model Review 9

Project D.A.R.E. Outcome Effectiveness Revisited

STEVEN L. WEST
Virginia Commonwealth University

KERI K. O'NEAL
University of North Carolina, Chapel Hill

OBJECTIVES. We provide an updated meta-analysis on the effectiveness of Project D.A.R.E. in preventing alcohol, tobacco, and illicit drug use among school-aged youths.

METHODS. We used meta-analytic techniques to create an overall effect size for D.A.R.E. outcome evaluations reported in scientific journals.

RESULTS. The overall weighted effect size for the included D.A.R.E. studies was extremely small (correlation coefficient = 0.011; Cohen's d = 0.023; 95% confidence interval = –0.04, 0.08) and nonsignificant (z = 0.73, NS).

CONCLUSIONS. Our study supports previous findings indicating that D.A.R.E. is ineffective.

From *American Journal of Public Health*, *94*, 1027–1029. Copyright © 2004 by American Journal of Public Health. Reprinted with permission.

In the United States, Project D.A.R.E. (Drug Abuse Resistance Education) is one of the most widely used substance abuse prevention programs targeted at school-aged youths. In recent years, D.A.R.E. has been the country's largest single school-based prevention program in terms of federal expenditures, with an average of three-quarters of a billion dollars spent on its provision annually.[1] Although its effectiveness in preventing substance use has been called into question, its application in our nation's schools remains very extensive.[2–6]

Given the recent increases in alcohol and other drug use among high school and college students,[7] the continued use of D.A.R.E. and similar programs seems likely. In a meta-analysis examining the effectiveness of D.A.R.E., Ennett et al.[3] noted negligible yet positive effect sizes (ranging from 0.00 to 0.11) when outcomes occurring immediately after program completion were considered. However, this analysis involved 2 major limitations. First, Ennett et al. included research from nonpeer-reviewed sources, including annual reports produced for agencies associated with the provision of D.A.R.E. services. While such an inclusion does not necessarily represent a serious methodological flaw, use of such sources has been called into question.[8]

Second, Ennett and colleagues included only studies in which postintervention assessment was conducted immediately at program termination. As noted by Lynam et al.,[6] the developmental trajectories of drug experimentation and use vary over time. Thus, if individuals are assessed during periods in which rates of experimentation and use are naturally high, any positive effects that could be found at times of lower experimentation will be deflated. Likewise, assessments made during periods in which experimentation and use are slight will exaggerate the overall effect of the intervention.

Ideally, problems such as those just described could be solved by the use of large-scale longitudinal studies involving extensive follow-up over a period of years. There have been several longer-term follow-ups, but the cost of such efforts may limit the number of longitudinal studies that can be conducted. In the present analysis, we attempted to overcome this difficulty by including a wider range of follow-up reports, from immediate posttests to 10-year postintervention assessments, in an updated meta-analysis of all currently available research articles reporting an outcome evaluation of Project D.A.R.E.

Methods

We conducted computer searches of the *ERIC*, *MEDLINE*, and *PsycINFO* databases in late fall 2002 to obtain articles for the present study. In addition, we reviewed the reference lists of the acquired articles for other potential sources. We initially reviewed roughly 40 articles from these efforts; 11 studies appearing in the literature from 1991 to 2002 met our 3 inclusion criteria, which were as follows:

1. The research was reported in a peer-reviewed journal; reports from dissertations/theses, books, and unpublished manuscripts were not included. We selected this criterion in an attempt to ensure inclusion of only those studies with rigorous methodologies. As noted, a previous meta-analysis of Project D.A.R.E. included research from nonreviewed sources, a fact that critics have suggested may have added error to the reported findings.[8]

2. The research included a control or comparison group (i.e., the research must have involved an experimental or quasi-experimental design).

Table 1
Primary Articles Included in the Meta-Analysis

Study (year)	Sample	r	d	95% confidence interval
Ringwalt et al. (1991)[18]	5th and 6th graders ($n = 1270$; 52% female/48% male; 50% African American/40% Anglo/10% other), posttested immediately	0.025	0.056	−0.06, 0.16
Becker et al. (1992)[19]	5th graders ($n = 2878$), posttested immediately	−0.058	−0.117	−0.19, −0.04
Harmon (1993)[20]	5th graders ($n = 708$), posttested immediately	0.015	0.030	−0.12, 0.18
Ennett et al. (1994)[21]	7th and 8th graders ($n = 1334$; 54% Anglo/22% African American/9% Hispanic/15% other), 2 years post-D.A.R.E.	0.000	0.000[a]	−0.11, 0.11
Rosenbaum et al. (1994)[22]	6th and 7th graders ($n = 1584$; 49.7% female/50.3% male; 49.9% Anglo/24.7% African American/8.9% Hispanic/16.5% other), 1 year post-D.A.R.E.	0.000	0.000[a]	−0.10, 0.10
Wysong et al. (1994)[23]	12th graders ($n = 619$), 5 years post-D.A.R.E.	0.000	0.000[a]	−0.16, 0.16
Dukes et al. (1996)[24]	9th graders ($n = 849$), 3 years post-D.A.R.E.	0.035	0.072	−0.06, 0.21
Zagumny & Thompson (1997)[25]	6th graders ($n = 395$; 48% female/52% male), 4–5 years post-D.A.R.E.	0.184	0.376	0.07, .68
Lynam et al. (1999)[6]	6th graders ($n = 1002$; 57% female/43% male; 75.1% Anglo/20.4% African American/0.5% other), 10 years post-D.A.R.E.	0.000	0.000[a]	−0.15, 0.15
Thombs (2000)[26]	5th through 10th graders ($n = 630$; 90.4% Anglo/5.5% African American/4.1% other), posttested at least 1 to 6 years post-D.A.R.E.	0.025	0.038	−0.15, 0.23
Ahmed et al. (2002)[14]	5th and 6th graders ($n = 236$; 50% female/50% male/69% Anglo/24% African American/7% other), posttested immediately	0.198	0.405	0.01, 0.80

Note. r = correlation coefficient; *d* = difference in the means of the treatment and control conditions divided by the pooled standard deviation. Negative signs for *r* and *d* indicate greater effectiveness of control/comparison group.
[a]Assumed effect size.

70 3. The research included both preintervention and postintervention assessments of at least 1 of 3 key variables: alcohol use, illicit drug use, and tobacco use. We chose to include only those effect sizes that concerned actual substance use behaviors, since the 75 true test of a substance use prevention effort is its impact on actual rates of use.

Using these criteria, we refined the original list of studies to 11 studies (Table 1). We calculated effect sizes using the procedures outlined by Rosenthal.[9] 80 Meta-analysis results are commonly presented in the form of either a correlation coefficient (r) or the difference in the means of the treatment and control conditions divided by the pooled standard deviation (Cohen's d).[10] Since both are ratings of effect size, they 85 can readily be converted to one another, and, if not provided in the original analyses, they can be calculated via F, t, and χ^2 statistics as well as means and standard deviations.[9]

We calculated both estimations for the individual 90 included studies and for the overall analysis. As discussed by Amato and Keith,[11] tests of significance used in meta-analyses require that effect sizes be independent; therefore, if 2 or more effect sizes were generated within the same outcome category, we used the mean 95 effect size. We also used the procedure for weighting effect sizes suggested by Shadish and Haddock[12] to ensure that all effect sizes were in the form of a com-

mon metric. In addition, we calculated 95% confidence intervals (CIs) for each study and for the overall 100 analysis.

Results

The average weighted effect size (r) for all studies was 0.011 ($d = 0.023$; 95% CI = −0.04, 0.08), indicating marginally better outcomes for individuals participating in D.A.R.E. relative to participants in control 105 conditions. The fact that the associated CI included a negative value indicates that the average effect size was not significantly greater than zero at $p < .05$. According to the guidelines developed by Cohen,[13] both of the effect sizes obtained were below the level nor- 110 mally considered small. Four of the included studies noted no effect of D.A.R.E. relative to control conditions, and 1 study noted that D.A.R.E. was less effective than the control condition.

Furthermore, the 6 reports indicating that D.A.R.E. 115 had more positive effects were for the most part small (Figure 1). The largest effect size was found in a report in which the only outcome examined was smoking. Finally, we conducted a test of cumulative significance to determine whether differences existed between 120 D.A.R.E. participants and non-D.A.R.E. participants. This test produced nonsignificant results ($z = 0.73$, NS).

180

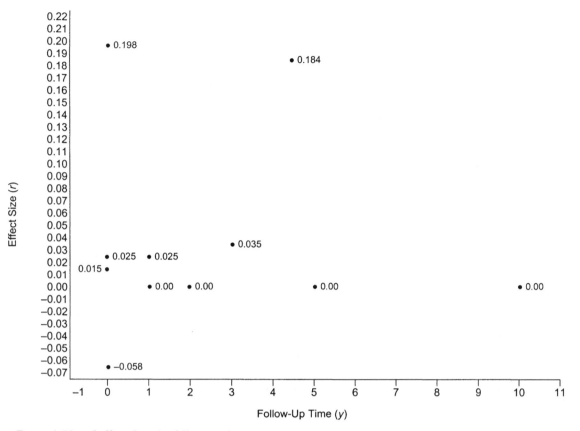

Figure 1. Plot of effect sizes, by follow-up time.

Discussion

Our results confirm the findings of a previous meta-analysis[3] indicating that Project D.A.R.E. is ineffective.
125 This is not surprising, given the substantial information developed over the past decade to that effect. Critics of the present analysis might argue that, despite the magnitude of our findings, the direction of the effect of D.A.R.E. was generally positive. While this is the case,
130 it should be emphasized that the effects we found did not differ significantly from the variation one would expect by chance. According to Cohen's guidelines,[13] the effect size we obtained would have needed to be 20 times larger to be considered even small. Given the
135 tremendous expenditures in time and money involved with D.A.R.E., it would appear that continued efforts should focus on other techniques and programs that might produce more substantial effects.

Our findings also indicate that D.A.R.E. was mini-
140 mally effective during the follow-up periods that would place its participants in the very age groups targeted. Indeed, no noticeable effects could be discerned in nearly half of the reports, including the study involving the longest follow-up period. This is an important con-
145 sideration for those involved in program planning and development.

As noted earlier, progression in regard to experimentation and use varies over time. Use of alcohol and other drugs reaches a peak during adolescence or

150 young adulthood and decreases steadily thereafter.[7,15] Such a developmental path would be expected of all individuals, regardless of their exposure to a prevention effort. Ideally, individuals enrolled in a program such as D.A.R.E. would report limited or no use during their
155 adolescent and young adult years. The fact that half of the included studies reported no beneficial effect of D.A.R.E. beyond what would be expected by chance casts serious doubt on its utility.

One shortcoming of our analysis should be noted.
160 In many of the studies we included, individual students were the unit of analysis in calculating effects. As noted by Rosenbaum and Hanson,[16] this practice tends to lead to overestimates of program effectiveness, since the true unit of analysis is the schools in which the stu-
165 dents are "nested." Because our meta-analysis was limited to the types of data and related information available from the original articles, the potential for such inflation of program effectiveness exists. However, the overall effect sizes calculated here were small and non-
170 significant, and thus it is unlikely that inclusion of studies making this error had a significant impact on the current findings.

An additional caveat is that all of the studies included in this analysis represent evaluations of what is
175 commonly referred to as the "old D.A.R.E.": programs generally based on the original formulations of the D.A.R.E. model. In response to the many critiques of

the program, the D.A.R.E. prevention model was substantially revamped in 2001, thanks in part to a $13.6 million grant provided by the Robert Wood Johnson Foundation.[17] The revisions to the model have since given rise to programs working under the "new D.A.R.E." paradigm. However, at the time of the writing of this article we were unable to find any major evaluation of the new D.A.R.E. model in the research literature, and the effectiveness of such efforts has yet to be determined.

References

1. McNeal RB, Hanson WB. An examination of strategies for gaining convergent validity in natural experiments: D.A.R.E. as an illustrative case study. *Eval Rev.* 1995;19:141–158.
2. Donnermeyer J, Wurschmidt T. Educators' perceptions of the D.A.R.E. program. *J Drug Educ.* 1997;27:259–276.
3. Ennett ST, Tobler NS, Ringwalt CL, Flewelling RL. How effective is Drug Abuse Resistance Education? A meta-analysis of Project D.A.R.E. outcome evaluations. *Am J Public Health.* 1994;84:1394–1401.
4. Hanson WB. Pilot test results comparing the All Stars Program with seventh-grade D.A.R.E.: Program integrity and mediating variable analysis. *Subst Use Misuse.* 1996;31:1359–1377.
5. Hanson WB, McNeal RB. How D.A.R.E. works: An examination of program effects on mediating variables. *Health Educ Behav.* 1997;24:165–176.
6. Lynam DR, Milich R, Zimmerman R, et al. Project D.A.R.E: No effects at 10-year follow-up. *J Consult Clin Psychol.* 1999;67:590–593.
7. Johnston LD, O'Malley PM, Bachman JG. *National Survey Results on Drug Use From the Monitoring the Future Study, 1975–1998. Volume 1: Secondary School Students.* Rockville, MD: National Institute on Drug Abuse; 1999. NIH publication 99–4660.
8. Gorman DM. The effectiveness of D.A.R.E. and other drug use prevention programs. *Am J Public Health.* 1995;85:873.
9. Rosenthal R. *Meta-Analytic Procedures for Social Research.* 2nd ed. Thousand Oaks, Calif: Sage Publications; 1991.
10. DasEiden R, Reifman A. Effects of Brazelton demonstrations on later parenting: A meta-analysis. *J Pediatr Psychol.* 1996;21:857–868.
11. Amato PH, Keith B. Parental divorce and well-being of children: A meta-analysis. *Psychol Bull.* 1991;110:26–46.
12. Shadish WR, Haddock CK. Combining estimates of effect size. In: Cooper H, Hedges LV, eds. *The Handbook of Research Synthesis.* New York. NY: Russell Sage Foundation; 1994:261–281.
13. Cohen J. *Statistical Power Analysis for the Behavioral Sciences.* 2nd ed. Hillsdale, NJ: Lawrence Erlbaum Associates; 1998.
14. Ahmed NU, Ahmed NS, Bennett CR, Hinds JE. Impact of a drug abuse resistance education (D.A.R.E.) program in preventing the initiation of cigarette smoking in fifth- and sixth-grade students. *J Natl Med Assoc.* 2002;94:249–256.
15. Shedler J, Block J. Adolescent drug use and psychological health: A longitudinal inquiry. *Am Psychol.* 1990;45:612–630.
16. Rosenbaum DP, Hanson GS. Assessing the effects of a school-based drug education: A six-year multilevel analysis of Project D.A.R.E. *J Res Crime Delinquency.* 1998;35:381–412.
17. Improving and evaluating the D.A.R.E. school-based substance abuse prevention curriculum. Available at: http://www.rwjf.org/programs/grantDetail.jsp?id=040371. Accessed January 8, 2003.
18. Ringwalt C, Ennett ST, Holt KD. An outcome evaluation of Project D.A.R.E. (Drug Abuse Resistance Education). *Health Educ Res.* 1991;6:327–337.
19. Becker HK, Agopian MW, Yeh S. Impact evaluation of drug abuse resistance education (D.A.R.E.). *J Drug Educ.* 1992;22:283–291.
20. Harmon MA. Reducing the risk of drug involvement among early adolescents: An evaluation of drug abuse resistance education (D.A.R.E.). *Eval Rev.* 1993;17:221–239.
21. Ennett ST, Rosenbaum DP, Flewelling RL, Bieler GS, Ringwalt CL, Bailey SL. Long-term evaluation of drug abuse resistance education. *Addict Behav.* 1994;19:113–125.
22. Rosenbaum DP, Flewelling RL, Bailey SL, Ringwalt CL, Wilkinson DL. Cops in the classroom: A longitudinal evaluation of drug abuse resistance education (D.A.R.E.). *J Res Crime Delinquency.* 1994;31:3–31.
23. Wysong E, Aniskiewicz R, Wright D. Truth and D.A.R.E.: Tracking drug education to graduation and as symbolic politics. *Soc Probl.* 1994;41:448–472.
24. Dukes RL, Ullman JB, Stein JA. Three-year follow-up of drug abuse resistance education (D.A.R.E.). *Eval Rev.* 1996;20:49–66.
25. Zagumny MJ, Thompson MK. Does D.A.R.E. work? An evaluation in rural Tennessee. *J Alcohol Drug Educ.* 1997;42:32–41.
26. Thombs DL. A retrospective study of D.A.R.E.: Substantive effects not detected in undergraduates. *J Alcohol Drug Educ.* 2000;46:27–40.

Acknowledgments: Portions of this research were presented at the Eighth Annual Meeting of the Society for Prevention Research, Montreal, Quebec, Canada, June 2000.

About the authors: Steven L. West is with the Department of Rehabilitation Counseling, Virginia Commonwealth University, Richmond. Keri K. O'Neal is with the Center for Developmental Science, University of North Carolina, Chapel Hill. Drs. West and O'Neal contributed equally to all aspects of study design, data analysis, and the writing of this article. No protocol approval was needed for this study.

Address correspondence to: Steven L. West, Ph.D., Virginia Commonwealth University, Department of Rehabilitation Counseling, 1112 East Clay St., Box 980330, Richmond, VA 23298-0330. E-mail: slwest2@vcu.edu

Exercise for Review 9

Directions: Answer the following questions based on your opinions. While there are no right or wrong answers, be prepared to explain the bases for your answers in classroom discussions.

1. Did the reviewers convince you that the topic of the review is important? Explain.

2. Is the review an essay organized around topics (as opposed to a string of annotations)? Explain.

3. Are there an adequate number of headings and subheadings? Explain.

4. Is the tone of the review neutral and nonemotional? Explain.

5. Overall, does the review provide a comprehensive, logically organized overview of the topic? Explain.

6. Is the conclusion/discussion at the end of the review appropriate in light of the material covered earlier? Explain.

7. Are the suggestions for future research, if any, appropriate in light of the material reviewed? Explain.

8. Are there any obvious weaknesses in this review? Explain.

9. Does this review have any special strengths? Explain.

10. What is your overall evaluation of this review on a scale from Excellent (10) to Very Poor (0)? Explain.

Appendix A

Qualitative versus Quantitative Research

Mildred L. Patten

The results of **quantitative research** are presented as quantities or numbers (i.e., statistics). In **qualitative research**, the results are presented as discussions of trends and/or themes based on words, not statistics. In addition to the difference in how results are presented, there are a number of characteristics that distinguish the two types of research. To understand some of the major ones, consider this research problem: A metropolitan police force is demoralized, with signs such as high rates of absenteeism, failure to follow procedures, and so on. Furthermore, the press has raised questions about the effectiveness of the force and its leadership. In response, the police commission is planning to employ a researcher to identify possible causes and solutions.

If a researcher with a quantitative orientation is retained, he or she would probably begin with a review of the research literature on demoralized police departments. From the review, the researcher would attempt to develop hypotheses to be tested by research. This is a *deductive approach* to planning the research. That is, the researcher is deducing from the literature possible explanations (i.e., hypotheses) to be tested. In contrast, a qualitative researcher would tend to use an *inductive approach* to planning the research. He or she might, for example, begin to gather data on the specific police force in question by making preliminary observations and conducting informal interviews. The resulting preliminary findings might be used as a basis for planning what additional types of information to collect and how to collect them. Thus, rather than approaching the research task with preconceived notions based on published theory and research, a qualitative researcher would emphasize induction from the preliminary data that he or she collected.

Note that qualitative researchers (like quantitative researchers) typically examine previously published literature and include reviews of it in their research reports. However, quantitative researchers use literature as the basis for planning research while qualitative researchers tend to deemphasize it.

When deciding what types of instruments (i.e., measuring tools) to use, quantitative researchers prefer those that produce data that can be easily reduced to numbers, such as structured questionnaires, or interview schedules with objective formats, such as multiple-choice questions. In contrast, qualitative researchers prefer instruments that yield words that are not easily reduced to numbers. These can be obtained using instruments such as unstructured interviews or direct, unstructured observations of police officers and their administrators.

When deciding how many members of the police force to use as participants,[1] quantitative researchers tend to select large samples. Quantitative researchers are able to work with large samples because objective instruments such as an anonymous, objective questionnaire usually are easy to administer to large numbers of participants in a short amount of time. In contrast, qualitative researchers tend to use smaller samples because of the amount of time required to use their instruments, such as extended, in-depth, one-on-one unstructured interviews and extensive observations over time.

When deciding which individuals to use as research participants, quantitative researchers prefer to select a *random sample* in which all participants have an equal chance of being selected. This can be done, for instance, by drawing names out of a hat. Qualitative researchers, on the other hand, are more likely to select a *purposive sample* of individuals that the researcher believes are key informants in terms of social dynamics, leadership positions, job responsibilities, and so on. In other words, qualitative researchers prefer to use informed judgment in selecting participants, while quantitative re-

---

[1] Note that the term "participants" implies that the individuals being studied have voluntarily agreed to participate in a given research project. When individuals are being observed without their consent, they are more likely to be called "subjects."

searchers prefer to leave the selection of participants to chance (i.e., random selection).

While working with the participants, qualitative researchers would be open to the possibility of making adjustments in the instrumentation, such as rewording questions or adding questions based on earlier responses by participants. On the other hand, quantitative researchers seldom make such adjustments during the course of a research project. Instead, quantitative researchers plan their research in detail in advance and follow the plan closely throughout the study because mid-stream deviations might be viewed as introducing subjectivity into the study. It is important to note that while quantitative researchers emphasize "objectivity," qualitative researchers believe all observational processes are inherently subjective and open to interpretation. Because of this, qualitative researchers sometimes mention relevant details of their personal backgrounds (such as having a mother who was a police officer) in order to inform readers of their research of possible sources of bias in collecting and interpreting the data.

For data analysis, quantitative researchers tend to summarize all responses with statistics and seldom report on the responses of individual participants. Qualitative researchers, on the other hand, tend to cite individuals' responses (such as quoting individual participants) in the Results section of a research report.

Finally, quantitative researchers tend to generalize the results to one or more populations, while qualitative researchers tend to limit their conclusions to only the individuals who were directly studied.

Should the police commission select a researcher with a "quantitative" *or* "qualitative" orientation? Some of the criteria that should be considered when making such a decision are:

A. Some research questions inherently lend themselves more to the quantitative than the qualitative approach. For instance, "What is the impact of terrorism on the U.S. economy?" is a question that lends itself to quantitative research because economic variables readily lend themselves to quantitative analysis. On the other hand, "What is the emotional impact of terrorism on at-risk health care workers?" is a question that lends itself more to the qualitative approach because this question focuses on emotional impact, which is more difficult to quantify. Note, however, that the second question could be ex-

amined with either qualitative or quantitative research.

B. When little is known about a topic, qualitative research should usually be initially favored. New topics are constantly emerging in all fields, such as new diseases like SARS, new criminal concerns such as domestic terrorism, and new educational techniques such as using the Internet for instructional purposes in classrooms. On new topics, there often is little, if any, previously published research. In its absence, quantitative researchers may find it difficult to employ the deductive approach (i.e., deduct hypotheses from previously published research). Also, quantitative researchers might find it difficult to write structured questions about a little-known topic. (How can a researcher know exactly what to ask when he or she knows little about a topic?) In contrast, qualitative researchers could start with broad questions and refine them during the course of the interviews as various themes and issues start to emerge. Based on the qualitative results, theories might be developed from which hypotheses could be deduced and subsequently tested by using quantitative research.

C. When the participants belong to a culture that is closed or secretive, qualitative research should usually be favored. A skilled qualitative researcher who is willing to spend considerable time breaking through the barriers that keep researchers out is more likely to be successful than a quantitative researcher who tends to spend much less time interacting with participants.

D. When potential participants are not available for extensive interactions or observation, the quantitative approach should be considered. For instance, it might be difficult to schedule extensive interviews with chief executives of major corporations. However, the chief executives might be willing to respond to a brief objective-type questionnaire, which would provide data that can be analyzed with statistics.

E. When time and funds are very limited, quantitative research might be favored. Although this is an arguable criterion for selecting between the two types of research, it is suggested because quantitative research can be used to provide quick, inexpensive snapshots of narrow aspects of research problems. Qualitative methods do not lend themselves to the more economical snapshot approach.

F. When audiences require "hard numbers" (such as legislators or funding agencies sometimes do), quantitative research should be favored or, at least, incorporated into a qualitative research project. When someone says, "Just the numbers, please," themes and trends illustrated with quotations are unlikely to impress them. For such an audience, one should start by presenting statistics when possible. This might open the door to consideration of more qualitative aspects of the findings. Notice that implicit in this criterion is the notion that both qualitative and quantitative approaches might be used in a given research project, with each approach contributing a different type of information.

Up to this point, quantitative and qualitative research have been presented as though they are opposites. However, some researchers conduct research that is a blend of the two approaches. For instance, a quantitative researcher who uses semi-structured interviews to collect data, reduces the data to statistics, but also reports quotations from participants to support the statistics, is conducting research that has some of the characteristics of both approaches.

Clearly, the hypothetical police commission needs to make a complex decision. How would you answer the question in the first paragraph of this topic? What is the basis for your answer? Arguably, a combination of both approaches might be the best answer.

Notes:

Appendix B

Quality Control in Qualitative Research

Mildred L. Patten

This topic describes some of the specific techniques that qualitative researchers use to establish the dependability and trustworthiness of their data.[1]

One technique is to use multiple sources for obtaining data on the research topic. The technical name for this is **data triangulation**. For instance, for a qualitative study of discrimination in an employment setting, a researcher might interview employees, their supervisors, and the responsible personnel officers. To the extent that the various sources provide similar information, the data can be said to be corroborated through data triangulation.

The methods used to collect data can also be triangulated. For instance, a researcher might conduct individual interviews with parents regarding their child-rearing practices and then have the same participants provide data via focus groups. This would be an example of **methods triangulation**.

Note that in *data triangulation*, typically two or more types of participants (such as employees and supervisors) are used to collect data on a research topic. In contrast, in *methods triangulation*, only one type of participant (such as parents) is used to provide data, but two or more methods are used to collect the data.

An important technique to assure the quality of qualitative research is to form a *research team*, with each member of the team participating in the collection and analysis of data. This can be thought of as **researcher triangulation**, which reduces the possibility that the results of qualitative research represent only the idiosyncratic views of one individual researcher.

Sometimes, it is helpful to form a **team of researchers with diverse backgrounds**. For instance, for a study on the success of minority students in medical school, a team of researchers that consists of both medical school instructors and medical school students might strengthen

the study by providing more than one perspective when collecting and analyzing the data.

The issue of having diversity in a research team is addressed in Example 1, which is from a qualitative research report on gender issues. The researchers point out that gender diversity in their research team helps to provide a "comprehensive view."

Oral interviews and focus groups are typically audiotaped and then transcribed. Sometimes, transcription is difficult because some participants might not speak distinctly. In addition, transcribers sometimes make errors. Therefore, checking the accuracy of a transcription helps to ensure the quality of the data. In Example 2, a sample of segments was checked.

In the analysis of data, each member of a research team should initially work independently (without consulting each other) and then compare the results of their analyses. To the extent that they agree, the results are dependable. This technique examines what is called **interobserver agreement**.[4] When there are disagreements, often they can be resolved by having the research-

---

[1] The terms "dependability" and "trustworthiness" in qualitative research loosely correspond to the terms "reliability" and "validity" in quantitative research.

[2] Rasera, E. F., Vieira, E. M., & Japur, M. (2004). Influence of gender and sexuality on the construction of being HIV positive as experienced in a support group in Brazil. *Families, Systems, & Health, 22,* 340–351.

[3] Lukens, E. P., Thorning, H., & Lohrer, S. (2004). Sibling perspectives on severe mental illness: Reflections on self and family. *American Journal of Orthopsychiatry, 74,* 489–501.

[4] In qualitative research, this is sometimes called *intercoder agreement*. In quantitative research, this concept is called *interobserver reliability*.

ers discuss their differences until they reach a consensus.

The use of an outside expert can also help to ensure the quality of the research. A researcher's peer (such as another experienced qualitative researcher) can examine the process used to collect data, the resulting data and the conclusions, and then provide feedback to the researcher. This process is called **peer review**. Under certain circumstances, the peer who provides the review is called an **auditor**.

The dependability of the results can also be enhanced by a process called **member checking**.

This term is based on the idea that the participants are "members" of the research team. By having the participants/members review the results of the analysis, researchers can determine whether their results "ring true" to the participants. If not, adjustments can be made in the description of the results.

Table 1

Table of Z-Values for r

r	Z	r	Z	r	Z	r	Z	r	Z
.000	.000	.200	.203	.400	.424	.600	.693	.800	1.099
.005	.005	.205	.208	.405	.430	.605	.701	.805	1.113
.010	.010	.210	.213	.410	.436	.610	.709	.810	1.127
.015	.015	.215	.218	.415	.442	.615	.717	.815	1.142
.020	.020	.220	.224	.420	.448	.620	.725	.820	1.157
.025	.025	.225	.229	.425	.454	.625	.733	.825	1.172
.030	.030	.230	.234	.430	.460	.630	.741	.830	1.188
.035	.035	.235	.239	.435	.466	.635	.750	.835	1.204
.040	.040	.240	.245	.440	.472	.640	.758	.840	1.221
.045	.045	.245	.250	.445	.478	.645	.767	.845	1.238
.050	.050	.250	.255	.450	.485	.650	.775	.850	1.256
.055	.055	.255	.261	.455	.491	.655	.784	.855	1.274
.060	.060	.260	.266	.460	.497	.660	.793	.860	1.293
.065	.065	.265	.271	.465	.504	.665	.802	.865	1.313
.070	.070	.270	.277	.470	.510	.670	.811	.870	1.333
.075	.075	.275	.282	.475	.517	.675	.820	.875	1.354
.080	.080	.280	.288	.480	.523	.680	.829	.880	1.376
.085	.085	.285	.293	.485	.530	.685	.838	.885	1.398
.090	.090	.290	.299	.490	.536	.690	.848	.890	1.422
.095	.095	.295	.304	.495	.543	.695	.858	.895	1.447
.100	.100	.300	.310	.500	.549	.700	.867	.900	1.472
.105	.105	.305	.315	.505	.556	.705	.877	.905	1.499
.110	.110	.310	.321	.510	.563	.710	.887	.910	1.528
.115	.116	.315	.326	.515	.570	.715	.897	.915	1.557
.120	.121	.320	.332	.520	.576	.720	.908	.920	1.589
.125	.126	.325	.337	.525	.583	.725	.918	.925	1.623
.130	.131	.330	.343	.530	.590	.730	.929	.930	1.658
.135	.136	.335	.348	.535	.597	.735	.940	.935	1.697
.140	.141	.340	.354	.540	.604	.740	.950	.940	1.738
.145	.146	.345	.360	.545	.611	.745	.962	.945	1.783
.150	.151	.350	.365	.550	.618	.750	.973	.950	1.832
.155	.156	.355	.371	.555	.626	.755	.984	.955	1.886
.160	.161	.360	.377	.560	.633	.760	.996	.960	1.946
.165	.167	.365	.383	.565	.640	.765	1.008	.965	2.014
.170	.172	.370	.388	.570	.648	.770	1.020	.970	2.092
.175	.177	.375	.394	.575	.655	.775	1.033	.975	2.185
.180	.182	.380	.400	.580	.662	.780	1.045	.980	2.298
.185	.187	.385	.406	.585	.670	.785	1.058	.985	2.443
.190	.192	.390	.412	.590	.678	.790	1.071	.990	2.647
.195	.198	.395	.418	.595	.685	.795	1.085	.995	2.994

Notes:

Notes:

Notes: